ESOTERIC CHRISTIANITY
and the Mission of
Christian Rosenkreutz

D1599265

ESOTERIC CHRISTIANITY
and the Mission of
Christian Rosenkreutz

Twenty-three lectures given between
17 September 1911 and 19 December 1912

RUDOLF STEINER

RUDOLF STEINER PRESS
LONDON

Lectures 13, 19, 21 and 22 translated by Matthew Barton, and
all others revised by him

6\08
MH

Rudolf Steiner Press
51 Queen Caroline Street
London W6 9QL

www.rudolfsteinerpress.com

Published by Rudolf Steiner Press 2000

Originally published in German under the title *Das esoterische
Christentum und die geistige Führung der Menschheit* (volume 130 in the
Rudolf Steiner Gesamtausgabe or Collected Works) by Rudolf Steiner
Verlag, Dornach. This authorized translation is published by kind
permission of the Rudolf Steiner Nachlassverwaltung, Dornach

Earlier English translations: *Esoteric Christianity and the Mission of
Christian Rosenkreutz*, Rudolf Steiner Press, London 1984 (13 lectures)
and *Faith, Love, Hope*, Steiner Book Centre, N. Vancouver, no date (2
lectures). Single lectures from this volume have also appeared in: *From
Buddha to Christ*, Anthroposophic Press, New York 1978; *The Etherisation
of the Blood*, Rudolf Steiner Press, London 1971; *Cosmic Ego and Human
Ego, The Nature of Christ the Resurrected*, Anthroposophic Press/Rudolf
Steiner Press, New York/London 1941; *Facing Karma*, Anthroposophic
Press, New York 1975; *Festivals and their Meaning*, Rudolf Steiner Press,
London 1996, and *The Mission of Christian Rosenkreutz*, Rudolf Steiner
Press, London 1950

Translation © Rudolf Steiner Press 2000

A catalogue record for this book is available from the British Library

ISBN 1 85584 083 9

Cover by Andrew Morgan Design
Typeset by DP Photosetting, Aylesbury, Bucks.
Printed and bound in Great Britain by Cromwell Press Limited,
Trowbridge, Wilts.

Contents

Publisher's Note

The previous English edition of this book contained only 13 of the 23 lectures which appear in the original German language edition. As the volume documents such a critical period in the development of Steiner's teaching—in particular his exposition of Christianity and its esoteric undercurrents—we felt it important that a complete edition should now be made available in English. We also felt that classic lectures such as 'The Etherisation of the Blood' should not be isolated to individual publications, but rather that readers should be given the chance of studying them in their original context.

In publishing an edition identical to the German, however, we have also included some repetition of content. This repetition was inevitable because Steiner was speaking on similar themes at different locations. We felt it justified, however, to publish the whole without further editing as there are also variations and important details which would otherwise be lost.

London, September 2000

Foreword

The Theosophical Society, founded by H.P. Blavatsky,[1] had the task of adding an occult element to the awakening European interest in oriental spirituality which had been greatly stimulated in the mid-nineteenth century by Schopenhauer and other major thinkers. *The Secret Doctrine*[2] by H.P. Blavatsky excited a good deal of interest and caused the rapid expansion of the Theosophical Society in the English-speaking world. It made no effort to take account of Christianity. An attempt by rosicrucian occultists, drawing on the author's mediumistic faculties, to place Christianity at the centre of the new movement, had already been previously deflected. And yet Western and Eastern wisdom needed to be brought into harmony. Ancient wisdom needed to live on in the future development of mankind, whose salvation was guaranteed by the Mystery of Golgotha. Similar to the way that Christianity in the past, still young and vigorous in belief, had assimilated science through a wave of Arabism, turning observation of nature into the science of nature, so present mankind, fallen prey to materialism and parched, had to be permeated with the knowledge of ancient wisdom in order to revive. This took place by way of Buddhist philosophy, with the result that the teaching of karma and reincarnation found entry to many souls and penetrated their understanding. The scientific works of Max Müller,[3] Deussen[4] and other significant philosophers opened up to Europeans a world of overwhelming spirituality and living imaginations. Intellectual knowledge and science, however, still needed to find a key to open its understanding of this world. The work done by Blavatsky and her pupils in this respect was insufficient.

There was as yet no one suitable for this task. Through the particular constitution of her physical organism H.P. Blavatsky had been an instrument particularly open to the influences of the spiritual world. Her strong will suited her for carrying out difficult tasks in the service of mankind; but her thinking was disjointed and her character often slipped back into emotionalism. When her emotions broke loose catastrophe ensued, and sometimes even her whole aim and direction were radically altered. It would not be wrong to say: as an instrument open to spiritual influence, occult forces fought over her.

In order to turn knowledge of the occult worlds into a science of the spirit which might in time be attained by others through serious study, someone was needed who could devote himself to this transformation with his character and temperament completely under control, a grasp of contemporary knowledge and command of all the various fields of knowledge—to an extent which enabled him to reply to the fiercest criticism. An iron and yet flexible physical constitution were required in order to withstand the onslaught against him.

Such a person was Rudolf Steiner.[5] His youth was spent in what might be called convivial seclusion and constant study. Hardly grown up, he supported himself by giving lessons, and then as an educator. On this foundation his lecturing and writing activity developed while he was still a young man. Since the life of spirit was quite natural to him, he quite consciously undertook the task of raising all the objections which the critical materialist brings to bear on revelations of the spirit, and to spare himself nothing which might be the smallest deviation from this line. This he called 'creeping into the skin of the dragon'. He felt this difficult task to be his duty. Otherwise he would have considered himself as lacking the right to fight the difficult battle for mankind to the end, of wresting victory from abstract intellectualism. Only then would he be able to present the deed of the Buddha and the deed of the Christ as a harmonious unity; only then, when he himself had gained victory over the inner adversary and his hidden ways, would he be able to point the path of salvation through Christ's deed. Thus armed, he made his appearance as representative of the ancient mystery teachings as they had been revealed to him in the light of Christ's deed.

The Theosophical Society was alarmed. It saw the deep effect of Steiner's teachings on souls in search of Christ. It did not want to expose its members to this, did not want to expose them to the danger of taking in Steiner's teachings, thus abandoning the 'orientalizing stream'. His lecture theme for the Congress of the Federation of European Sections, arranged to take place in Genoa,[6] was on Buddhist wisdom and Western esotericism. They opposed this subject with an Indian boy, according to them the incarnation in the flesh of Christ Jesus. No common ground for serious debate, as should have taken place at the Congress in Genoa, could be found to cover such a gaping divergence; and now that Rudolf Steiner's significance had been recognized such a debate was deemed much too dangerous an undertaking. It was better to avoid such hot issues altogether. The congress was cancelled at the last minute for reasons which never became clear.

And Steiner, who had already set out for Italy—as had many others—was able to speak only to group meetings, to small circles. There was no time to arrange for stenographers. But not everything was lost, due to the devotion of a number of members who were taking notes. However their note-taking quite naturally became more perfunctory towards the end, as they were caught up increasingly in the spirited fire of Rudolf Steiner's words. The Locarno lecture and those given in Neuchâtel in particular give us cause to remember our dear Agnes Friedländer, who died of pneumonia in 1942 in a concentration camp. She was among those whose souls were particularly deeply affected by the transforming impulses alive in the Christ Mystery.

The lectures themselves have only been preserved as fragments. No satisfactory transcripts exist. It seems like a counter-attack by adversary forces that no experienced stenographer was present. They exist—apart from the shortened Kassel lectures—partly as fragments and partly as notes which have been pieced together. Nevertheless, the essential framework has been preserved and the effort was made to place them in context. This effort is not always successful as far as stylistic form is concerned; but the spirit is challenged and stimulated all the more to sharpen its powers of thought and embark on their study.

Besides emphasizing the particular character of spiritual science after the advent of Christ, the aim of the lectures given in 1911 and 1912[7] was to bring out the significance of karma, the course of our destiny, and to enable us to penetrate into its intimate nature. Even if the overall course of those reflections has been preserved only as a series of remembered images—the notes were frequently too brief to convey logical progression, and the haphazard collection of notes and headings tend to be little more than indications—the direction of spiritual impulses given by Dr. Steiner has been preserved and perhaps justifies this attempt at a compilation: these impulses can deepen the soul through meditative work and continue to be active within us.

Marie Steiner

The Christ Impulse and Historical Development

1. Lugano, 17 September 1911

We shall begin by discussing something of a general character. And since we are a small intimate circle, we can then elaborate on any aspect that especially interests you. I would like to make some general statements about the being of man in connection with World Being, with the macrocosm. And I will not approach it so much in the style of my book *Theosophy*—you can all gain what you need to from that—but I invite you to consider especially man's inner nature.

If now and then we contemplate ourselves as human beings, we are immediately struck by the fact that we experience the world about us through our senses, and then think about the impressions we have received. We constantly observe these two attributes of man's being. If, for instance, we have put the light out at night and review the day's impressions before going to sleep, we are conscious that all day long the world has worked upon us. Now only the memory pictures of the day's impressions surge up and down in our souls. We know that we are thinking about them, our soul now inhabits the after-effects of what has taken place in us through outer impressions. Leaving more ordinary, trivial matters on one side, we see these memories of the day as individual to us. It is only because we are intelligent, individual human beings, beings with an intellect, that we are capable of receiving impressions of the world in this way.

Now, in our spiritual life this individual aspect is closely connected with external impressions. During the day, whilst we observe the world, our sense impressions and our thoughts intermingle. And at bedtime, when we no longer have any fresh sense impressions, but let those we have had pass through our soul, then we know very well that these are our pictures of what is outside. Our impressions of the outer world merge with what we are as individuals. They become one. Now, as we all know, one can make this inner, individual element within us more and more alive, more and more exact, by the means already known to us and described for instance in my book *How to Know Higher Worlds*. What you can experience first of all in your inner life, is that you feel you are not absolutely dependent in your thoughts on the external world. If, for instance, someone can think about what happened on Saturn, Sun and Moon, then he has higher thoughts of this kind. For of course nobody can have *external* impressions of what happened on old Saturn, old Sun and old Moon. We do not even need to go so far. If we ask ourselves in a quiet moment: 'How many of my concepts have changed since my youth?' this in itself is taking an independent, individual stand with regard to the world. When we form views about life, we feel ourselves becoming more independent in our intellect. Becoming independent in the individual element of the intellect is of great importance for human beings. For what does this mean? What does it mean for the human being to grasp general truths about life—not just in theory but through experience—even of things that are independent of external impressions? It means that he is becoming more independent in his etheric body. That is the first step in a long process. At the beginning he does not even notice that he is freeing his etheric body a little; ultimately he can make it completely independent of the physical body.

Whilst the beginning is just a tiny step towards becoming independent, the end is a total drawing out of the etheric body and a perceiving with it. We then have perceptions in the environment with this independent etheric body. We can even perceive in this way when we are not yet very advanced in inner mystical experience. We can grasp this and to a certain extent understand it if we remember what our perception is like in the physical body. With our physical body we perceive by means of our senses, which are independent of each other. Our eyes function separately and so do our ears. We can perceive the world of colour and the world of sound separately. We can no longer do this when we perceive with our intelligence. In the case of intelligence everything is a unity, nothing is divided into separate spheres. Likewise we cannot perceive with etheric eyes and etheric ears as though they were separate sense realms, but we perceive the etheric world in general. And when we begin to say something about it we can describe how etheric experience works as a comprehensive whole. I will not discuss how much further this experience can lead, but only point out that when we perceive how our intelligence forms general truths, then we can perceive something of the etheric elements.

Whoever perceives the etheric world and can gradually realize that a higher world of this kind exists, can have an inner conviction that an etheric body is the basis of the physical body. As soon as we speak of such a thing as the etheric body we must take our lead from important things we can learn through direct experience. As soon as we know that the physical body is interpenetrated by an etheric body we will readily understand the occultist describing how paralysis is an abnormal occurrence of what otherwise happens through normal training. It can happen that a person's etheric body withdraws from his physical body. Then the physical body becomes independent. Paralysis could possibly result, for the physical body has been deprived of its enlivening etheric body. But we do not need to go as far as the appearance of paralysis, for we can understand its appearance in everyday life even better. For example, what is a lazy person? He is someone who has a weak etheric body from birth or who has let it grow weak through neglect. We try to correct it by relieving the physical body of its leaden heaviness and by some means making it lighter. A thorough cure, however, can only arise by way of the astral body, for this can stimulate the etheric body to fresh life. But you have to realize something else. The etheric body is actually the bearer of our whole intellect. When we go to sleep at night all our thought pictures and memories actually remain in the etheric body. The human being leaves his thoughts behind in the etheric body and does not return to them until morning. By laying aside the etheric body we lay aside the whole web of our experiences.

The nature of this etheric body, however, is such that when we investigate it in a spiritual scientific way we can quite clearly perceive that we are subject to a far greater number of changes in the course of time than we would imagine. We all know, of course, that man has passed through a series of incarnations. It is not for nothing that we are incarnated again and again. Man's vision is limited. It is a general belief that our organization has always been as it is today. In fact, the human organization changes from one century to another, only we cannot perceive this externally. In the frontal lobe of the brain there is an organ with delicate convolutions, that has only developed since the fourteenth to fifteenth centuries. It is an organic form for the purely intellectual life of present centuries. We can well imagine that it is impossible for a detail of this kind to alter in the brain without, in fact, the whole human organization altering, even if only slightly. So that the human organization does indeed show signs of changes as the centuries pass by. But it is only through reading the Akashic Record that these changes can be confirmed, which is where changes in the etheric body can be best observed. We see that the people of ancient

Greece or ancient Egypt had etheric bodies that were quite different. All the etheric streams in them were different.

Now in order to arrive at a thought that can be useful and productive for us, I would like to make a short digression and draw your attention to the fact that even in ordinary life you can assume the existence of more than one world. The human being goes to sleep without knowing that he is passing into another world. But the fact that he is asleep and does not know anything about it does not prove that this other world does not exist. Other worlds do impinge in a certain way. The human being perceives with his senses when he is in the physical world but not when he withdraws into himself: then he has a thought world which borders on the physical. And he finds within himself, in addition to the already developed element of intellect, two other elements as well that are quite different again. Can the human being develop these other elements?

A simple reflection can show that something else is more characteristic of our inner life than merely having thoughts. This is present whenever we feel ourselves to be moral human beings. That is the world where we connect a feeling of sympathy or antipathy with certain definite experiences. This goes beyond intellectual experience. Someone shows goodwill to another and we are pleased, or he shows ill will and we are displeased. That is something quite different from what is experienced purely intellectually. Mere reflection does not produce in us the feeling of whether a deed is moral or not. A person can be highly intelligent in an intellectual way, without feeling the repulsive nature of a purely egotistical action. That is another realm of experience, which we also become aware of when we admire what is beautiful and elevating in works of art, or are repulsed by what is ugly. What elevates us in works of art cannot be grasped by the intellect but only by our life of soul. So we can say: something comes into our life in this way which is beyond the intellect. If an occultist observes a soul at the moment when it is experiencing aversion from an immoral deed, or pleasure in a moral one, he perceives a higher level of soul life. The mere having of thoughts is on a lower level of soul life than pleasure in or aversion from moral or immoral deeds. If the human being strengthens his etheric body and so develops a more intense feeling for what is moral or immoral, this can be seen not only as increased strength in his etheric body but as an increase of strength in his astral body too, an especial intensification of the astral forces. So that we can say: a person who has particularly sensitive feelings about moral and immoral deeds will acquire especially strong forces in his astral body, whilst a person who only improves his etheric body intellectually—with exercises, say, that strengthen the memory—can certainly develop his clairvoyance a great deal, but he will not get beyond the etheric-astral world, because the intellectual element alone is active within him. If we want to get beyond the astral world we must do the kinds of exercise in which we develop sympathy for moral deeds and antipathy for immoral deeds. Then we do indeed ascend to a world that is behind our world in more than just an astral sense. We then ascend to the heavenly world. So that we can say: in the great invisible world the heavenly world of the macrocosm corresponds to our response to moral or immoral impressions, and the astral world of the macrocosm corresponds to our intellectual-sense perception of the physical world. All that develops within the intellectual element corresponds to the astral world, whilst what can be developed in relation to moral or immoral deeds corresponds to the heavenly world, the world of devachan.

Then there is yet another element in the human soul. There is a difference between feeling *happy* about moral deeds and feeling *responsible* enough to carry out what thus appeals to you, and to withstand doing what is not moral. A feeling of responsibility for our actions is the highest level we can reach in the world today.

So the human being's soul stages can be set out like this:

1. The sense person.
2. The intellectual person, who relates to the first invisible world.
3. The aesthetic person with moral feelings, who is attracted or repelled by moral and immoral deeds. This corresponds externally to the lower devachanic world.
4. The morally active person.

Actually carrying out what we feel within ourselves to be the highest moral ideals corresponds externally to the higher devachanic world, the world of reason, ruled by those beings who represent absolute reason in the world. When the human being can grasp that his moral impulses give a shadow picture of the highest world from which he comes, he has understood a great deal about the macrocosm.

So we have the physical world and the world of the intellect, the moral world or the heavenly world of lower devachan, and the world of reason or higher devachan. Cosmic worlds cast in us shadow pictures of the sense world—the intellectual world: intellectual clairvoyance; the aesthetic world: moral feeling; the world of reason: moral impulses for deeds. Through a kind of self-knowledge man can perceive these different stages within himself.

Now this whole configuration of the human being has altered in the course of time. In ancient Greek or Egyptian times the human being was not at all as he is today. In the Greek age man was so constituted that higher beings ruled over the soul element within him, and so he felt a kind of natural obligation towards those beings. We now live in the age when man is ruled by his intellect, and so he feels something like an aesthetic-moral obligation. In those olden times however, it would have been impossible for anyone to have conceived of acting in a way contrary to a moral impulse that presented itself. In Greece they still felt pleasure and displeasure so strongly that they had to act accordingly.

Then came the modern age, when people do not even feel an obligation towards the aesthetic element, as one can see from the saying: 'There's no accounting for tastes'—though people who have a developed taste can probably agree among themselves.

What was felt in earlier times to be a necessity in the moral and aesthetic sphere is nowadays felt to be so in the intellectual sphere: to have a certain standard in thinking—not thinking as you like but conforming to the laws of logic. This brings us, however, to the lowest point of human experience. At the moment we are at a transitional stage, as we can well see. For if we look at past millennia we see the physical body of man drying up more and more, until he has become quite different. One and a half millennia ago the physical body was considerably softer and more pliable. It has become harder and harder. On the other hand something quite different has occurred in the etheric body, something that the human being could have less experience of because this etheric body has passed through an upward development. It is significant that we stand at the important moment when the human being must grow aware that his etheric body should become different. That is the event that will take place in this twentieth century. Whilst on the one hand an intensification of the intellectual element is making itself felt, on the other hand the etheric body will become so much more independent that human beings are bound to become aware of it. For a period of time after the Christ Event people did not think as intellectually as they do today. Strengthening the intellectual element causes the etheric body to become more and more independent, so that it can also be used as an independent instrument. And during this process it can be seen to have gone through a hidden development which makes possible the perception of the Christ in the etheric body. Just as the Christ could formerly be seen physically, He can now be seen etherically, so that in this twentieth century a beholding of the Christ will occur like a natural event, in the way Paul saw Him. A number of people will be able to see Christ in the etheric, which means that we shall know Him even if all Bibles are destroyed. We shall not need any records then, for we shall see Him. And that is an event equal in importance to what occurred on Golgotha. In the centuries to come a greater and greater number of people will reach the stage where they can see the Christ. The next three millennia on earth will be devoted to the kind of development whereby the etheric body becomes more and more sensitive, so that certain people will experience this and other events. I will just mention *one* more thing to come: there will be more and more people who want to do something and then have an urge to hold back. Then a vision will follow, and these people will perceive increasingly clearly that what happens in the future is the karmic result of what they have previously done. A few people who are ahead of the rest already feel such things. It happens especially with children.

There is a tremendous difference between what trained clairvoyants experience and what I have described here as something that will come about in the natural course of events. Since time immemorial the trained clairvoyant experienced the Christ by means of certain exercises. On the physical plane, if I meet someone he is there in front of me; with clairvoyant vision, on the other hand, I can perceive him in quite different places and we do not actually meet. It has always been possible to see the Christ clairvoyantly. But to meet Him, now that He stands in a different relationship to humanity—helping us from the etheric world—is something which is independent of our clairvoyant development. From the twentieth century onwards, in the next three thousand years, certain people will be able to meet Him, meet Him objectively as an etheric form. That is very different from experiencing a vision of Him through inner development.

This places the exalted Being we call the Christ in an altogether different sequence of evolution from that of the Buddha. The bodhisattva who became Buddha was born into the royal house of Suddhodana and became Buddha in the twenty-ninth year of his life, so that he did not need to undergo further incarnations. When such a being, a bodhisattva, becomes a Buddha or Master, this signifies a higher form of inner development, that any human being can pass through. The esoteric training of a human being is a start in the direction that can lead to Buddha-hood. That has nothing to do with what happens around us. Such people appear at certain times to help the world forward. But those events are different from the Christ Event. Christ did not develop out of another human individuality. He came from the macrocosm, whilst all the bodhisattvas have always been connected with the earth.

So we have to be clear that in so far as we speak about bodhisattvas or Buddhas we do not come near to the Christ. For Christ is a macrocosmic being who became connected with the earth for the first time through the baptism by John. That was His physical manifestation. Now the etheric manifestation is coming, then will come the astral one and a higher one still after that. Human beings will first have to be far advanced before they experience that higher stage. What human beings can experience belongs to the general laws of the earth. The Being whom we call by the name of Christ or by other names will also bring about what we can describe as the saving of all souls on earth for Jupiter existence, whilst everything else will fall away with the earth. Anthroposophy is not something arbitrary, but something of importance that had to come into the world. The world must learn to understand the Christ Being who lived for three years on the earth at the beginning of our present era.

In my book *The Spiritual Guidance of Man and Humanity* you will find details about the two Jesus boys. The Christ Event was prepared for by an individuality connected with the sect of the Essenes, Jeshu ben Pandira, who was born a hundred years before the two Jesus boys were born in Palestine. So you have to distinguish between them and Jeshu ben Pandira, of whom Haeckel,[8] among others, has spoken in a most derogatory way. The Matthew Gospel,[9] in the main, originated from this most exalted person, Jeshu ben Pandira, as a preparation for what was to come.

In what way should we understand the relationship of Jeshu ben Pandira to Jesus of Nazareth?

The individualities have nothing to do with one another initially, except that one prepared the way for the other; as individualities they are in no way related. The facts are that in one of the Jesus boys, the one described in the Luke Gospel, we have a somewhat indefinable individuality, so far difficult to understand in that He could speak immediately after birth in a way His mother could not understand. He was not intellectual, this individuality of the Luke Gospel, but tremendously vital and elemental in the realm of moral feelings. The astral body of this being was influenced by the individuality of the Buddha.

When he had reached the Buddha stage, Buddha did not need to incarnate on earth any further. As long as he was a bodhisattva he continued to incarnate. After he had become Buddha he was active from the higher worlds, and his activity flowed through the astral body of the Jesus of the Luke

Gospel. The forces emanating from Buddha are in the astral body of this Jesus boy. Thus the Buddha stream is contained within the Jesus of Nazareth stream.

On the other hand, what is told in Eastern writings and is also known to be correct by Western occultists, is that at the moment the bodhisattva becomes Buddha a new bodhisattva appears. In the moment when Gautama Buddha became Buddha this bodhisattva individuality was taken from the earth, and a new bodhisattva became active. He is the bodhisattva who is to become a Buddha in due time. In fact the time is exactly determined when the successor of Gautama Buddha, Maitreya, will become a Buddha: five thousand years after the enlightenment of Buddha beneath the bodhi tree. Roughly three thousand years after our time the world will experience the Maitreya Buddha incarnation, which will be the last incarnation of Jeshu ben Pandira. This bodhisattva, who will come as Maitreya Buddha, will also come in a physical body in our century in his reincarnation in the flesh—but not as Buddha—and he will make it his task to give humanity true concepts about the Christ Event.

Genuine occultists recognize the incarnations of the bodhisattva, the Maitreya Buddha-to-be. In the same way as other human beings, this individuality will also go through a development of the etheric body. When humanity becomes more like him who is to become the Maitreya Buddha, then this individuality will go through a special development that in a certain respect, in its highest stages, will be something like the baptism of Jesus of Nazareth: he will undergo an exchange of individuality. In both cases another individuality comes in. They grow up as children in the world, and after a certain number of years their individuality is exchanged. It is not a continuous development, but a development that undergoes a break, as was the case with Jesus. In His case there was an exchange of individuality of this kind in the twelfth year and then again at the baptism by John. This kind of exchange occurs, too, with the bodhisattva who is to become the Maitreya Buddha. These individualities are suddenly as it were fructified by another. The Maitreya Buddha, in particular, will live with a certain individuality until his thirtieth year, and then an exchange will occur in him, as we find with Jesus of Nazareth during the baptism in Jordan. We will always recognize the Maitreya Buddha, however, from the fact that nothing will be known of him prior to this exchange of individuality, even though he is present. And then he will suddenly reveal himself.

Leading an unknown life is characteristic of all bodhisattvas who are to become Buddhas. The human individuality in the future will have to be more and more self-reliant. It will be a characteristic of his that he will pass unknown in the world for many years, and it will only be possible to recognize him then through the fact that he works from out of his own inner strength as a self-reliant individual. It has been known for thousands of years past, and is now recognized by occultists of the present day, that the nature of his being needs to remain unknown throughout his youth until the time of the birth of the intellectual soul, indeed even until the birth of the consciousness soul, and that he will come into his own with the help of nobody but himself.

Any true occultist would find it strange for a Buddha to appear in the twentieth century, as every occultist knows that he can only come five thousand years after Gautama Buddha. However a bodhisattva can and will be incarnated.

It is part of an occultist's basic armoury to know that the Maitreya Buddha will be unknown in his youth. That is why I have been emphasizing for years that we should bear this principle of occultism in mind: before a certain age nobody should be obliged by any central office or organization to speak about occult matters. I have stressed this for years.

When younger people speak, they may do this for good reasons, but they do not do it as an occult duty.

The Maitreya Buddha will make himself known through his own power. He will appear in such a way that he can receive no help except from the power of his own soul being.

To approach true theosophy, understanding for the whole of earth evolution is a necessity. Those who do not develop this understanding will destroy the life of the modern theosophical movement.[10]

The Christ Impulse and Historical Development

2. Locarno, 19 September 1911

I am very happy to be speaking to you today—among these peaceful mountains and within view of that wonderful lake—about matters appealing to our deepest interests, that is, revelations, realities of the life of the spirit. And the most obvious fact that strikes those of us who have gathered here today to visit our Alpine friends, is this: that a number of our friends have withdrawn up here, not necessarily for the sake of solitude, but at least for the peace and charm of the mountains. And if they ask themselves what their hearts are looking for, they might find that it is something very similar to man's present-day longing for the spirit. And perhaps it is no illusion to assume that in the wider world the same impulse is at work as the one that has spurred people on to come up here into the solitude of the mountains.

Man knows, or senses dimly, that there is spirituality in all that surrounds us in nature, in forest and crag, wind and storm; the kind of spirituality which, according to a well-known Western figure, is more consistent than man's actions, feelings and thinking. We cannot help sensing that in everything that surrounds us as forest and crag, mountain and lake, the spirit is coming to expression. And in spiritual science we become more and more aware that there is spirit in everything that expresses itself in nature round about us and in the firm earth beneath us. Looking back into the ancient past we can tell ourselves that we descend from a spiritual past and are the children of ancient times. Just as we create our works of art, exploring what we can make of the material to hand, in just such a way did our ancestors create their implements and tools. And the phenomena of nature are the product of the work of the ancient gods in times long past. And if we permeate ourselves with such a feeling, the whole of nature will gradually become for us what it has always been for spiritual knowledge through the ages. Even though it will seem a maya, it will become the kind of maya that is beautiful and great, for the very reason that it is divine-spiritual creation. So when we go out into nature we are among memorials reminding us of the spiritual activity that took place in ancient, pre-earthly times. Then we are filled with that tremendous enthusiasm that deepens our feeling for nature and can fill us with warmth.

When we can enhance our feeling for nature through spiritual science we should also feel that it is in a certain respect a privilege to dwell within the spirit of nature. And it *is* a privilege. For we can and ought to bear in mind how many people there are who are unable to get close to the creations of nature in their present incarnation. How many people there are today, especially in cities, who no longer have the chance of feeling the uplifting quality of the divine in nature! And when we look at nature with a power of observation enhanced by spiritual science, then we know the intimate connection that exists between what we feel for nature and what we call morality—moral life being the highest thing we can strive for in this life.

It is a paradox perhaps, but it is true to say that those people who live in towns and have to forget what oats, wheat and barley look like, unfortunately get separated in their hearts, too, from the deepest moral sources of their existence. If we bear this in mind, then we will certainly regard it as a privilege to be able to be close to the sources of nature's spirit, for a feeling like this of itself leads to another which, supported by spiritual science, must become known in the world: that is, the truth of reincarnation. To begin with we take it on trust, this truth concerning man's repeated earth lives. But how can a soul retain composure at the present time, when it sees what very different paths of life people tread, and experiences all the glaring but inevitable inequalities in the world? The human being who is privileged to be near the well-springs of nature, not only feels that he has every reason to be happy in knowing the truths of spiritual science, but also feels a great responsibility, a great obligation towards this knowledge of the spirit. For what is the greatest thing that these souls will be able to bring to the gate of death, these souls who today have the privilege of enjoying peace and health in nature? What will be their finest contribution?

If we look for a moment at what is taught us by the spiritual powers that are closer to us now than they were in the nineteenth century, what can we learn? We can learn, without any doubt, that we can take something different with us into our following incarnations, in our deepest soul, in our deepest feeling, if we imbue ourselves with spiritual science, than we could if we kept aloof from it. Nowadays we are certainly not expected to take what spiritual science can give us as an abstract theory. What your souls receive, what enters into you as theory, is there so that it can come alive in you. *WHERE ARE WE GOING WITH THIS* And this happens with some people in this incarnation and with others in the next. It will become real, immediate life, the life we cannot conceive of unless we devote ourselves to that prophetic vision which prompts us to ask: Where does this development lead? With all its fruits it leads straight into outer life. And what we can only express in the form of words today, will become vision, vision in the young, vision in the old, vision that brings blessing.

All those people who have not yet been able to approach the warmth and light of spiritual science and to acquire the fruits of spiritual science for themselves, will feel the blessing of such vision! Everything that can exist in the way of outer personality will in the future have that fire in it for which our present-day theories are the fuel. It is just a handful of people who have the will to be the real bearers of what, in the future, will have to reach all those who are in need of it, that is the real, genuine fruits of human love and human compassion. We do not study spiritual science for the sake of our own satisfaction but so that we can acquire gentle hands that have the power to bless, and gentle eyes whose look alone works upon others, so that we can give out all that springs forth from the eyes, all that we call spiritual vision. Those people in particular who have this attitude, and who have the good fortune to live so close to nature should pay heed right now to the way everything is changing at present! It *is* changing, in fact it is changing throughout the cosmos.

It is wrong to say nature makes no leaps. Nature is perpetually making leaps, from leaf to blossom, from blossom to fruit. When the chick develops out of the egg, that is a leap. To say that nature makes no leaps could not be further from the truth. There are leaps everywhere, sudden transitions. And we are living in such a time of transition. During our lifetime there has been a year of great importance:[11] the year 1899. The turn of the twentieth century is significant for the whole of cultural development because it is the time when the stream that came from the East and mingled with Western culture ceased in order to make way for what can be drawn from the life of nature to enliven the deepest levels of our life of soul.

Those whose spirit is awakened will be able to see beings of a new order in the processes of nature. The human being who has not yet become clairvoyant will increasingly be able to experience that despite all his melancholy feelings concerning all that continually dies away there is something of a rejuvenating quality in nature. The human being, though, whose clairvoyant faculties have awakened, will see new elemental beings issuing out of dying nature. Whilst in outer physical nature relatively little will be seen of the great change at the turn of the twentieth century, the spiritually awakened soul will feel: times are changing, and we human beings have the task of preparing spirit knowledge. It will become more and more important to observe such things and carry them in our consciousness. For people are free either to take up such things for the salvation of humanity or to pass them by, which will lead to disaster.

That is to say, at the turn of the century a relatively new kingdom of nature-beings will come to life, arising from nature like a spiritual spring, and human beings will be able to see and experience this. And, though it would show great apathy of soul if a person were unable to perceive the sprouting forth of springtime, there is still more than this to come. Those people who will grow able to experience as a fact of nature what has just been described, will preserve these impressions in quite a different way than through ordinary memory. They will carry beyond the threshold what streams towards them in the form of new elemental spirits, as the seeds carry their life through the winter into spring. What was experienced in spring and what was experienced in autumn, this bursting forth of nature in the spring and this melancholy in autumn, had no connection one with the other in the past. What issues from the memory of the cosmos enables us to carry over something of what we have experienced in the autumn into the spring. If we let the elemental forces of autumn work in us, then we can feel in a new way what will be given us in the future. Everything will acquire something new in the future, and it is our duty to prepare ourselves through our knowledge of the spirit to understand it. For spiritual science has not come into the world through the personal whims of human beings, but because new things are happening in the heavens, that can only be perceived when people take up the results of spiritual research. This is why the theosophical movement has come into being.

In moral life it is the same as it is in nature: the life of the soul will experience a transformation. Certain things will happen of which people have as yet no idea. I would just like to mention one example. There will be more and more people, especially children, who will have the experience that when they intend doing something or other in the future, a voice will speak in their souls urging them to be still and listen to what is to be told them from the spiritual world. Something will come to meet them, appearing before their eyes like a vision. First of all they will be strangely touched by these visions. When they have made a greater contact with spiritual science they will then realize that they are seeing the karmic counterpart of the deeds they have just done. The soul is being shown: you must strive to take yourself in hand so that you can take part in future evolution. And it is also being shown that there is no such thing as a deed without consequence. And this will be a driving force bringing order into our moral life. Moral impulses will be planted in our souls like a karma, in the course of time, if we prepare ourselves to open our spiritual eyes and our spiritual ears to what can speak to us from the spiritual world.

We know that it will take a long time before people learn to see in spirit. But it will begin in the twentieth century, and a greater and greater number of people will acquire this capacity in the course of three thousand years. Humanity will devote itself to such things during the next three millennia. In order that these things can happen, however, the main streams of development—again directed by beings who oversee the spiritual guidance of humanity—will take their course in such a way that human beings will be able to come to an understanding of occult life as I have described it today.

There are two main streams. The first is known through the fact that there is a so-called school of Western philosophy, and that the most elementary concepts of the spiritual world arise from the purest depths of philosophy. And it is remarkable what we see when we make a survey of what has gradually taken place within the science of Western culture. We see how some people become purely intellectual, whilst others are rooted in the religious life, yet at the same time are filled with what can only be given through vision of the spiritual world underlying all existence. On all sides we see spiritual life flowing out of Western philosophy. I will only mention Vladimir Soloviev,[12] the Russian philosopher and thinker, a real clairvoyant, though he only saw into the spiritual world three times in his life: once when he was a boy of nine, the second time in the British Museum, and the third time in the Egyptian desert under the starry heavens of Egypt. On these occasions there was revealed to him what can only be seen by clairvoyant vision. He had a prevision of the evolution of humanity. There welled up in him what Schelling[13] and Hegel[14] also achieved through sheer spiritual effort. They stood alone on the heights of thinking, and so we may now place them on the summit which all educated people will eventually reach. All this has come to expression in the course of previous centuries, particularly the last four centuries. When we survey this and work on it with the methods of practical occultism, as has been done recently in order to make a special investigation into what purely intellectual thinkers from Hegel to Haeckel[15] have worked out, we can see occult forces at work here too. And a very remarkable thing comes to light: we can speak of pure inspiration in the case of just those people who appear to have least of it. Who inspired all the thinkers who are rooted in pure intellectualism? Who gave the stimulus for this life of thought that speaks out of every book to be found even in the lowliest cottage? Where does all this abstract thought-life in Europe come from, that has had such a remarkable outcome?

We all know, of course, how the following great event took place. An important individuality in the evolution of mankind, one of the individualities that we call a bodhisattva, incarnated in the royal house of Suddhodana. We all know that this individuality was destined to ascend to the next rank after that of bodhisattva. Each human being who progresses and reaches the rank of bodhisattva must become a Buddha in his final incarnation. What does this rank of Buddha signify? What does it signify in the case of the particular bodhisattva who attained the rank of Buddha as Gautama Buddha? It signifies that Buddha—as with every other Buddha—does not need to incarnate on earth any more in a body of flesh. And therefore Gautama Buddha was destined, like every Buddha, to work henceforth from the spiritual world. He must not appear again on the earth in physical form, but his achievements in the course of incarnations enabled him henceforth to send his influence into our civilization.

The first great deed that the Buddha had to accomplish as a purely spiritual being was, as I indicated in Basle,[16] to send his forces down into the astral body of the Jesus boy described in the Luke Gospel, which came to significant expression in the Christmas message: Divine beings are revealing themselves in the heights, and peace shall come to men of good will on earth.

If our souls are stirred by this message that angel beings hovered in the aureole above the angelic child, we should know that in this aura around Jesus the forces of the Nirmanakaya[17] of the Buddha were active. Since then, the spiritual forces of the Buddha have been incorporated in the highest individualities involved in the events of which the Mystery of Golgotha speaks. His forces thus work also in the world view of western philosophers. He himself is the driving force working out of the spiritual world, stimulating a life that has penetrated as far as intelligence and has then gone astray.

If we read Leibniz,[18] Schelling and Soloviev today, and ask ourselves how they have been inspired, we find that it was by the individuality who was born in the palace of Suddhodana, ascended from bodhisattva to Buddha and then continued to work selflessly. In fact he continued to work in such a selfless way that we can go back in time today to a point when not even the name of Buddha was mentioned in the West. You do not find the name of the bodhisattva who became Buddha, not even in Goethe! You know, though, that he lives in everything. He has met with so much understanding that he works on unnamed in Western literature. The Middle Ages knew about this, too, but did not speak about it in this way then. They tell us something different.

In the eighth century there lived a man called John of Damascus[19] who wrote a book in the form of a narrative. What was it about? He relates that there once lived a great teacher who became the teacher of Josaphat, instructing Josaphat in the secret doctrine and the great Christian truths. And if you investigate all this you find truths concerning those things. You also find narratives from Buddhist literature. When we follow up our theme we come upon a legend, the one that relates that Buddha went on living, not in an earthly human form but in an animal form, that of a hare. And when a Brahman once happened to find a hare—which was the disguised Buddha—the Brahman complained to him about the misery of mankind outside in the world, and Buddha made a fire and roasted himself, in order to help mankind. The Brahman took him and transported him to the moon. When you know that the moon is the symbol of eternal wisdom, which lives in the human breast, then you see there is a consciousness of Buddha's sacrifice, which has been developed and presented in these old legends.

What is Buddha's task out there in the spiritual world? It is his task now and for evermore to kindle those forces in our hearts that can give birth to great wisdom. This is how we must understand one force streaming through our world; it is the Buddha force. It is also represented in the form it has taken in our century, even though here it has been reduced to abstraction. We have to try, however, to understand the occult significance of every spiritual form. Alongside this force is the other one, whose source was the Mystery of Golgotha, and which combined with the Buddha force to make a necessary whole. Of this force too we must partake in earthly life. This force, emanating from Golgotha, with which all people have to connect themselves, not only affects man's inner life but involves our whole earthly existence.

Whilst the Buddha stream, like any other such stream, concerns all of us as human beings, in the case of the Christ Being we have a cosmic intervention. All bodhisattvas are individualities who go through life here on earth, who belong to the earth. The Christ individuality comes from the sun, and walked the earth for the first time at the baptism in the Jordan, dwelling in the physical body of Jesus of Nazareth for only three years. The uniqueness of the Christ individuality was that He was destined to work for only three years in the earthly world. He is the same being to whom Zarathustra referred when he called Him Ahura Mazda, He who is behind the visible sun, the same whom the Holy Rishis announced, and whom the Greeks spoke of as the being behind the pleroma. This is the being who has gradually become the spirit of our earth, the aura of our earth, since His blood flowed on Golgotha. The first person to whom it was granted to see Him without witnessing the physical event, was Paul.

Thus through the Mystery of Golgotha something took place that has brought a completely new course of events into our earthly evolution. Before that time, the greatest variety of concepts could be assimilated through all the different religions. What crossed over from the Buddha religion, when the being of Buddha streamed into the astral aura of Jesus, and what I told you concerning the soul seeing and feeling new things in nature, means nothing short of this: that just as the Christ being descended into a physical body through the Jordan baptism, dwelt within it until the Mystery of Golgotha, and was therefore here physically on the physical plane, He will now, in the same way, begin working in the etheric world. So we can speak of a physical incarnation from the time of the baptism by John until Golgotha; and now of an etheric reappearance.

The etheric Christ will come to be perceived through the development of the etheric body, and also through impressions of autumn which the human being weaves into himself. Why was Christ here in a physical body? It was so that man could evolve further in order increasingly to acquire the capacity to perceive the Christ in the etheric.

To sum up: we began this lecture with the elemental spirits manifesting in nature. We continued with those particular visions that impel us to pause in our actions and listen to the inner word. And in all these occurrences, grouping themselves round a central point, we see that those human beings who find the right path to the spiritual world—and this does not mean trained clairvoyants, who have always been able to find the Christ, but human beings on their natural path of development—will be able to see the Christ as an etheric vision: see Him who will only take part in world events from the etheric realm. We see that all these occurrences group themselves around the future Christ event. And if we look at the whole of spiritual development in its progressive stages, we see that the Buddha who sacrificed himself in the fire of love is the inspirer of our spiritual science.

Those people who give careful thought to reading such books as *The Soul's Probation*,[20] which I was able to have performed in Munich, and who become aware of where all the mysterious forces lie that tell us of what surrounds us in nature, and who also pay heed to the wisdom of the future— even if the wisdom of the future is often the folly of the present, as the wisdom of the present is often the folly of the future—these people will become aware that there will be a kind of chemistry pervaded by the Christ impulse, and a kind of botany pervaded by the Christ impulse, and so on. The world does not consist of lifeless molecules. All that is spread out in nature comes from the spirit. Even a flower is an etheric being, and on the other hand the spirit has entered the earth from outside through this flower. In all the forms that spring forth out of the earth we can see meaning of the highest order. Then we shall not only know by faith, but we shall understand.

Thus we have conjured up the second stream which has to unite with the first. The coming years will bring many surprises to the earth. In everything that will occur in this way we shall be able to see the Christ principle, whilst we shall become aware of the Buddha impulse in a more inward way. This is why, unless we have an understanding of those sublime measures through which the world is spiritually guided, we shall not see clearly how to seek the Christ impulse, nor perceive that it is He who, in the course of history, develops one individuality from another. What is it that slakes the thinking man's thirst for knowledge in the sort of phenomenon found in the West, where all thinking is expressed more in the style of—let us say Galileo, to name an example—or again, in the East, where it is expressed in the manner of Vladimir Soloviev? When we see what it is, we acknowledge how objectively the Christ works. Similarly, we can see the Christ impulse in everything that happens outside in the world.

Great things will happen in the next epochs of culture. What only arose as a dream[21] of the great martyr Socrates in the fourth epoch, will become reality. What was this mighty impulse of Socrates? He wanted anyone experiencing a moral precept and understanding it so thoroughly that it becomes one with his feeling to be a moral person also, carrying his morality into his actions. Consider what a long way from this we still are, what a lot of people can say: such and such *must* happen—but how few have the inner power, the moral strength to do it! Moral principles will have to be so clearly understood and moral feelings so positively developed that we cannot inwardly know something without having the impulse to carry it out enthusiastically. For this really to mature in the human soul, so that a moral impulse does not stop at the stage of understanding, but has inevitably to become a deed, people will have to live their way into these two particular streams. Then, under the influence of the two streams, human beings will develop in increasing numbers who are capable of carrying feeling for, and recognition of morality through into action.

How can it come about that these two streams unite in humanity so that through Buddha the Christ can be taken up from within? Through the fact that the position of bodhisattva has never been left empty. As soon as the bodhisattva became Buddha, another attained to the rank of bodhisattva. And this was the particular individuality who is known to have lived as an Essene about a hundred years before Jesus of Nazareth. This individuality has been sadly slandered and misunderstood, by the writer Celsus,[22] for example, and particularly by Haeckel in his *Riddles of the World*. He was the one who carried out his task a full hundred years before the Mystery of Golgotha, and is known as Jeshu ben Pandira, one of the incarnations of the bodhisattva succeeding the bodhisattva Gautama who became Buddha. He will continue to work as a bodhisattva until three thousand years have gone by, and then, when about five thousand years have taken their course after the Buddha became enlightened under the bodhi tree, he will become a Buddha also. Every serious occultist knows that five thousand years after the enlightenment of Gautama Buddha under the bodhi tree that individuality who lives on as bodhisattva will have become Maitreya Buddha. He will have incarnated frequently before that time comes. And then, when the five thousand years are over, a teaching will arise that will be the teaching of Maitreya Buddha, Buddha of the Good, where the spoken word works at the same time morally. Words are not powerful enough at the present time to describe the reality of this. It can only be perceived in the spiritual world, and human beings will first of all have to be mature enough to receive it. What will be special about the Maitreya Buddha is that he will have to repeat in a certain way what took place at the event of Golgotha.

We know that the Buddha individuality entered into Jesus of Nazareth and now only works into earth evolution from outside. All those individuals who live as bodhisattvas and will later on become Buddhas have the particular destiny on earth, as every serious occultist can see, of being in a certain respect unknown in their youth. Those who do know something of them may see them as gifted people, but do not see that the being of the bodhisattva is working in them. It has always been like this, and it will be like this in the twentieth century too. It will only become recognizable during the time that lies between their thirtieth and the thirty-third year—the same span of time as there was between the baptism in Jordan and Golgotha. Then a change takes place in the human being, and to a certain degree he sacrifices his individuality and becomes the vehicle for another, as the Jesus individuality made way for the Christ.

The bodhisattva incarnations, which are those of the future Maitreya Buddha, occur in unknown people. They work as individuals relying on their own inner strength. The Maitreya Buddha will also work out of his own inner strength, and against the stream of general opinion. He will remain unknown in his youth. And when in his thirtieth year he has sacrificed his individuality, he will appear in such a way that morality will work through his words. Five thousand years after the Buddha was enlightened beneath the bodhi tree his successor will ascend to the rank of Buddha, and will be the bringer of the word that works morally. We now say: 'In the beginning was the Word'. We shall then be able to say: 'In the Maitreya Buddha the greatest teacher has been given us, and he has appeared in order to make apparent to human beings the full extent of the Christ Event. His unique quality will be that he, the greatest of teachers, will be the bringer of the most exalted Word.'

As it happens so often that great things that should be brought into the world in the right way are so badly misunderstood, we must try to prepare ourselves for what should come. And if we want to approach the spirit at the point where the spirit of nature also speaks to us morally, then we may say to ourselves: all spiritual science is in a certain respect a preparation to help us understand what has been said in relation to that Event at the turning point of time.

New times were dawning when John proclaimed the Christ. In a certain sense we can also speak today of new times, in preparation for which it is necessary for our hearts to change. Despite all the machinery of civilization that will appear in the outside world, human hearts must change so that souls care about the spiritual world making itself known in a new way at this precise time in which we live. Whether a glimpse of it will become visible here in this life, or at the gate of death, or at a new birth—we shall not only see this new world but work through and out of this new world. And the best that is often in us will come to realization because, from beyond the gates of death, beings send these forces into us from the other world. And we shall also be able to send these forces, if we go through the gate of death having acquired what we recognize to be the necessary changes for our time, about which I have permitted myself to speak to you today.

Buddha and Christ. The Sphere of the Bodhisattvas

Milan, 21 September 1911

Today I want to speak of certain facts belonging essentially to the ethical and moral domain, that help us to understand the mission of spiritual science in our time.

We are all deeply convinced of the great truth of reincarnation, and so must realize that this repetition of earthly lives has its own good purpose in the evolution of the earth. Occult research answers the question as to why we reincarnate by saying that our experiences differ in each of the epochs in which we are reborn on the earth. In incarnations immediately following the Atlantean catastrophe the experiences of the human soul were entirely different from those of later pre-Christian epochs and in our own age.

I need only briefly mention that in the times directly after the Atlantean catastrophe, souls were endowed with a certain elementary clairvoyance in the bodies they then inhabited. This clairvoyance, once a natural faculty in man, was gradually lost, mainly as a result of the conditions prevailing during the Graeco-Roman epoch of culture. Since then, man has developed in such a way that great progress has been achieved on the physical plane, and during the course of the present post-Atlantean epoch clairvoyance will gradually be re-acquired.

We are living in the fifth post-Atlantean epoch of culture. The ancient Indian was the first, the ancient Persian the second, the Babylonian-Chaldean the third and the Graeco-Roman the fourth. The sixth and seventh epochs will follow our own, at which time another great catastrophe will befall the earth and humanity as was the case at the end of the Atlantean epoch.

Occult research is able to indicate the characteristic trend of human evolution in each of these post-Atlantean epochs of civilization, including the fifth, sixth and seventh. The essential characteristic of our present fifth epoch is the development of intellect and reason. The main characteristic of the sixth will be that definite feelings regarding what is moral and what is immoral will arise in human souls. Delicate feelings of sympathy will be aroused by compassionate, kindly deeds and feelings of antipathy by malicious actions. Nobody today has the faintest conception of the intensity of these feelings.

In the seventh epoch the moral life will be still further deepened. Whereas in the sixth epoch man will take pleasure in good and noble actions, in the seventh the natural outcome of such pleasure will be a moral impulse. In other words, there will be a firm resolve to do what is moral. There is a great difference between taking pleasure in a moral action and the *doing* of it. So we can say that our own epoch is the epoch of intellectualism; the essential characteristic of the following epoch will be aesthetic pleasure in good, and aesthetic displeasure in evil; the seventh will be characterized by an active moral life.

Today only the seeds of what will become part of mankind in future epochs are contained in the human soul and it can be said that all these intellectual aptitudes or predispositions in man leading to feelings of sympathy or antipathy toward moral impulses, aroused by certain actions, are related to the higher worlds. Every moral action has a definite connection with the higher worlds. Our intellectual aptitudes have a supersensible connection with the astral plane. Our sympathies and antipathies for good or evil are connected with the sphere of lower devachan, and the domain of moral impulses in the soul is connected with higher devachan. Hence, we can also say that in our present age it is mainly the forces of the astral world that penetrate the human soul and take effect there. In the sixth epoch it will be the forces of lower devachan that penetrate more deeply into the soul, and in the seventh, the forces of higher devachan will work with special strength into humanity.

From this it is understandable that in the preceding fourth post-Atlantean epoch it was the forces of the physical plane that exercised the strongest influence on the soul of man. That is why Greek culture was able to produce such wonderful sculptures in which the human form was given such magnificent expression on the physical plane. Conditions in that epoch were especially suitable for people to experience the Christ in a physical body. In our present fifth epoch, which will last until the fourth millenium, souls will gradually become able, from the twentieth century onward, to experience the Christ Being in an etheric form on the astral plane, just as in the fourth epoch He was visible in a physical form on the physical plane.

To understand the nature of development in the sixth epoch, it is well to consider the characteristic qualities of the soul in future incarnations. In our intellectual age today intellectuality and morality are practically separate spheres in the life of the soul. It is quite possible for someone to be clever and at the same time immoral or, vice versa, to be deeply moral and anything but clever.

In the fourth epoch the future juxtaposition of morality and intellectuality was prophetically foreseen by the Hebrews. They endeavoured to bring about an artificial harmony between morality and intellectuality, whereas among the Greeks it was a more natural matter of course. Today we can learn from the Akashic Records how the leaders of the ancient Hebrews strove to establish this harmony between intellectuality and morality. They wore symbols, which they understood so profoundly that when they concentrated their attention on them, making themselves receptive to their influences, a certain harmony was established between what was good in a moral sense and what was wise. The ancient Hebrew priests wore these symbols on their breast-plates. The symbol for morality was called Urim, and for wisdom, Thummim.[23] When a Hebrew priest wanted to learn whether or not a certain action was both good and wise, he made himself receptive to the forces of Urim and Thummim, with the result that a certain harmony between morality and intellectuality was induced. Magical effects were produced by means of these symbols and a magical link thus established with the spiritual world. Our task in future incarnations is to achieve through inner development of the soul the effect that in earlier times was produced by means of these symbols.

Let us think once again of the fifth, sixth and seventh post-Atlantean epochs in order to grasp the way in which intellectuality, aestheticism and morality will come to expression in man's soul life.

In the present fifth epoch intellectuality can remain unimpaired even if no pleasure is taken in moral actions. In the sixth epoch it will be quite different in that from about the third millennium onward, immorality will have a paralysing effect on intellectuality. The mental abilities of someone who is intellectual and at the same time immoral will definitely deteriorate and this condition will become gradually more pronounced as man evolves. A person who has no morals will then have no intellectual power since this will depend entirely on moral actions. In the seventh epoch, cleverness without morality will be non-existent.

It will be well to consider here the nature of moral forces in souls in their present incarnations. How can it be that at our stage of evolution a person can become immoral? It is because in earlier incarnations we have gradually descended into the physical sensory world. The more forcefully the impulses belonging to the descending phase of evolution work upon a soul, the more immoral it tends to become. This fact is confirmed by an interesting finding of occult research. You know that when we pass through the gate of death we lay aside our physical and etheric bodies and for a short time have a retrospective view of our past life on earth. A kind of sleep then ensues and after a few months or perhaps years we waken on the astral plane in kamaloka. The earthly life just departed is lived over again in backward order, three times as fast. At the beginning of this life in kamaloka everyone undergoes a significant experience. Most Europeans or, speaking generally, people of modern civilization experience this as follows.

At the beginning of life in kamaloka a spiritual individuality shows us a kind of register of our transgressions, in which is inscribed everything we have done out of selfish motives. The more concretely you picture this experience, the better. At the beginning of the kamaloka period it is actually as though an individual were presenting you with the record of your physical life. The important fact, for which, naturally, there can be no further proof because it can be confirmed only by occult experience, is that the majority of Europeans recognize this individual to be Moses. This has been known to rosicrucian research since the Middle Ages and it has been confirmed in recent years by very painstaking, delicate investigations. You can gather from this that at the beginning of life in kamaloka one feels a great responsibility toward the pre-Christian powers inasmuch as they have drawn us downward. The powers and forces that draw us upward again to the spiritual world fall into two categories. The one path is that of wisdom, the other that of morality.

The forces to which intellectual progress is mainly due all proceed from the impulse given by a great individuality of the fourth post-Atlantean epoch who is known to all of you, namely Gautama Buddha. It is a remarkable discovery of spiritual investigation to find that the most penetrating and significant thoughts conceived in our present epoch originated with Gautama Buddha. This is all the more remarkable inasmuch as his name was almost unknown in the West before Schopenhauer's[24] time, by no means long ago.

As we know, Siddartha, the son of King Suddhodana, rose from the rank of a bodhisattva to that of Buddha when he was twenty-nine years old. An individual who has been raised to Buddhahood does not incarnate again on earth in a physical body. The bodhisattva individuality who became Buddha five or six centuries before the Christian era has not reincarnated, nor can he incarnate again in a physical body. Instead, he sends his forces down from the higher, supersensible worlds, inspiring all those cultured individuals who are not yet permeated by the Christ impulse.

Consciousness of this truth was demonstrated in a beautiful legend written by John of Damascus in the eighth century and well-known throughout Europe in the Middle Ages. This legend of Barlaam and Josaphat related how the successor of Buddha, Josaphat, whose name is a phonetic variation of bodhisattva, received instructions from Barlaam about the Christ impulse. The legend was subsequently forgotten but it told how the bodhisattva who succeeded Gautama Buddha was instructed by Barlaam, and his soul was fired by the Christ impulse. In addition to the impulse of Buddha, this Christ impulse, which is connected with the future ascent of man to morality, also continued to work in man's evolution. Although Buddha's teaching is in a particular sense moral *teaching*, the Christ impulse is not a teaching but actual *power.* It works as such and to an increasing degree imbues man with moral strength.

In the fourth post-Atlantean epoch the Christ Being who descended from cosmic heights had first to appear in a physical body. In our fifth epoch the intense consolidation of intellectual forces will make it possible for human beings to behold the Christ in an etheric form. This is beginning even now in our century. From the thirties to the forties of this century onward, individuals will appear who have developed in a way that will enable them to see the etheric form of Christ, just as they saw the physical Christ at the time of Jesus of Nazareth. During the next three thousand years those able to behold the etheric Christ will steadily increase until, about three thousand years from now, a plentiful number of human beings on earth will not need gospels or such records. They will possess in their own soul lives an actual vision of the Christ.

We must clearly understand that in the fourth post-Atlantean epoch people were only capable of beholding the physical Christ and so He came in a physical body. In our own epoch and on into the third millenium they will gradually become able to behold the etheric Christ. He will never come again in a physical body.

If we bear in mind the fact that when a person of the present age, who has united himself deeply with the Christ impulse, passes into kamaloka and is called to account by a figure personifying a moral force, by Moses, we shall understand how a transformation of the Moses individuality can be brought about. What does Moses show us when he confronts us with the record of our sins and transgressions? He reveals the debit side of our karmas. For a soul of our epoch it is of great significance that the doctrine of karma can be comprehended through the inspiration of Buddha. The reality of the working of karma after death, however, is revealed to us by Moses of the Old Testament. As the influences of the supersensible Christ increasingly pervade human souls, the figure of Moses will be replaced after death by that of Christ Jesus. This means that human karma will be linked with Christ; Christ will unite with our karmas.

It is interesting to realize that in the teachings of Buddha, karma is an abstract matter having an impersonal character. In the future incarnations of human beings, as Christ comes into ever closer connection with karma, it will acquire the quality of *being*, that is, of potential life.

Our earlier stages of evolution, our lives in the past, may be related to the words *Ex Deo nascimur.*[25] If we direct our development in such a way that we meet Christ after death instead of Moses, Christ with whom our karmas are then united, we can express it in the words used in rosicrucian Christianity since the thirteenth century, *In Christo morimur.*

Buddhahood can be attained only on the physical plane. The qualification for meeting Christ in death can likewise be acquired by the human soul only on the physical plane. A Buddha is first a bodhisattva and rises to the rank of Buddha during a physical incarnation. It is then no longer necessary for him to return to the earth. Understanding of Christ in the sense just explained can be acquired only on the physical plane. Hence, during the next three thousand years people will have to acquire in the physical world the power to behold the supersensible Christ. It is the mission of the spiritual science movement to create, first of all, the conditions that make understanding of Christ possible on the physical plane, and then to make possible the power to behold Him.

If on the physical plane we have acquired the capacity to behold Christ, we can then do so while living in a physical body or when we are between death and a new birth. Let us suppose, for example, that someone died before it was possible to behold Christ in His present etheric form. Nevertheless, if during his life in the physical world he had acquired the necessary understanding, vision of the Christ would be possible for him between death and rebirth. Someone, however, who keeps aloof from spiritual life and acquires no understanding of Christ will have to wait until his next incarnation to acquire it.

What has just been said will indicate that as humanity lives on through the fifth, sixth and seventh epochs of civilization, the Christ impulse will gain increasing power on the earth. We have heard that in the sixth epoch intellectuality will be impaired by immorality. The other aspect is that someone who has paralysed his intellectual faculty as a result of immorality must turn to Christ with all the greater determination so that He may imbue him with the moral strength to return to morality.

What I have told you here has been carefully investigated by rosicrucians ever since the thirteenth century. It is a truth, however, that has always been known to many occultists. If it were to be asserted that Christ could appear again on earth in a physical body, it would, according to occultism, be equivalent to asserting that a pair of scales works more efficiently when supported at two points rather than one. The three years of Christ's life on earth in the body of Jesus of Nazareth truly constitutes the fulcrum of earth evolution. Just as there can be only one point at which the scale-beam is attached, so there can be only one fulcrum of earth evolution.

The teaching of moral development is not the same as the impulse for such development. Before the Event of Golgotha occurred, the bodhisattva who is the successor to Buddha was incarnated on earth to teach and prepare those around him for that Event. He incarnated in the personality of Jeshu ben Pandira one century before the birth of Jesus of Nazareth. Thus we must distinguish between the Jeshu ben Pandira incarnation of the bodhisattva who succeeded Gautama

Buddha, and the incarnation of Jesus of Nazareth who for three years was permeated by the cosmic being we call the Christ. This bodhisattva who incarnated in Jeshu ben Pandira, and also in others, returns repeatedly. About three thousand years hence he will attain Buddhahood and, as the Maitreya Buddha, will live through his final incarnation.

The Christ individuality was on earth in the body of Jesus of Nazareth for only three years and will not come again in a physical body. In the fifth post-Atlantean epoch He will come in an etheric body, in the sixth, in an astral body, and in the seventh, in a mighty cosmic ego that will be like a great group soul of humanity. When a person dies, his physical, etheric and astral bodies fall away from him, and his ego passes over to the next incarnation. It is exactly the same with the earth. What is physical in our earth falls away at the end of the earth period and human souls in their totality pass over into the Jupiter condition, the next planetary embodiment. Just as the ego of an individual person is the centre of his further evolution, so for the whole of future humanity the Christ ego in human astral and etheric bodies goes on to ensoul the Jupiter existence. So we see how, starting from physical existence on earth, the Christ gradually evolves as etheric Christ, astral Christ and ego Christ to become the spirit of the earth who then rises to even higher stages together with all mankind.

What are we doing when we profess spiritual science today but teaching what Oriental wisdom so clearly proclaimed when the bodhisattva, the son of King Suddhodana, attained Buddhahood. The realization was expressed in those Oriental teachings that it was the task of the next bodhisattva, who would also eventually become a Buddha, to spread over the earth the knowledge that would reveal Christ to us in His true light. Thus the bodhisattva who incarnated in Jeshu ben Pandira and in others became the great teacher of the Christ impulse. This is clearly indicated in the legend of Barlaam and Josaphat that tells how Josaphat, the bodhisattva, is instructed by Barlaam, the Christian teacher. Oriental occult teachings call this bodhisattva who will become the Maitreya Buddha, 'the Bringer of the Good'. We know from occult investigations that the power of the Word will be present in Maitreya Buddha in a degree which people today can as yet have no conception of. Through higher clairvoyant perception of the process of world evolution it is possible to discover how the Maitreya Buddha will teach three thousand years from now. Much of his teaching can also be expressed in symbolic forms. But because mankind today is insufficiently mature, it is not yet possible to speak words such as those that will come from the lips of the Maitreya Buddha.

In the Eightfold Path, Gautama Buddha gave the great intellectual teachings of right speech, right thinking, right action, etc. The words of the Maitreya Buddha will contain a magic power that will become *moral impulses* in those who hear them. Should there be a gospel telling of the Maitreya Buddha, it would have to use different words than those used by Christ in the Gospel of St. John, 'And the Word was made *Flesh*.' The evangelist of the Maitreya Buddha would have to testify, 'And the Flesh was made *Word*.'

The pronouncements of the Maitreya Buddha will be permeated in a miraculous way with the power of Christ. Occult investigations today show that in a certain respect even the external life of the Maitreya Buddha will be patterned on the life of Christ. When in ancient times a great individuality appeared who was to become a teacher of humanity, it was indicated by signs, special talents and qualities of soul evident in his early youth. But there is also a different development in which a complete change in personality becomes apparent at a certain point in life. In such instances, when the individual has reached a certain age his ego is removed from his bodily sheaths and is replaced by another. Jesus is the most outstanding example of this development, in that, in his thirtieth year, the Christ individuality took possession of him. All the incarnations of the bodhisattva who will become the Maitreya Buddha have shown that in this sense his life, too, will resemble that of Christ.

It is never known during the childhood or youth of an individual that he will become a bodhisattva at the age of thirty or thereabouts. Also, whenever a bodhisattva reaches Buddhahood there is evidence that at the age of thirty or thirty-one another individuality takes possession of his body. Such a bodhisattva will never reveal himself in his early youth, but in his thirtieth or thirty-first year he will manifest quite different qualities because another being has taken possession of his body. Other individualities who will not incarnate as children but who will take possession of the personality of some human being in this way are, for example, Moses, Abraham and Ezekiel.

Today it is the same in the case of the bodhisattva who, in three thousand years, will become the Maitreya Buddha. It would be sheer occult dilettantism to assert that this being would be recognizable in his early years as the bodhisattva, but between his thirtieth and thirty-first years he will reveal himself through his own power without having to be proclaimed by others. He will convince the world through his own power and if he were alleged by some to reveal himself in someone under the age of thirty, that fact alone would be evidence of the fallacy of such a statement. Claims like this have frequently been made. In the seventeenth century, for example, Shabbetai Tzevi in Smyrna proclaimed himself to be an incarnation of the messiah or Christ. Hosts of people from all over Europe made pilgrimages to him in Smyrna.

It is certainly true that today there is a rooted disinclination to recognize genius in people. But, on the other hand, the sort of mental laziness is prevalent which leads to people being only too ready to acknowledge some individual or other as a great soul merely on authority. It is important for the science of the spirit to be presented in such a way as to be based to the smallest possible extent on belief in authority. Much that I have said today can be substantiated only by means of occult investigation. Yet I beg you not to give credence to these things because I say them, but to test them by everything known to you from history, and above all by what you can learn from your own experience. I am absolutely certain that the more closely you examine them, the more confirmation you will find. In this age of intellectualism I do not appeal to your belief in authority but to your capacity for intelligent examination. So let me repeat what I have already said. The bodhisattva of the twentieth century will not rely upon a herald to announce him as the future Maitreya Buddha, but upon the power of his own words; he will stand on his own feet in the world.

What has been said here may perhaps be summed up as follows. In our period of evolution two streams of spiritual life are at work. One of them is the stream of wisdom, or the Buddha stream, containing the most sublime teaching of wisdom, goodness of heart and peace on earth. To enable this teaching of Buddha to permeate the hearts of all human beings, the Christ impulse is indispensable. The second stream is the Christ stream itself that will lead humanity from intellectuality, by way of aesthetic feeling and insight, to morality. The greatest teacher of the Christ impulse will be that bodhisattva who incarnates again and again and who in three thousand years will become the Maitreya Buddha. The statement contained in Oriental chronicles is true! Exactly five thousand years after Gautama Buddha attained enlightenment under the bodhi tree, the Maitreya Buddha will incarnate on earth for the last time.

The succession of bodhisattvas and Buddhas has no relation to the cosmic being we call Christ. It was a bodhisattva, not the Christ, who incarnated in the body of Jeshu ben Pandira. Christ incarnated in a physical body only once, for a period of three years. The bodhisattva appears in every century until he becomes the Maitreya Buddha.

The mission of spiritual science today is to bring about a synthesis of religions. We can conceive of one form of religion in Buddhism, another form in Christianity. As evolution proceeds, the more closely do the different religions unite in the way that Buddha and Christ themselves are united in our hearts. This vista of the spiritual development of humanity brings home to us the need for the vitalizing impulse of spiritual science as a preparation for understanding the progress of culture and events in the great process of our evolution.

Rosicrucian Christianity

1. Neuchâtel, 27 September 1911

It gives me great joy to be here for the first time in this newly founded group bearing the great name of Christian Rosen-kreutz,[26] which gives me the opportunity for the first time of speaking about Christian Rosenkreutz at greater length. What is contained in the mystery of Christian Rosenkreutz? I cannot tell you all about this individuality in one evening, so we shall speak about Christian Rosenkreutz himself today, and tomorrow we shall talk about his work.

To speak about Christian Rosenkreutz presupposes great trust in the mysteries of spiritual life, trust not only in the person himself but in the great secrets of the life of the spirit. The founding of a new group likewise also always pre-supposes faith in spiritual life.

Christian Rosenkreutz is an individual who is active both when he is in incarnation and when he is not incarnated in a physical body; he works not only as a physical being and through physical forces, but above all spiritually, through higher forces.

As we know, man lives not only for himself but also in connection with human evolution as a whole. Usually when someone passes through death his etheric body dissolves into the cosmos. A part of this dissolving etheric body always stays intact, however, and so we are always surrounded by these remaining parts of the etheric bodies of the dead, for our good, or also to our detriment. They affect us for good or ill according to whether we ourselves are good or bad. Far-reaching effects emanate also from the etheric bodies of great individualities. Great forces emanating from the etheric body of Christian Rosenkreutz can work into our soul and also into our spirit. It is our duty to get to know these forces, for we work with them as rosicrucians.

Strictly speaking the rosicrucian movement began in the thirteenth century. At that time these forces worked extraordinarily strongly, and a Christian Rosenkreutz stream has been active in spiritual life ever since. There is a law that this spiritual stream of force has to become especially powerful every hundred years or so. This is to be seen now in the theosophical movement. Christian Rosenkreutz himself gave an indication of this in his last exoteric statements.[27]

In the year 1785 the collected esoteric revelations of the rosicrucians appeared in the work: *The Secret Symbols of the Rosicrucians*[28] by Hinricus Madathanus Theosophus.[29] In a certain limited sense this publication contains references to the rosicrucian stream active in the previous century, which was revealed for the first time in the works collected and put together by Hinricus Madathanus Theosophus. Another hundred years later we see the influence of the rosicrucian stream coming to expression again in the work of H.P. Blavatsky, especially in the book *Isis Unveiled*.[30] A considerable amount of Western occult wisdom is contained in this book that is still a long way from being improved upon, even though the composition is sometimes very confused. It is interesting to compare *The Secret Symbols of the Rosicrucians* by Hinricus Madathanus Theosophus with the works of H.P. Blavatsky. We must think especially of the first part of the publication, which is written in 'symbolic' form. In the second part Blavatsky deviates a little from the rosicrucian stream. In her later works she departs entirely from it, and we must be able to distinguish between her early and her later publications, even though something of her uncritical spirit already appears in the early ones. That this is said is no more than the wish of H.P. Blavatsky herself, who is not in incarnation now.

When we look at the characteristic quality of human consciousness in the thirteenth century we see that primitive clairvoyance had gradually disappeared. We know that in earlier times everybody had an elementary clairvoyance. In the middle of the thirteenth century this reached its lowest point, and there was suddenly no more clairvoyance. Everyone experienced a spiritual eclipse. Even the most enlightened spirits and the most highly developed individuals, including initiates, had no further access to the spiritual worlds, and when they spoke about the spiritual worlds they had to confine themselves to what remained in their memories. People only knew about the spiritual world from tradition or from those initiates who awakened their memories of what they had previously experienced. For a short time, though, even these minds could not see directly into the spiritual world.

This short period of darkness had to take place at that time to prepare for what is characteristic of our present age: today's intellectual, rational development. That is what is important today in the fifth post-Atlantean cultural epoch. In the Graeco-Roman cultural epoch the development of the intellect was not as it is today. Direct perception was the vital factor, not intellectual thinking. Human beings identified with what they saw and heard, in fact even with what they thought. They did not produce thoughts from out of themselves then as we do today, and as we ought to do, for this is the task of the fifth post-Atlantean cultural epoch. Man's clairvoyance gradually begins again after this time, and the clairvoyance of the future can now develop.

The rosicrucian stream began in the thirteenth century. During that century individuals particularly suitable for initiation had to be specially chosen. Initiation could take place only after the short period of darkness had run its course.

In a place in Europe that cannot be named yet[31]—though this will be possible in the not very distant future—a lodge of a very spiritual nature was formed comprising a council of twelve men who had received into themselves the sum of the spiritual wisdom of olden times and of their own time. Thus we are concerned with twelve men who lived in that dark era, twelve outstanding individualities, who united to help the progress of humanity. None of them could see directly into the spiritual world, but they could awaken to life in themselves memories of what they had experienced through earlier initiations. And the karma of mankind brought it about that everything that still remained to mankind of the ancient Atlantean epoch was incarnated in seven of these twelve. In my *Outline of Esoteric Science* it has already been stated that in the seven Holy Rishis of old, the teachers of the ancient Indian cultural epoch, all that was left of the Atlantean epoch was preserved. These seven men who were incarnated again in the thirteenth century, and who were part of the council of twelve, were those who could look back into the seven streams of the ancient Atlantean cultural epoch of mankind and the further course of these streams. Each of these seven individualities could bring one stream to life for their time and our present time. In addition to these seven there were another four who could not look back into times long past but could look back to the occult wisdom mankind had acquired in the four post-Atlantean epochs. The first could look back to the ancient Indian period, the second to the ancient Persian cultural period, the third to the Egyptian-Chaldean-Assyrian-Babylonian cultural period and the fourth to the Graeco-Roman culture. These four joined the seven to form a council of wise men in the thirteenth century. A twelfth had the fewest memories as it were, however he was the most intellectual among them, and it was his task to foster external science in particular. These twelve individualities not only lived in the experiences of Western occultism, but these twelve different streams of wisdom worked together to make a whole. A remarkable reference to this can be found in Goethe's poem *The Mysteries*.[32]

We shall be speaking, then, of twelve outstanding individualities. The middle of the thirteenth century is the time when a new culture began. At this time a certain low point of spiritual life had been reached. Even the most highly developed could not approach the spiritual worlds. Then it was that the council of these most spiritually advanced people assembled. These twelve men, who represented the sum of all the spiritual knowledge of their age and the twelve schools of thought, came together in a place in Europe that cannot as yet be named.

This council of the twelve only possessed clairvoyant memory and intellectual wisdom. The seven successors of the seven Rishis remembered their ancient wisdom, and the other five represented the wisdom of the five post-Atlantean cultures. Thus the twelve represented the whole of Atlantean and post-Atlantean wisdom. The twelfth was a man who attained the intellectual wisdom of his time in the highest degree. He possessed intellectually all the knowledge of his time, whilst the others, to whom direct spiritual wisdom was also then denied, acquired their knowledge by returning in memory to their earlier incarnations.

The beginning of a new culture was only possible, however, because a thirteenth came to join the twelve. The thirteenth did not become a scholar in the accepted sense of that time. He was an individuality who had been incarnated at the time of the Mystery of Golgotha. In the incarnations that followed he prepared himself for his mission through humility of soul and through a fervent life devoted to God. He was a great soul, a pious, deeply mystical human being, who had not just acquired these qualities but was born with them. If you imagine a young man who is very pious and who devotes all his time to fervent prayer to God, then you can have a picture of this thirteenth individuality. He grew up entirely under the care and instruction of the twelve, and he received as much wisdom as each one could give him. He was educated with the greatest care, and every precaution was taken to see that no one other than the twelve exercised an influence on him. He was kept apart from the rest of the world. He was a very delicate child in that incarnation of the thirteenth century, and therefore the education that the twelve bestowed upon him worked right into his physical body. Now the twelve, being deeply devoted to their spiritual tasks and inwardly permeated with Christianity, were conscious that the external Christianity of the Church was only a caricature of real Christianity. They were permeated with the greatness of Christianity, although in the outside world they were regarded as its enemies. Each individuality worked his way into just one aspect of Christianity. Their endeavour was to unite the various religions into one great whole. They were convinced that the whole of spiritual life was contained in their twelve streams, and each one influenced the pupil to the best of his ability. Their aim was to achieve a synthesis of all the religions, but they knew that this was not to be achieved by means of any theory but only through active spiritual life. And for this a suitable education of the thirteenth was essential.

Whilst the spiritual forces of the thirteenth increased beyond measure, his physical forces drained away. It came to the point when he almost ceased to have any further connection with external life, and all interest in the physical world disappeared. He lived entirely for the sake of the spiritual development which the twelve were bringing about in him. The wisdom of the twelve was reflected in him. It reached the point where the thirteenth refused to eat and wasted away. Then an event occurred that could only happen once in history. It was the kind of event that can take place when the forces of the macrocosm co-operate for the sake of what they can bring to fruition. After a few days the body of the thirteenth became quite transparent, and for days he lay as though dead. The twelve now gathered round him at certain intervals. At these moments all knowledge and wisdom flowed from their lips. Whilst the thirteenth lay as though dead, they let their wisdom flow towards him in short prayer-like formulae. The best way to imagine them is to picture the twelve in a circle round the thirteenth. This situation ended when the soul of the thirteenth awakened like a new soul. He had experienced a great transformation of soul. Within him there now existed something that was like a completely new birth of the twelve streams of wisdom, so that the twelve wise men could also learn something entirely new from the youth. His body, too, came to life now in such a way that this revival of his absolutely transparent body was beyond compare. The youth could now speak of quite new experiences. The twelve could recognize that he had experienced the event of Damascus: it was a repetition of the vision of Paul on the road to Damascus. In the course of a few weeks the thirteenth reproduced all the wisdom he had received from the twelve, but in a new form. This new form was as though given by Christ Himself. What he now revealed to them, the twelve called true Christianity, the synthesis of all the religions, and they distinguished between this true Christianity and the Christianity of the period in which they lived. The thirteenth died relatively young, and the twelve then devoted themselves to the task of recording what the thirteenth had revealed to them, in imaginations— for it could only be done in that way. Thus came the symbolic figures and images contained in the collection of Hinricus Madathanus Theosophus, and the communications of H.P. Blavatsky in the work *Isis Unveiled*. We have to see the occult process in such a way that the fruits of the initiation of the thirteenth remained as the residue of his etheric body, within the spiritual atmosphere of the earth. This residue inspired the twelve as well as their pupils who succeeded them, so that they could form the occult rosicrucian stream. Yet it continued to work as an etheric body, and it then became part of the new etheric body of the thirteenth when he incarnated again.

The individuality of the thirteenth reincarnated as early as half-way through the fourteenth century. In this incarnation he lived for over a hundred years. He was brought up in a similar way, in the circle of the pupils and successors of the twelve, but not so secluded as in his previous incarnation. When he was twenty-eight years old he conceived a remarkable ideal. He had to leave Europe and travel. First he went to Damascus, and what Paul had experienced there happened again to him. This event can be described as the fruits of what took place in the previous incarnation. All the forces of the wonderful etheric body of the individuality of the thirteenth century had remained intact, none of them dispersed after death into the general world ether. This was a permanent etheric body, remaining intact in the ether spheres thereafter. This same highly spiritual etheric body again radiated from the spiritual world into the new incarnation, the individuality in the fourteenth century. Therefore he was led to experience the event of Damascus again. This is the individuality of Christian Rosenkreutz. He was the thirteenth in the circle of the twelve. He was named thus from this incarnation onwards. Esoterically, in the occult sense, he was already Christian Rosenkreutz in the thirteenth century, but exoterically he was named thus only from the fourteenth century. And the pupils of this thirteenth are the successors of the other twelve in the thirteenth century. These are the rosicrucians.

At that time Christian Rosenkreutz travelled through the whole of the known world. After he had received all the wisdom of the twelve, fructified by the mighty Being of the Christ, it was easy for him to receive all the wisdom of that time in the course of seven years. When, after seven years, he returned to Europe, he took the most highly developed pupils and successors of the twelve as his pupils, and then began the actual work of the rosicrucians.

By the grace of what radiated from the wonderful etheric body of Christian Rosenkreutz they could develop an absolutely new world conception. What has been developed by the rosicrucians up to our time is work of both an outer and an inner nature. The outer work was for the purpose of discovering what lies behind the maya of the material world. They wanted to investigate the maya of matter. Just as man has an etheric body, so does the whole of the macrocosm have an etheric macrocosm, an etheric body. There is a certain point of transition from the coarser to the finer substance. Let us look at the boundary between physical and etheric substance. What lies between physical and etheric substance is like nothing else in the world. It is neither gold nor silver, lead nor copper. It is something that cannot be compared with any other physical substance, yet it is the essence of all of them. It is a substance that is contained in every other physical substance, so that the other physical substances can be considered to be modifications of this one substance. To see this substance clairvoyantly was the endeavour of the rosicrucians. The preparation, the development of such vision they saw to require a heightened activity of the soul's moral forces, which would then enable them to see this substance. They realized that the power for this vision lay in the moral power of the soul. This substance was really seen and discovered by the rosicrucians. They found that this substance lived in the world in a certain form both in the macrocosm and in man. In the world outside man they revered it as the mighty garment of the macrocosm. They saw it arising in man when there is a harmonious interplay between thinking and willing. They saw the will forces as being not only in man but in the macrocosm also, for instance in thunder and lightning. And they saw the forces of thought on the one hand in man and also outside in the world, in the rainbow and the rosy light of dawn. The rosicrucians sought the strength to achieve such harmony of willing and thinking in their own soul, in the forces radiating from this etheric body of the thirteenth, Christian Rosenkreutz.

It was established that all the discoveries they made had to remain the secret of the rosicrucians for a hundred years, and that not until a hundred years had passed might these rosicrucian revelations be divulged to the world, for not until they had worked at them for a hundred years might they talk about them in an appropriate way. Thus what appeared in 1785 in the work *The Secret Symbols of the Rosicrucians*[33] was being prepared from the seventeenth to the eighteenth century.

Now it is also of great importance to know that in any century the rosicrucian inspiration is given in such a way that the name of the one who receives the inspiration is never made public. Only the highest initiates know it. Today, for instance, only those occurrences can be made public that happened a hundred years ago, for that is the time that must pass before it is permissible to speak of it in the outside world. The temptation is too great that people would fanatically idealize a person bearing such authority, which is the worst thing that can happen. It would be too near to idolatry. This silence, however, is not only essential in order to avoid the outer temptations of ambition and pride, which could probably be overcome, but above all to avoid occult astral attacks which would be constantly directed at an individuality of that calibre. That is why it is an essential condition that a fact like this can only be spoken of after a hundred years.

Through the works of the rosicrucians the etheric body of Christian Rosenkreutz became ever stronger and mightier from century to century. It worked not only through Christian Rosenkreutz but through all those who became his pupils. From the fourteenth century onwards Christian Rosenkreutz has been incarnated again and again. Everything that is made known in the name of theosophy is strengthened by the etheric body of Christian Rosenkreutz, and those who make theosophy known let themselves be overshadowed by this etheric body, that can work on them both when Christian Rosenkreutz is incarnated and when he is not in incarnation.

The Count of Saint Germain was the exoteric name of Christian Rosenkreutz' incarnation in the eighteenth century.[34] This name was given to other people, too, however; therefore not everything that is told about Count Saint Germain here and there in the outside world applies to the real Christian Rosenkreutz. Christian Rosenkreutz is incarnated again today. The inspiration for the work of H.P. Blavatsky, *Isis Unveiled*, came from the strength radiating from his etheric body. It was also Christian Rosenkreutz' influence working invisibly on Lessing[35] that inspired him to write *The Education of the Human Race* (1780). Because of the rising tide of materialism it became more and more difficult for inspiration to come about in the rosicrucian way. Then in the nineteenth century came the high tide of materialism. Many things could only be given very incompletely. In 1851 the problem of the immortality of the soul was resolved by Widenmann[36] through the idea of reincarnation. His text was awarded a prize. Even around 1850 Drossbach[37] wrote from a psychological point of view in support of reincarnation.

Thus the forces radiating from the etheric body of Christian Rosenkreutz continued to be active in the nineteenth century too. And a renewal of theosophical life could come about because by 1899 the short Kali Yuga had run its course. That is why it is now easier to approach the spiritual world and spiritual influence is possible to a far greater degree. The etheric body of Christian Rosenkreutz has become very powerful, and, through devotion to this, man will be able to acquire new clairvoyance, and invoke lofty spiritual forces. This will only be possible, however, for those people who follow the training of Christian Rosenkreutz correctly. Until now an esoteric rosicrucian preparation was essential, but the twentieth century has the mission of enabling this etheric body to become so mighty that it can also work exoterically. Those affected by it will be granted experience of the event that Paul experienced on the road to Damascus. Until now this etheric body has only worked upon the rosicrucian school; in the twentieth century more and more people will be able to experience the effect of it, and through this they will come to experience the appearance of Christ in the etheric body. It is the work of the rosicrucians that makes possible the etheric vision of Christ. The number of people who will become capable of seeing it will grow and grow. We must attribute this re-appearance to the important work of the twelve and the thirteenth in the thirteenth and fourteenth centuries.

If you can become an instrument of Christian Rosenkreutz, then you can be assured that the tiniest soul-steps you take will be there for eternity.

Tomorrow we will come to speak about the work of

Christian Rosenkreutz. A vague longing for spiritual science is present in mankind today. And we can be sure that wherever students of rosicrucianism are striving seriously and conscientiously, they are working creatively for eternity. Every spiritual achievement, however small, brings us further. It is essential to understand and revere these holy matters.

Rosicrucian Christianity

2. Neuchâtel, 28 September 1911

My task today will be to tell you something about the work of Christian Rosenkreutz. This work began in the thirteenth century, is still going on today, and will continue on into eternity. The work began, of course, with what I told you yesterday of the initiation of Christian Rosenkreutz, and all that took place between the council of the twelve and the thirteenth. When Christian Rosenkreutz was born again in the fourteenth century, in an incarnation lasting more than a hundred years, his main task was instructing the pupils of the twelve. At that time hardly anyone else came to know Christian Rosenkreutz apart from these twelve. This is not to be understood as if Christian Rosenkreutz did not meet other people, but only that the other people did not recognize him for what he was. Fundamentally this has remained the same until today. However, the etheric body of Christian Rosenkreutz has been constantly active in the circle of his pupils, its forces working in ever growing circles, until today many people are actually able to be influenced by the forces of his etheric body.

Christian Rosenkreutz selects those whom he wants to have as his pupils in a remarkable way. The one chosen has to pay attention to a certain kind of event, or several events in his life of the following kind: Christian Rosenkreutz chooses people so that, for instance, someone comes to a decisive turning-point, a karmic crisis in his life. Let us assume that a person is about to commit an action that would lead him to his death. These things can be very different one from the other. This man goes along a path which, without noticing it, can lead him into great danger. It leads to the edge of a precipice, perhaps. Then the man, now only a step or two from the precipice perhaps, hears a voice saying 'Stop!'—so that he has to stop without knowing why. There could be a thousand similar situations. I should say, of course, that this is only the external sign of being outwardly qualified for a spiritual calling. To be inwardly qualified, the chosen person has to have an interest in something spiritual, theosophy or some other form of spiritual science. The external event I have described is a fact of the physical world, though it does not come by means of a human voice. The event always occurs in such a way that the person concerned knows quite clearly that the voice comes from the spiritual world. He may at first imagine that the voice has come from a human being who is hidden somewhere, but when the pupil is mature enough he discovers that it was not a physical person inter-vening in his life. In short, this event convinces the pupil that there are messages from the spiritual world. Such events can occur once or many times in life. We have to understand what effect this has on the soul of the pupil. The pupil tells himself: I have received another life through grace; the first one was forfeited. This new life given him through grace sheds light on the whole of the pupil's further life. He has a definite feeling which can be described in this way: without this rosicrucian experience of mine I should have died. My sub-sequent life would not have had the same value but for this event.

It can happen, of course, that even though someone has already experienced this once or even several times he does not come to theosophy or spiritual science at once. Later on, however, the memory of the event can come back. Many of you here can examine the past course of your lives and you will find that similar occurrences have happened to you. We give too little attention to such things today. We ought to realize how very important occurrences pass by without us noticing them. This is an indication of the way the more advanced pupils of rosicrucianism are called.

This kind of occurrence will either pass a person by without being noticed at all, in which case the impression is blotted out and he attaches no importance to it; or, assuming the person to be attentive, he will appreciate its significance, and he will then perhaps realize that he was actually facing a crisis then, a karmic crisis; his life should actually have ended at that moment. He had forfeited his life, and was only saved by something resembling chance. Since that hour a second life has been grafted on to the first, as it were. You must look on this life as a gift and live it accordingly.

When such an event awakens in a person the inner sense of looking at his life from that time onwards as a gift, this makes him, nowadays, a follower of Christian Rosenkreutz. For that is his way of calling these souls to him. And whoever can recall having had such an experience can tell himself: Christian Rosenkreutz has given me a sign from the spiritual world that I belong to his stream. Christian Rosenkreutz has added the possibility of such an experience to my karma. That is the way in which Christian Rosenkreutz makes his choice of pupils. He chooses his community like this. Whoever experiences this consciously, knows: a path has been shown me, and I must follow it and see how far I can use my forces to serve rosicrucianism. Those who have not understood the sign, however, will do so at a later time, for whoever has received the sign will not be free of it again.

That a person can have an experience of the kind described is due to his having met Christian Rosenkreutz in the spiritual world between his last death and his latest birth. Christian Rosenkreutz chose us then, and he put an impulse of will into us that now leads us to such experiences. This is the way in which spiritual connections are brought about.

To go further, let us discuss the difference between Christian Rosenkreutz' teaching in earlier times and in later times. This teaching used to be more in the nature of natural science, whereas today it is more like spiritual science. In earlier times, for instance, people observed natural processes and called this science alchemy; and when such processes took place beyond the earth they called it astrology. Today we start from a more spiritual perspective. If we consider, for instance, the successive post-Atlantean cultural epochs, the culture of ancient India, ancient Persia, the Egyptian-Chaldean-Assyrian-Babylonian culture and the Graeco-Roman culture, we learn about the nature of the development of the human soul. The rosicrucians of the Middle Ages studied natural processes, regarding them as the earth processes of nature. They distinguished, for instance, three different natural processes which they regarded as the three great processes of nature.

The first important process is the salt process. Everything in nature that can form a deposit of hard substance out of a solution was called salt by the medieval rosicrucian. When the medieval rosicrucian saw this salt formation, however, his conception of it was entirely different from that of modern man. For if he wanted to feel he had understood it, the witnessing of such a process had to work like a prayer in his soul. Therefore the medieval rosicrucian tried to make clear to himself what would have to happen in his own soul if the formation of salt were to take place there too. He arrived at the thought: human nature is perpetually destroying itself through instincts and passions. Our life would be nothing but a decomposition, a process of putrefaction, if we only followed our instincts and passions. And if man really wants to protect himself against this process of putrefaction, then he must constantly devote himself to noble thoughts that turn him towards the spirit. It was a matter of bringing his thoughts to a higher level of development. The medieval rosicrucian knew that if he did not combat his passions in one incarnation he would be born with a predisposition for illness in the next one, but that if he purified his passion he would enter life in the next incarnation with a predisposition for health. The process of overcoming, through spirituality, the forces that lead to decay, is microcosmic salt formation. So we can understand how a natural process like this occasioned the most reverent prayer. When observing salt formation the medieval rosicrucians told themselves, with a feeling of deepest piety: Divine spiritual powers have been working in this process for thousands of years in the same way as noble thoughts work in me. I am praying to the thoughts of the gods, the thoughts of divine spiritual beings that are behind the maya of nature. The medieval rosicrucian knew this, and he said to himself: When I let nature stimulate me to develop feelings like this, I make myself like the macrocosm. If I observe this process in an external way only, I cut myself off from the gods, I fall away from the macrocosm. Such were the feelings of the medieval theosophist or rosicrucian.

The process of dissolution gave a different experience: it was a different natural process that could also lead the medieval rosicrucian to prayer. Everything that can dissolve something else was called by the medieval rosicrucian quicksilver or mercury. Now he asked again: What is the corresponding quality in the human soul? What quality works in the soul in the same way in which quicksilver or mercury works outside in nature? The medieval rosicrucian knew that all the forms of love in the soul are what correspond to mercury. He distinguished between lower and higher processes of dissolution, just as there are lower and higher forms of love. And thus the witnessing of the dissolution process again became a pious prayer, and the medieval theosophist said to himself: God's love has been at work out there for thousands of years in the same way as love works in me.

The third important natural process for the medieval theosophist was combustion, that takes place when material substance is consumed by flames. And again the medieval rosicrucian sought the inner process corresponding to this combustion. This inner soul process he saw to be ardent devotion to the deity. And everything that can go up in flames he called sulphur. In the stages of development of the earth he beheld a gradual process of purification similar to a combustion or sulphur process. Just as he knew that the earth will at some time be purified by fire, he also saw a combustion process in fervent devotion to the deity. In the earth processes he beheld the work of those gods who look up to mightier gods above them. And permeated with great piety and deeply religious feelings at the spectacle of the process of combustion, he told himself: Gods are now making a sacrifice to higher gods. And then when the medieval theosophist produced the combustion process in the laboratory himself, he felt: I am doing the same as the gods do when they sacrifice themselves to higher gods. He only considered himself worthy to carry out such a process of combustion in his laboratory when he felt himself filled with the mood of sacrifice, when he himself was filled with the desire to devote himself in sacrifice to the gods. The power of the flame filled the medieval theosophist with lofty and deeply religious feelings, and he told himself: When I see flames outside in the macrocosm I am seeing the thoughts and the love of the gods, and the gods' willingness to sacrifice, to make offerings.

The medieval rosicrucian produced these processes himself in his laboratory and then he entered into contemplation of these salt formations, solutions and processes of combustion, letting himself at the same time be filled with deeply religious feelings in which he became aware of his connection with all the forces of the macrocosm. These soul processes called forth in him divine thoughts, divine love and divine sacrifice. And then the medieval rosicrucian discovered that when he produced a salt process, noble, purifying thoughts arose in him. With a solution process love was stimulated in him, he was inspired by divine love; and with a combustion process the desire to make a sacrifice was kindled in him, it urged him to sacrifice himself on the altar of the world.

These were the experiences of one who did these experiments. And if you had attended these experiments yourself in clairvoyant vision, you would have perceived a change in the aura of the person carrying them out. The aura that was a mixture of colours before the experiment began, being full of instincts and desires to which the person in question had perhaps succumbed, became single-hued as a result of the experiment. First of all, during the experiment with salt formation, it became the colour of copper—pure, divine thoughts—then, in the experiment with a solution, the colour of silver—divine love—and finally, with combustion, the colour of gold—divine sacrifice. And then the alchemists said they had made subjective copper, subjective silver and subjective gold out of the aura. And the outcome was that the person who had undergone this, and had really experienced such an experiment inwardly, was completely permeated by divine love. Such was the way these medieval theosophists became permeated with purity, love and the will to sacrifice, and by means of this sacrificial service they prepared themselves for a certain clairvoyance. This is how the medieval theosophist could see behind maya into the way spiritual beings helped things to come into being and pass away again. And this enabled him to realize which forces of aspiration in our souls are helpful and which are not. He became acquainted with our own forces of growth and decay. The medieval theosophist Heinrich Khunrath,[38] in a moment of enlightenment, called this process the law of growth and decay.

Through observing nature the medieval theosophist learnt the law of ascending and descending evolution. The science he acquired from this he expressed in certain signs, imaginative pictures and figures. It was a kind of imaginative knowledge. One of the outcomes of this was *The Secret Symbols of the Rosicrucians* mentioned yesterday.

This is the way the best alchemists worked from the fourteenth to the eighteenth and until the beginning of the nineteenth century. About this truly moral, ethical, intellectual work nothing has been published. What has been written about alchemy concerns purely external experiments only, and was only written by those who performed alchemy as an end in itself. The false alchemist wanted to create physical substance. When he experimented with the burning of substances he saw the material results as the only thing gained, whereas the genuine alchemist attached no importance to these material results. For him it all depended on the inner soul experiences he had whilst the substance was forming, the thoughts and experiences within him. Therefore there was a strict rule that the medieval theosophist who produced gold and silver from his experiments was never allowed to profit from it himself. He was only allowed to give away the metals thus produced. People today no longer have the correct conception of these experiments. We have no idea what the experimenter could experience. The medieval theosophist was able to experience whole dramas of the soul in his laboratory when, for example, antimony was extracted; the experimenters saw significant moral forces at work in these processes.

If these things had not taken place at that time, we would not be able to practise spiritual scientific rosicrucianism today. What the medieval rosicrucian experienced when he beheld the processes of nature was a holy science. The mood of spiritual sacrifice, the tremendous joys, the great natural events, the pain and sadness too, as well as the events that uplifted him and made him happy, all these experiences that he had during the experiment he performed, worked on him in a liberating and redeeming way. All that was planted in him then, however, is now hidden in the innermost depths of man.

How shall we rediscover these hidden forces that used to lead to clairvoyance? We shall find them by studying spiritual science and by devoting ourselves deeply to the soul's inner life in serious meditation and concentration. By means of inner development of this kind, work with nature will gradually become a sacrificial rite again. For this to come about human beings must go through what we now call spiritual science. Human beings in their thousands must devote themselves to the science of the spirit; they must cultivate an inner life, so that in the future the spiritual reality behind nature will be perceptible again, and we learn to understand again the spirit behind maya. Then, in the future, although it will only happen to small numbers to begin with, people will be able to experience Paul's vision on the road to Damascus and to perceive the etheric Christ, who will come among us in supersensible form. But before this happens man will have to return to a spiritual view of nature. If we did not know the whole significance of rosicrucianism we could believe that humanity was still at the same stage as it was two thousand years ago. Until man has gone through this process, which is only possible by means of spiritual science, he will not come to spiritual vision. There are many good and pious people who are theosophists at heart, although they are not followers of spiritual science.

Through the event of the baptism in Jordan, when the

Christ descended into the body of Jesus of Nazareth, and through the Mystery of Golgotha, mankind became capable of later beholding and recognizing the Christ in the etheric body—in our century in fact, from 1930 onwards. Christ has only walked the earth once in a physical body, and we should learn to understand this. 'The second coming of Christ' means seeing Christ supersensibly in the etheric. Therefore everyone who wants to tread the right path of development must work to acquire the capacity to see with spiritual eyes. It would not signify human progress for Christ to appear again in a physical body. His next appearance will be a revelation in the etheric body.

What was given in the different religious creeds has been gathered into one whole by Christian Rosenkreutz and the council of the twelve. This means that everything that the separate religions had to give and all that their followers strove and longed for will be found in the Christ impulse. Development during the next three thousand years will consist in this: the establishing and furthering of an under-standing of the Christ impulse. From the twentieth century onwards all religions will come to be reconciled in the mys-tery of rosicrucianism. And in the course of the next three thousand years this will become possible because it will no longer be necessary to teach from records or documents; for through beholding Christ human beings will themselves learn to understand the experience Paul had on the way to Damascus. Mankind itself will pass through the experience of Paul.

The Maitreya Buddha will appear five thousand years after Buddha was enlightened under the bodhi tree, that is, about three thousand years from now. He will be the successor of Gautama Buddha. Among true occultists this is no longer in doubt. Occultists of both the West and the East are in agreement about it. So two things are beyond question:

Firstly, that the Christ could appear only *once* in a physical body; secondly that He will appear in the twentieth century in etheric form. Great individualities will certainly appear in the twentieth century, like the bodhisattva, the successor of Gautama Buddha, who will become the Maitreya Buddha in about three thousand years. But no true occultist will give to any human being physically incarnated in the twentieth century the name of Christ, and no real occultist will expect Christ to be incarnated physically in the twentieth century. Every genuine occultist would find such a statement mistaken. It is to Christ especially, however, that the bodhisattva will point.

Secondly, it will be three thousand years before the bodhisattva who appeared in Jeshu ben Pandira appears as the Maitreya Buddha. The real occultists of India, in particular, would be horrified if we were to maintain that the Maitreya Buddha could appear before then. There could well be the kind of occultists in India, of course, who are not real occultists and who, for reasons of their own, speak of a Maitreya Buddha already in incarnation. Proper devotion to rosicrucian theosophy and to Christian Rosenkreutz can protect anyone from falling into these errors.

All these things are stated in rosicrucianism in such a way that they can be tested by reason. Ordinary common sense can test all these things. Do not believe anything on my authority, but just take what I say as stimulus and then test it for yourselves. I am sure that the more you examine theosophy or spiritual science the more sensible you will find it. The less you take on authority, the more understanding you will have for Christian Rosenkreutz. We know Christian Rosenkreutz best when we enter properly into his individuality and become conscious that his spirit lives on and on. And the closer we approach to his great spirit the stronger we shall become. We can hope for a great deal of strength and help from the etheric body of this great leader, who will always be there if we ask him to help us.

We will also be able to understand the strange event of Christian Rosenkreutz falling ill if we absorb ourselves properly in the work of spiritual science. In the thirteenth century this individuality lived in a physical body that grew weak to the point of transparency, so that for several days he lay as though dead, and during this time he received from the twelve their wisdom and also experienced the event of Damascus.

May the spirit of true rosicrucianism be with you and inspire you in this group, then the mighty etheric body of Christian Rosenkreutz will be all the more active here.

May this group be one of the building stones in the temple we wish to raise. We have begun it in the spirit of Christian Rosenkreutz; let us try to carry our work further in the same spirit.

The Etherisation of the Blood

Basle, 1 October 1911

Wherever we human beings strive for knowledge—whether as mystics or realists or in any way at all—the need to acquire *self-knowledge* is ever-present through the ages. But as has been repeatedly emphasized on other occasions, self-knowledge is by no means as easy to achieve as many people believe—anthroposophists sometimes among them. The anthroposophist should be constantly aware of the hindrances he will encounter in his efforts. But the acquisition of self-knowledge is absolutely essential if we are to reach a worthy evolutionary goal and if our life and actions are to be worthy of us as human beings.

Let us ask ourselves why the achievement of self-knowledge is so difficult. Man is a very complicated being. If we mean to speak truly of his inner life, his life of soul, we shall not begin by regarding it as something simple and elementary. We shall rather have the patience and perseverance, the will, to penetrate more deeply into that marvellous creation of divine-spiritual powers known to us as man.

Before we investigate the nature of self-knowledge, two aspects of the life of the human soul may present themselves to us. Just as the magnet has North and South poles, just as light and darkness are present in the world, so there are two poles in man's life of soul. These two poles become evident when we observe a person placed in two contrasting situations. Suppose we are watching someone who is entirely absorbed in the contemplation of some strikingly beautiful and impressive natural phenomenon. We see how still he is standing, moving neither hand nor foot, never turning his eyes away from the spectacle presented to him, and we are aware that he is inwardly picturing what he sees before him. That is one situation. Another is the following: someone is walking along the street and feels another has insulted him. Without thinking, he is roused to anger and gives vent to it by striking the person who insulted him. There we are witnessing a manifestation of forces springing from anger, a manifestation of impulses of will, and it is easy to imagine that if the action had been preceded by thought no blow need have been struck. We have now pictured two contrasting situations: in the one there is only ideation, a process in the life of thought from which all conscious will is absent; in the other there is no thought, no ideation, and immediate expression is given to an impulse of will. Here we have examples of the two extremes of human behaviour. The first pole is complete surrender to contemplation, to thought, in which the will has no part; the second pole is the impelling force of will without thought. These facts are revealed simply by observation of external life.

We can go into these things more deeply and we come then into spheres in which we can find our bearings only by summoning the findings of occult investigation to our aid. Then another polarity confronts us—that of sleeping and waking. From elementary anthroposophical concepts we know that in waking life the four members of man's being—physical body, etheric body, astral body and ego—are organically and actively interwoven, but that in sleep physical and etheric bodies remain in the bed, while astral body and ego are poured out into the great world bordering on physical existence. These facts could also be approached from a different point of view. What, for instance, is there to be said about ideation, contemplation, thinking; and about the will and its impulses: on the one hand during waking life, and during sleep on the other?

When we penetrate more deeply into this question it becomes evident that in his present physical existence man is, in a certain sense, always asleep, only there is a difference between sleep during the night and sleep during the day. Of this we can be convinced in a purely external way, for we know that we can wake in the occult sense during the day, that is to say, we can become clairvoyant and see into the spiritual world. The physical body in its ordinary state is asleep to such perception, and we can rightly speak of an *awakening* of our spiritual senses. In the night, of course, we are asleep in the normal way. It can therefore be said that ordinary sleep is sleep in relation to the outer physical world, while daytime consciousness at the present time is sleep in relation to the spiritual world.

These facts can be considered in still another light. On deeper scrutiny we realize that in the ordinary waking condition of physical life, man has, as a rule, very little power or control over his will and its impulses. The will is very detached from daily life. Only consider how little of all you do from morning to evening is really the outcome of your own thinking, of your personal resolutions. When someone knocks at the door and you say 'Come in!', that cannot be called a decision of your own thinking and will. If you are hungry and seat yourself at table, that cannot be called a decision made by the will, because it is occasioned by your circumstances, by the needs of your organism. Try to picture your daily life and you will find how little the will is directly influenced from the centre of your being. Why is this? Occultism shows us that in respect of our will we actually sleep by day; that is to say we are not in the real sense present in our will-impulses at all. We may evolve better and better concepts and ideas; or we may become more highly moral, more cultured, individuals, but we can do nothing as regards the will. By cultivating better thoughts we can work *indirectly* upon the will but as far as life is concerned we can do nothing *directly* to it, for in the waking life of day, our will is influenced in an indirect way only, namely through *sleep*. When we are asleep we do not think; ideation passes over into a state of sleep. The will, however, awakes, permeates our organism from outside, and invigorates it. We feel strengthened in the morning because what has penetrated into our organism is of the nature of will. That we are not aware of this activity of the will becomes comprehensible when we remember that all conceptual activity ceases when we ourselves are asleep. To begin with, therefore, let me give you this stimulus for further contemplation, further meditation. The more progress you make in self-knowledge, the more you will find confirmation of the truth of the words that man sleeps in his will when he is awake and sleeps in his conceptual life when he is asleep. The life of will sleeps by day; the life of thought sleeps by night.

Man is unaware that the will does not sleep during the night because he only knows how to be awake in his life of thought. The will does not sleep during the night but it then works as it were in a fiery element, works upon his body in order to restore what has been used up by day.

Thus there are two poles in man, the life of observation and ideation, and the impulses of will; and man is related in entirely opposite ways to these two poles. The whole life of soul moves in various nuances between these two poles, and we shall come nearer to understanding it by bringing this microcosmic life of soul into relation with higher worlds.

From what has been said we have learnt that the life of thought and ideation is one of the poles of man's life of soul. This life of thought is something which seems unreal to materialistically-minded individuals. Do we not often hear it

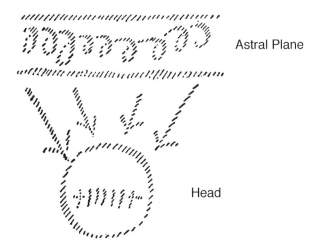

Astral Plane

Head

said: 'Oh, ideas and thoughts are *only* ideas and thoughts!' This is intended to imply that if someone has a piece of bread or meat in his hand it is real because it can be eaten, whereas a thought is *only* a thought, is not a reality. Why is this said? It is because what man *calls* his thoughts are related to what thoughts really are as a shadow-image is to the actual thing. The shadow-image of a flower points you to the flower itself, to the reality. So it is with thoughts. Human thinking is the shadowing forth of ideas and beings belonging to a higher world, the world we call the astral plane. And you represent thinking rightly to yourself when you picture the human head thus [see diagram]—it is not absolutely correct but simply diagrammatic. In the head are thoughts but these thoughts must be pictured as living beings on the astral plane. Beings of the most varied kinds are at work there in the form of teeming concepts and activities which cast their shadow-images into us, and these processes are reflected in the human head as thinking.

As well as the life of thought in the human soul, there is also the life of feeling. Feelings fall into two categories: those of pleasure and sympathy and those of displeasure and antipathy. The former are aroused by good deeds, bene-volent deeds, while antipathy is aroused by unjust, malevo-lent deeds. Here there is something more than and different from the mere forming of concepts. We form concepts of things irrespective of any other factor. But our soul experi-ences sympathy or antipathy only in respect of what is beautiful and good, or of what is ugly and evil. Just as everything that takes place in man in the form of thoughts points to the astral plane, so everything connected with sympathy or antipathy points to the realm we call lower devachan. Processes in the heavenly world, or devachan, are projected, mainly into our breast, as feelings of sympathy or antipathy for what is beautiful or ugly, for what is good or evil. So that in our feelings for the moral-aesthetic element, we bear within our souls shadow-reflections of the heavenly world or lower devachan.

There is still a third province in the life of the human soul which must be strictly distinguished from mere *preference* for good deeds. There is a difference between standing by and taking pleasure in witnessing some kindly deed, and setting the will in action, to actually perform some such deed. I will call pleasure in good deeds or displeasure in evil deeds the *aesthetic* element as against the *moral* element which impels a person to perform some good deed. The moral element is at a higher level than the purely aesthetic; mere pleasure or dis-pleasure is at a lower level than the will to do something good or bad. In so far as our soul feels constrained to give expression to moral impulses, these impulses are the shadow-images of higher devachan, of the higher heavenly world.

It is easy to picture these three stages of activity of the human soul—the purely intellectual (thoughts, concepts), the aesthetic (pleasure or displeasure), and the moral (revealed in impulses to good or bad deeds)—as *microcosmic* images of the three realms which in the macrocosm, the great universe, lie one above the other. The astral world is reflected in the world of thought; the devachanic world is reflected in the aesthetic sphere of pleasure and displeasure; and the higher devachanic world is reflected as morality.

Thoughts: Shadow-images of beings of the astral plane (waking)

Sympathy and antipathy: shadow-images of beings of lower devachan (dreaming)

Moral impulses: shadow-images of beings of higher devachan (sleeping)

If we connect this with what was said previously concerning the two poles of soul-life, we shall take the pole of intellect to be that which dominates waking life, the life in which we are mentally awake. During the day we are awake in respect of our intellect; during sleep we are awake in respect of our will. It is because at night we are asleep in respect of intellect that we are unaware of what is happening to our will. The truth is that what we call *moral principles, moral impulses*, are working indirectly into the will. And in point of fact man needs the life of sleep in order for the moral impulses he takes into himself through the life of thought to become active and effective. In his ordinary life today man is capable of accomplishing what is right only on the plane of intellect; he is less able to accomplish anything on the moral plane for there he is dependent upon help coming from the macrocosm.

What is already within us can bring about the further development of intellectuality, but the gods must come to our aid if we are to acquire greater moral strength. We go to sleep in order that we may plunge into the divine will where the intellect does not intervene and where divine forces transform into power of will the moral principles we accept, where they instil into our will that which we could otherwise receive only into our thoughts.

Between these two poles, that of the will which wakes by night and of the intellect which is awake by day, lies the sphere of aesthetic appreciation which is continuously present in man. During the day man is not fully awake—at least only the most prosaic, pedantic individuals are always fully awake in waking life. We must always be able to dream a little even by day when we are awake; we must be able to give ourselves up to the enjoyment of art, of poetry, or of some other activity that is not concerned wholly with mundane reality. Those who can give themselves up in this way form a connection with something that can enliven and invigorate the whole of existence. To give oneself up to such imaginings is like a dream making its way into waking life. You know well that dreams enter our sleep-life; these are dreams in the usual sense, dreams which permeate sleep-consciousness. Human beings also need to dream by day if they do not wish to lead an arid, empty, unhealthy waking life. Dreaming takes place during sleep at night in any case and no proof of this is required. Midway between the two poles we have spoken of, come night dreaming and day dreaming: the condition that can come to expression in imagination.

So here again there is a threefold life of soul. The intellectual element in which we are really awake brings us shadow-images of the astral plane when by day we give ourselves up to thought—wherein the most fruitful ideas for daily life and great inventions originate. Then during sleep, when we dream, these dreams play into our life of sleep and shadow-images from lower devachan are reflected into us. And when we work actively during sleep, impressing morality into our will—we cannot be aware of this actual process but certainly we can of its effects—when we are able to imbue our life of thought during the night with the influence of divine spiritual powers, then the impulses we receive are reflections from higher devachan, the higher heavenly world. These reflections are the moral impulses and feelings which are active within us and lead to the recognition that human life is vindicated only when we place our thoughts at the service of the good and the beautiful, when we allow the very heart's blood of divine spiritual life to stream through our intellectual activities, permeating them with moral impulses.

The life of the human soul as presented here, first from external, exoteric observation and then from observation of a more mystical character is revealed by deeper (occult) investigation. The processes that have been described in their more external aspect can also be perceived in man through clairvoyance. When someone stands in front of us today in his waking state and we observe him with the eye of clairvoyance, certain rays of light are seen streaming continually from the heart towards the head. Within the head these rays play around the organ known in anatomy as the pineal gland. These streams arise because human blood, which is a physical substance, is perpetually resolving itself into etheric substance. In the region of the heart there is a continual trans-

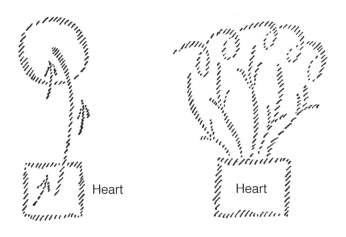

Heart   Heart

formation of the blood into this delicate etheric substance which streams upwards towards the head and glimmers around the pineal gland. This process—the etherisation of the blood—can be perceived in the human being all the time during his waking life.

But during sleep it is different. Then the occult observer is able to see a continual streaming from outside into the brain, and also back from the brain to the heart. These streams, which in sleeping man come from outside, from cosmic space, from the macrocosm, and flow into the inner constitution of the physical body and etheric body lying in bed, reveal something very remarkable when they are investigated. The rays vary greatly in different individuals. Sleeping human beings differ very drastically from one another, and if those who are a little vain only knew how badly they betray themselves to occult observation when they go to sleep during public gatherings, they would try their level best not to let this happen!

Moral qualities are revealed very distinctly in the particular colouring of the streams which flow into human beings during sleep; in an individual of lower moral principles, the streams are quite different from what can be seen in an individual of noble principles. Efforts to dissemble are useless. In the face of cosmic powers no dissembling is possible. In the case of someone who has only a slight inclination towards moral principles the rays streaming into him are a brownish red in colour—various shades tending towards brownish red. In someone of high moral ideals the rays are lilac-violet in colour. At the moment of waking or of going to sleep a kind of struggle takes place in the region of the pineal gland between what streams down from above and what streams upwards from below. When a person is awake the intellectual element streams upwards from below in the form of currents of light; and what is of moral-aesthetic nature streams downwards from above. At the moment of waking or of going off to sleep, these two currents meet, and in someone who is especially clever but of low morality a violent struggle between the two streams takes place in the region of the pineal gland. In someone of high morality there is as it were a little sea of light around the pineal gland. Moral nobility is revealed when a calm glow surrounds the pineal gland at these moments of falling asleep or waking. In this way a person's moral disposition is reflected in him, and this calm glow of light often extends as far as the heart. Two streams can therefore be perceived in man—one macrocosmic, the other microcosmic.

To estimate the significance of how these two streams meet in man is possible only by considering on the one hand what was said previously in a more external way about the life of the soul and how this life reveals the threefold polarity of the intellectual, the aesthetic, and the moral element that streams downwards from above, from the brain towards the heart; and if, on the other hand, we grasp the significance of what was said about turning our attention to the corresponding phenomenon in the macrocosm. This corresponding phenomenon can be described today as the result of the most scrupulously careful occult investigations of recent years, undertaken by certain truly genuine rosicrucians. These investigations have shown that something similar to what has been described in connection with the microcosm also takes place in the macrocosm. You will understand this more fully as time goes on.

Just as in the region of the human heart the blood is continually being transformed into etheric substance, a similar process takes place in the macrocosm. We understand this when we turn our minds to the Mystery of Golgotha—to the moment when the blood flowed from the wounds of Jesus Christ.

This blood must not be regarded simply as chemical substance, but by reason of all that has been said concerning the nature of Jesus of Nazareth it must be recognized as something altogether unique. When it flowed from His wounds, a substance was imparted to our earth, which in uniting with it, constituted an Event of the greatest possible significance for all future ages of the earth's evolution—and it could take place only once. What came of this blood in the ages that followed? Nothing different from what otherwise takes place in the heart of man. In the course of earth evolution this blood passes through a process of 'etherisation'. And just as our human blood streams upwards from the heart as ether, so since the Mystery of Golgotha the etherized blood of Christ Jesus has been present in the earth's ether. The etheric body of the earth is permeated by the blood—now transformed—which flowed on Golgotha. This is supremely important. If what has thus come to pass through Christ Jesus had not taken place, man's condition on the earth could only have been as previously described. But since the Mystery of Golgotha it has always been possible for the etheric blood of Christ to flow together with the streams flowing from below upwards, from heart to head.

Because the etherised blood of Jesus of Nazareth is present in the etheric body of the earth, it accompanies the etherised human blood streaming upwards from the heart to the brain, so that not only those streams of which I spoke earlier meet in man, but the human blood-stream unites with the blood-stream of Christ Jesus. A union of these two streams can, however, come about only if a person is able to unfold true understanding of what is contained in the Christ impulse. Otherwise there can be no union; the two streams then mutually repel each other, thrust each other away. In every epoch of earth evolution understanding must be acquired *in the form suitable for that epoch*. At the time when Christ

Jesus lived on earth, preceding events were rightly understood by those who came to His forerunner, John, and were baptized by him through the rite described in the Gospels. They received baptism in order that their sin, that is to say, the karma of their previous lives—karma which had come to an end—might be changed; and in order that they might realize that the most powerful impulse in earth evolution was about to descend into a physical body. But the evolution of humanity progresses and in our present age what matters is that people should recognize the need for the knowledge contained in spiritual science and be able so to fire the streams flowing from heart to brain that this knowledge can be understood.

If this comes to pass, individuals will be able to receive and comprehend the event that has its beginning in the twentieth century: this event is *the appearance of the etheric Being of Christ as opposed to the physical Christ of Palestine.* For we have now reached the point of time when the etheric Christ enters into the life of the earth and will become visible—at first to a small number of individuals through a form of natural clairvoyance. Then in the course of the next three thousand years, He will become visible to greater and greater numbers of people. This will inevitably come to pass in the natural course of evolution. That it will come to pass is as true as were the achievements involving electricity in the nineteenth century. A number of individuals will see the etheric Christ and will themselves experience the event that took place at Damascus. But this will depend upon such people learning to be alert to the moment when Christ draws near to them. In only a few decades from now it will happen, particularly to those who are young—already there are many signs of this—that some individual here or there has certain experiences. If he has sharpened his vision through studying anthroposophy, he may become aware that suddenly someone has come near to help him, to make him alert to this or that. The truth is that Christ has come to him, although he believes that what he saw was a physical human being. He will come to realize that what he saw was a supersensible being, because it immediately vanishes. Many a person will have this experience when sitting silent in his room, heavy-hearted and oppressed, not knowing which way to turn. The door will open, and the etheric Christ will appear and speak words of consolation to him. The Christ will become a living comforter to human beings. However strange it may as yet seem, it is true nevertheless that many a time when people— even in considerable numbers—are sitting together, not knowing what to do, and waiting, they will see the etheric Christ. He will Himself be there, will confer with them, will make His voice heard in such gatherings. These times are approaching, and the positive, constructive aspect now described will take real effect in the evolution of mankind.

No word shall be said here against the great cultural advances of our times; these achievements are essential for human welfare and freedom. But whatever can be gained in the way of outer progress, in mastering the forces of nature, is something small and insignificant compared with the blessing bestowed upon the individual who experiences the awakening through Christ, the Christ who will now be operative in human culture and its concerns. People will thereby acquire unifying, positive forces. Christ brings nurturing, up-building forces into human culture and civilization.

If we look into early post-Atlantean times, we find that people built their dwelling-places by methods very different from those used in modern life. In those days they made use of all kinds of growing things. Even when building palaces they summoned nature to their aid by utilizing plants interlaced with branches of trees and so on, whereas today people must build with broken fragments. All external culture is contrived with the aid of products of fragmentation. And in the course of the coming years you will realize even more clearly how much in our civilized life is the outcome of destruction.

Light destroys itself in this post-Atlantean age. Until the time of Atlantis the earth was part of an upward, progressive process. Since then it has been in a process of decay.* What is light? Light decays and the decaying light is *electricity*. What we know as electricity is light that destroys itself within matter. And the chemical force that undergoes a transformation in the process of earth evolution is *magnetism*. Yet a third force will become active; and if electricity seems to work wonders today, this third force will affect civilization in a still more miraculous way. The more of this force we employ, the faster will the earth become a corpse so that its spiritual part can work its way through into Jupiter embodiment. Forces have to be applied for the purpose of destruction, in order that man may become free of the earth and that the earth's body may fall away. As long as the earth was involved in progressive evolution, no such destruction took place, for the great achievements of electricity can only serve a decaying earth. Strange as this sounds, it must gradually become known. By understanding the process of evolution we shall learn to assess our culture in the right way. We shall also learn that it is necessary for the earth to be destroyed, for otherwise the spiritual could not become free. We shall also learn to value what is positive, namely the penetration of spiritual forces into our existence on earth.

Thus we realize what a tremendous advance was signified by the fact that Christ lived for three years on the earth in a specially prepared human body so that He might be visible to physical eyes. Through what came to pass during those three

---

* See also the section at the end of the text, containing answers given by Rudolf Steiner to questions.

years people have grown ready to behold the Christ who will move among them in an etheric body, who will participate in earthly life as truly and effectively as did the physical Christ in Palestine. If people observe such happenings with undimmed senses they will know that this is an etheric body taking its way through the physical world, but is also the *only* etheric body able to appear in the physical world as a human physical body appears. It will differ from a physical body in this respect only, that it can be in two, three, nay even in a hundred, a thousand places at the same time. This is possible only for an etheric, not for a physical form. What will be accomplished in humanity through this further advance is that the two poles of which I have spoken, the intellectual and the moral, will more and more become one; they will merge into a unity. This will come about because in the course of the next millennia human beings will become aware of the presence of the etheric Christ in the world; more and more they will be influenced in waking life too by the direct working of the good in spiritual worlds. Whereas at the present time, the will is asleep by day, and man is only able to influence it indirectly through thought, in the course of the next millennia, through what works into us from our time onwards under the aegis of Christ, a direct influence for the good will also affect our waking deeds.

The dream of Socrates that virtue can be taught, will come true;[39] more and more it will be possible on earth not only for the intellect to be stimulated and energized by this teaching but for moral impulses to be disseminated. Schopenhauer has said: 'To preach morality is easy; to establish it is very difficult.' Why is this? Because no morality has yet been truly spread by preaching. It is quite possible to recognize moral principles and yet not abide by them. For most people the Pauline saying holds good, that the spirit is willing but the flesh is weak. This will change, because the moral fire streaming from the figure of Christ will intensify recognition of the need for moral impulses. Man will transform the earth by feeling with ever-increasing strength that morality is an essential part of it. In the future, to be immoral will be possible only for individuals who are goaded in this direction, who are possessed by evil demons, by ahrimanic, asuric powers, and moreover aspire to be so.

In time to come there will be on earth a sufficient number of individuals who teach morality and at the same time sustain its principles; but there will also be those who by their own free decision surrender themselves to the evil powers and thus enable an army of evil to be pitted against a good humanity. Nobody will be forced to do this; it will lie in the free will of each individual.

Then will come the epoch when the earth passes into conditions of which, as in so much else, oriental occultism and mysticism alone give some idea. The moral atmosphere will by then have gathered strength. For many thousands of years oriental mysticism has spoken of this epoch, and since the coming of Gautama Buddha it has spoken with special emphasis about that future condition when the earth will be bathed in a 'moral-ether-atmosphere'. Ever since the time of the ancient Rishis it was the great hope of oriental mysticism that this moral impulse would come to the earth from Vishva-Karman or, as Zarathustra proclaimed, from Ahura Mazda. Thus oriental mysticism foresaw that this moral impulse, this moral atmosphere, would come to the earth from the Being we call the Christ. And it was upon Him, upon the Christ, that the hopes of oriental mysticism were set.

Oriental mysticism was able to picture the consequences of that event but not the actual form which it would take. The mind could picture that within a period of 5,000 years after the great Buddha achieved enlightenment, pure akashic forms, bathed in fire, lit by the sun, would appear in the wake of One beyond the ken of oriental mysticism. Truly a wonderful picture: something would happen to make it possible for the sons of fire and of light to move about the earth, not in physical embodiment but as pure akashic forms within the earth's moral atmosphere. But then, so it was said, in 5,000 years after Gautama Buddha's enlightenment, the teacher will also be there to make known to men the nature of these wonderful forms of pure fire and light. This teacher—the Maitreya Buddha—will appear 3,000 years after our present era and will be able to teach the Christ impulse.

Thus oriental mysticism unites with western Christian knowledge to form a wonderful, beautiful unity. We are also clearly told that he who will appear three thousand years after our era as the Maitreya Buddha will have incarnated again and again on the earth as a bodhisattva, as the successor of Gautama Buddha. One of his incarnations was that of Jeshu ben Pandira, who lived a hundred years before the Christian era. The being who incarnated in Jeshu ben Pandira is he who will one day become the Maitreya Buddha, and who from century to century returns ever and again in a body of flesh, not yet as Buddha, but as bodhisattva. Even now there proceed from him who later on will be the Maitreya Buddha, the most significant teachings concerning the Christ Being and the sons of fire—the Agnishvattas—of Indian mysticism.

The indications by which the being who is to become the Maitreya Buddha can be recognized are common to all genuine eastern mysticism and Christian gnosis. The Maitreya Buddha who, in contrast to the sons of fire, will appear in a physical body as bodhisattva, can in the first instance be recognized by the fact that his early development gives no intimation of the nature of the individuality within him. Only those possessed of understanding will recognize the presence of a bodhisattva in such a human being between the ages of thirty and thirty-three, and not before. Something akin to a change of personality then takes place. The Maitreya Buddha will reveal his identity to humanity in the thirty-third year of his life. As Christ Jesus began His mission in His thirtieth year, so do the bodhisattvas, who will continue to proclaim the Christ impulse, reveal themselves in the thirty-third year of their lives. And the Maitreya Buddha himself, as transformed bodhisattva, speaking in powerful words of which no adequate idea can be given at the present time, will proclaim the great secrets of existence. He will speak in a language that has first to be created, for no human being today could formulate words such as those in which the Maitreya Buddha will address humanity. The reason why human beings cannot be addressed in this way at the present time is that the physical instrument for this form of speech does not yet exist. The teachings of the enlightened one will not stream into human beings as teachings only, but will pour moral impulses into their souls. Words such as will then be spoken cannot yet be uttered by a physical larynx; in our time they can be present only in the spiritual worlds.

Anthroposophy is the preparation for everything that the future holds in store. Those who take the process of man's evolution seriously resolve not to allow the soul's development to come to a standstill but to ensure that this development will eventually enable the spiritual part of the earth to become free, leaving the grosser part to fall away like a corpse—for man could frustrate the whole process. Those who desire evolution to succeed must acquire understanding of the life of the spirit through what we now call anthroposophy. The cultivation of anthroposophy thus becomes a duty; knowledge becomes something that we actually feel, something towards which we have responsibility. When we are inwardly aware of this responsibility and have this resolve, when the mysteries of the world arouse in us the wish to become anthroposophists, then our feeling is true and right. But anthroposophy must not be something that merely satisfies our curiosity; it must rather be something without which we cannot live. Only then are our feelings what they ought to be, only then do we live as building stones in that great work of construction which must be carried out in human souls and can embrace all mankind.

Anthroposophy is a revelation of world-phenomena which will confront people of the future, will confront our own souls whether still in the physical body or in the life between death and a new birth. The coming changes will affect us, no matter whether we are still living in the physical body or whether it has been laid aside. Understanding of these events must however be acquired during life in the physical body if they are to take effect after death. To those who acquire some understanding of the Christ while they are still living in the physical body, it will make no difference, when the moment comes for vision of the Christ, whether or not they have already passed through the gate of death. But if those who now reject any understanding of the Christ have already passed through the gate of death when this moment arrives, they must wait until their next incarnation, for such understanding cannot be acquired between death and re-birth. Once the foundation has been acquired, however, it endures, and then the Christ becomes visible also during the period between death and the new birth.

And so anthroposophy is not only something we learn for our physical life but is of essential value when we have laid aside the physical body at death.

This is what I wished to offer you today as a help in understanding man and answering many questions. Self-knowledge is difficult because man is such a complex being. The reason for this complexity is that he is connected with all the higher worlds and beings. We have within us shadow-images of the great universe and all the members of our constitution—physical, etheric, astral bodies and ego—are worlds for divine beings. Our physical body, etheric body, astral body and ego form one world; the other is the higher world, the heaven world. Divine-spiritual worlds are the bodily members of the beings of the higher spheres of cosmic existence.

Man is the complex being he is because he is a mirror-image of the spiritual world. Realization of this should make him conscious of his intrinsic worth. But from the knowledge that, although we are reflected images of the spiritual world, we nevertheless fall far short of what we ought to be—from this knowledge we also acquire, as well as consciousness of our worth as human beings, the right attitude of modesty and humility towards the macrocosm and its gods.

Answers given to questions at the end of the lecture

Question: How are the words used by St. Paul, 'to speak with tongues' (Cor. I. 12) to be understood?
Answer: In exceptional human beings it can happen that not only is the phenomenon of speaking present in the waking state, but that something otherwise present in sleep-consciousness only, flows into this speaking. This is the phenomenon to which St. Paul refers. Goethe refers to it in the same sense; he has written two very interesting treatises on the subject.

Question: How are Christ's words of consolation received and experienced?
Answer: People will feel these words of consolation as though arising in their own hearts. The experience may also seem like physical hearing.

Question: What is the relation of chemical forces and substances to the spiritual world?
Answer: There are in the world a number of substances which

can combine with or separate from each other. What we call chemical action is projected into the physical world from the world of devachan—the realm of the harmony of the spheres. In the combination of two substances according to their atomic weights, we have a reflection of two tones of the harmony of the spheres. The chemical affinity between two substances in the physical world is like a reflection from the realm of the harmony of the spheres. The numerical ratios in chemistry are an expression of the numerical ratios of the harmony of the spheres, which has become dumb and silent owing to the densification of matter. If man were able to etherealize material substance and to perceive the inner formative principle in the atomic numbers, he would be hearing the harmony of the spheres.

We have the physical world, the astral world, the lower devachan and the higher devachan. If the body is thrust down lower even than the physical world, one comes into the sub-physical world, the lower astral world, the lower or evil lower devachan and the lower or evil higher devachan. The evil astral world is the province of Lucifer, the evil lower devachan the province of Ahriman, and the evil higher devachan the province of the Asuras. When chemical action is driven down beneath the physical plane—into the evil devachanic world—*magnetism* arises. When light is thrust down into the sub-material—that is to say a stage lower than the material world—*electricity* arises. If what lives in the harmony of the spheres is thrust down farther still, into the province of the Asuras, an even more terrible force—which it will not be possible to keep hidden very much longer—is generated. It can only be hoped that when this force comes to be known—a force we must conceive as being far, far stronger than the most violent electrical discharge—it can only be hoped that before some inventor gives this force into the hands of humankind, human beings will no longer have anything immoral left in them.

Question: What is electricity?
Answer: Electricity is light in the sub-material state. Light is there compressed to the utmost degree. An inward quality too must be ascribed to light; light is *itself* at every point in space. Warmth can expand in the three dimensions of space. In light there is a fourth; it is of fourfold extension—it has the quality of inwardness as a fourth dimension.

Question: What happens to the earth's corpse?
Answer: As the residue of Moon evolution we have our present moon which circles around the earth. Similarly there will be a residue of the earth which will circle around Jupiter. Then these residues will gradually dissolve into the universal ether. On Venus there will no longer be any residue. Venus will manifest, to begin with, as pure warmth, then it will become light and then pass over into the spiritual world. The residue left behind by the earth will be like a corpse. This is a path along which man must not accompany the earth, for he would thereby be exposed to dreadful torments. But there are beings who accompany this corpse, since they themselves will by that means develop to a higher stage.

Reflected as *sub-physical* world:

    Astral world........... the province of Lucifer
    Lower devachan ...... the province of Ahriman
    Higher devachan ...... the province of the Asuras

Life ether
Chemical ether
Light ether
sub-physical astral world: electricity
sub-physical lower devachan: magnetism
sub-physical higher devachan: terrible
       forces of destruction

Jeshu ben Pandira and the Christ Impulse

1. Leipzig, 4 November 1911

When we bring the science of the spirit to bear upon other spiritual worlds in addition to our physical world, and declare that the human being has a relationship not only to this physical world but also to supersensible realms, we may ask what is to be found within the human soul—without calling on any sort of clairvoyant capacity—which is supersensible, which gives an indication that the human being is connected with supersensible worlds. In other words, can even the ordinary person, with no clairvoyant capacity, observe something in the soul, experience something which bears a relationship to higher realms? The lectures today and tomorrow will endeavour to answer this question.

When we observe the life of the human soul, it divides clearly into three parts which are in a certain way independent of one another, and yet which are also, on the other hand, closely linked.

What first confronts us when we direct attention to ourselves as souls is our conceptual life, which in certain respects also includes our thinking, our memory. Memory and thought are not physical. They belong to the invisible, supersensible world: in our thought-life we have something which points to higher worlds. The nature of this conceptual world may be grasped in the following way: we bring before someone an object which he observes, and from which he then turns away. He has not immediately forgotten the object but preserves within himself a living picture of it. Thus we have concepts of the world surrounding us, and we may speak of the conceptual life as a part of our soul life.

We can observe a second part of our soul life if we inquire whether there is something within us related to objects and other beings in addition to our concepts. We do indeed have something else. It is what we call feelings of love and hate, what our thinking terms *sympathy, antipathy.* We consider one thing beautiful, another ugly; perhaps, we love one thing and hate another; one we feel to be good, the other evil. If we wish to sum up what thus appears in our inner life we may call it movements of feeling. The life of the heart is something quite different from conceptual life. In the life of the heart we have a far more intimate indication of the invisible than in conceptual life. This life of emotions, then, is a second component of our soul organism.

We become aware of a third by realizing that we not only consider a thing beautiful or ugly, good or evil, but that we feel impelled to do this or that, we have an impulse to act. When we undertake anything, perform a relatively important act or even merely take hold of an object, there must always be an impulse within us which induces us to do this. These impulses, moreover, are gradually transformed into habits, and we do not always need to bring conscious impulses to bear when we do something. When we go out, for instance, intending to go to the railway station, we do not have to resolve to take the first, second, and third steps; we simply go to the station. Behind all this lies the third member of our soul life, our will impulses, as something often wholly invisible to us.

If we now connect these three impulses characteristic of the human being with our initial question—whether the ordinary person can infer the existence of higher worlds—we must consider dream life, and how this is related to the three soul elements of thinking, feeling and willing.

These three components of our soul life—our thought life, emotions, and will impulses—can be clearly differentiated in our outward lives. Let us first take our conceptual life. The life of thought follows its course throughout the day—if we are not actually void of thought. Throughout the day we have concepts; and, when we grow tired in the evening, these concepts first become hazy. It is as if they become transmuted into a kind of fog. They become hazier and hazier, finally vanishing altogether, and we can then go to sleep. Thus this conceptual life, as we possess it on the physical plane, persists from our waking till our falling asleep, and disappears the moment we fall asleep. No one will suppose that his thought life can continue during sleep just as it does while he is awake—unless he is clairvoyant during sleep. The life of thought—or the conceptual life—which engrosses us fully from our waking till our falling asleep, must be extinguished, and only then can we go to sleep.

But the human being must recognize that the concepts he has, which have so fully taken up his attention during the day, and which he always has unless he merely drowses along, are no *hindrance* to his falling asleep. That this is so is best seen when we surrender ourselves to particularly vigorous concepts before falling asleep—for instance, by reading a very difficult book. When we have been thinking really intensely, we most easily fall asleep; and so if we cannot go to sleep, it is good to pick up a book, or occupy ourselves with something which requires concentrated thinking—study a book of mathematics, for instance. This will help us to fall asleep; but not something, on the other hand, in which we are deeply interested, such as a novel containing much that captivates our interest. Here our emotions become aroused, and the life of the emotions is something that hinders us from falling asleep. When we go to bed with our feelings vividly stirred, when we know that we have burdened our soul with something or when there is a special joy in our heart which has not yet subsided, it frequently happens that we turn and toss in bed and are unable to fall asleep. In other words, whereas concepts unaccompanied by emotions weary us, so that we easily fall asleep, things which strongly affect our feelings prevent us from falling asleep. It then becomes impossible to bring about the separation within ourselves which is necessary if we are to enter into the state of sleep. We can thus see that our emotional life has a different relationship to our whole existence from that of our life of thinking.

If we wish, however, to make the distinction quite clearly, we must take something else into account: our dreams. It might be supposed at first that, when the variegated life of dreams works upon us, it consists of concepts continuing their existence into the state of sleep. But if we test the matter quite accurately, we can observe that our conceptual life does not continue in our dreams. The activity which by its very nature wearies us does not continue during our dreams, except when our concepts are linked with intense emotions.

It is emotions that manifest in dream pictures. But to realize this it is necessary, of course, to test these things adequately. Take an example: someone dreams that he is young again and has some experience or other. Immediately the dream is transformed and something occurs which he may not have experienced at all. A kind of event is manifest to him which is foreign to his memory, because he has not experienced it on the physical plane. But persons known to him appear. How often it happens during dreams that one finds oneself involved in actions in the company of friends or acquaintances whom one has not seen for a long time. But if we examine this carefully we shall be forced to the conclusion that emotions are behind what emerges in dreams. Perhaps we still feel attached to the friend of that time, have not yet quite separated from him; there must still be some kind of emotion in us which is connected with him. Nothing occurs in dreams that is not connected with emotions. Accordingly we must draw a certain conclusion here—that when concepts of our waking life do not appear in dreams, this proves that they do not accompany us into sleep. When emotions keep us from sleeping, this proves that they do not release us, that they remain with us so as to be able to appear in dream pictures. It is the emotions which bring us dream images. This is due to the fact that the emotions are far more intimately connected with man's real being than is the life of thought. We carry emotions over into sleep. In other words, they are a soul element that remains united with us even during sleep. In contrast with ordinary concepts, the emotions accompany us into sleep; they are far more closely, more intensely, connected with the human individuality than is ordinary thinking when it is not pervaded by emotion.

What about the third soul component of will impulses? There also we can give a sort of example. Of course this can be observed only by people who pay attention to the moment of falling asleep in a rather subtle way. If someone has through training acquired a certain capacity to observe this moment, he will find it extremely interesting. At first, our concepts appear to us to be enveloped in mist; the external world vanishes, and we feel as if our soul-being were extended beyond our bodily limits, as if we were no longer confined within our skin but were flowing out into the elements of the cosmos. A profound feeling of satisfaction may be associated with falling asleep. Then comes a moment when a certain memory arises. Only very few people have this experience probably, but we can perceive this moment if we are sufficiently attentive. Before our vision appear the good and also the bad will impulses we have had; and the strange thing is that one feels about the good impulses: 'This is something connected with all wholesome will forces, something that invigorates me.' If the good will impulses present themselves to the soul before we fall asleep, we feel so much fresher and more filled with life-forces, and may often feel: 'If only this moment could last forever! If only this moment could endure throughout eternity!' Then one feels, also, how our bodily nature is deserted by the soul. Finally there comes a jerk, and one falls asleep. One does not need to be a clairvoyant in order to experience this, but only to observe our life of soul.

We must infer from this something extremely important. Our will impulses work before we fall asleep, and we feel that they fructify us. We experience extraordinary invigoration. With regard to emotions *per se*, we had to say that these are more closely connected with our individuality than our ordinary thinking, our ordinary act of conceiving. So we must now say of our will impulses: 'This is not merely something that remains with us during sleep, but something which becomes a strengthening, an empowering, of the life within us.' Will impulses are still more intimately connected with our life than are our emotions; and whoever frequently observes the moment of falling asleep feels in this moment that, if he cannot look back upon any good will impulses during the day, it is as though something of what enters into the state of sleep had been killed in him. In other words, will impulses are connected with health and disease, with the life force in us.

Thoughts cannot be seen. We see the rose bush at first through ordinary physical perception; but when the beholder turns aside or goes away, the image of the object remains in him. He no longer sees the object but he can form a mental image of it. Thus our thought life is somewhat supersensible. Completely supersensible are our emotions; and our will impulses, although they are transmuted into actions, are none the less supersensible. But taking into consideration everything which has now been said, we can see that our thought life, when not permeated by will impulses, is least closely connected with us.

Now, it might be supposed that what has just been said is refuted by the fact that on the following day our concepts of the preceding day arise before us again; that we can recollect them. Indeed, we are *obliged* to recollect. We must, in a supersensible way, call our concepts back into memory.

With our emotions, the situation is different; they are more intimately united with us. If we have gone to bed in a mood of remorse, we shall sense upon awaking the next morning a feeling of dullness—or something of the sort. If we experienced remorse, we sense this the next day in our body as weakness, lethargy, numbness; joy we sense as strength and elevation of spirits. In this case we do not need first to remember the remorse or the joy, to reflect upon them; we feel them in our body. We do not need to recollect what has been there: it *is* there, it has passed into sleep with us and has lived with us. Our emotions are more intensely, more closely, bound up with the eternal part of us than are our thoughts.

But anyone able to observe his will impulses feels that they are simply present again; they are always present. It may be that at the moment of waking we note that we experience again in its immediacy, in a certain sense, what we experienced as joy in life on the preceding day through our good moral impulses. In reality nothing so refreshes us as that which we cause to flow through our souls on the preceding day in the form of good moral impulses. We may say, therefore, that what we call our will impulses are most intimately bound up with our existence.

Thus the three soul components are different from one another; and we shall understand, if we clearly grasp these distinctions, that occult knowledge confirms that our thoughts, which are supersensible, bring us into relationship with the supersensible world, our emotions with another supersensible world, and our will impulses with still another, even more intimately bound up with our own real being. Thus we can say that when we perceive with the outer senses, we thereby perceive everything that is in the physical world. When we think or conceive, our life of concepts, our thought life, is in relationship to the astral world. Our emotions bring us into connection with what we call the heavenly world or lower devachan. And our moral or will impulses brings us into connection with the higher devachan, or the 'world of reason'. Man thus stands in relationship with three worlds through the impulses of thinking, feeling and willing. To the extent that he belongs to the astral world he can carry his thoughts into the astral world; he can carry his emotions into the world of devachan; he can carry into the higher heavenly world all that he possesses in his soul as will impulses.

When we consider the matter in this way, we shall see how right occult science is to speak of the three worlds. And when we take this into consideration, we shall view the realm of morality in an entirely different way; for the realm of good will impulses gives us a relationship to the highest of the three worlds into which the being of man extends.

Our ordinary thought life reaches only up to the astral world. No matter how brilliant our thoughts may be, if they are not sustained by feelings they penetrate no further than the astral world; they have no significance for other worlds. You will certainly understand what is meant in regard to external science, dry, matter-of-fact external science when we say that thoughts not permeated by emotion cannot express anything about realms other than the astral. Under ordinary circumstances, the thinking of the scientist, the chemist, the mathematician, proceeds without any accompanying feeling. It only scratches the surface. Indeed, scientific research even demands that it shall proceed in this way, and because of this it penetrates only into the astral world.

Only when delight or repugnance are associated with the thoughts of the research scientist is there added to these thoughts the element needed in order to penetrate the world of devachan. Only when emotions enter into thoughts, into concepts, when we feel one thing to be good and another evil, do we link thoughts with something which carries them into the heavenly world. Only then can we get a glimpse into deeper layers of existence. If we wish to grasp something belonging to the world of devachan, theories are no help to us at all. The only thing that helps us is to unite feelings with our thoughts. Thinking alone carries us only into the astral world.

When the geometrician, for example, grasps the relationships pertaining to the triangle, this lifts him only into the astral element. But, when he grasps the triangle as a symbol, and draws out the inherent meaning in it about the participation of the human being in three worlds, his threefold nature, this helps him to a higher level. One who sees in symbols the expression of soul forces, who inscribes this in his heart, who connects feelings with everything that people generally merely know, brings his thoughts into connection with devachan. For this reason, in meditating we must feel our way through what is given us, for only thus do we bring ourselves into connection with the world of devachan. Ordinary science, therefore, void of such feeling, can only ever bring us into connection with the astral world, however sharp-witted we may be.

On the other hand, art, music, painting and so on, lead us into the lower devachan world. One might object that if it is true that the emotions really lead us into the lower devachan world, passions, appetites and instincts would also do this. Indeed, they do. But this only shows that we are more intimately bound up with our feelings than with our thoughts.

Our sympathies may be associated with our lower nature also; an emotional life is aroused by appetites and instincts also, and this leads into lower devachan. Whereas we absolve in kamaloka whatever false thoughts we have, we carry with us into the world of devachan all that we have developed into emotions; and this imprints itself upon us right into the next incarnation, so that it comes to expression in our karma. Through our life of feeling, so far as this can have these two aspects, we either raise ourselves into the world of devachan, or we offend it.

Through our will impulses, on the other hand, which are either moral or immoral, we either have a good relationship with the higher world or we injure it, and have to compensate for this in our karma. If a person is so bad and degenerate that he actually injures the higher world through his evil impulses, he is cast out. But the impulse must nevertheless originate in the higher world. The significance of moral life becomes clear to us in all its greatness when we view the matter in this way.

From the worlds with which the human being is in such a close relationship through his threefold soul nature and also through his physical nature—from these realms proceed those forces which can lead man through the world. That is, we cannot observe an object belonging to the physical world without eyes to see it with, and thus we have a relationship with the physical world. Through our life of thought we are in relationship with the astral world; through our life of feeling we are connected with the world of devachan; and through our moral life with the world of upper devachan.

Four worlds	Participation of the human being
Upper devachan	Will: moral impulses
Lower devachan	Feelings: aesthetic ideals
Astral world	Thought: etheric nature
Physical world	Corporeality: physical-material nature

Man has four relationships with four worlds therefore. But this means nothing other than having a relationship with the *beings* of these worlds. From this point of view it is interesting to reflect upon man's evolution, to look into the past, the present, and the immediate future.

From the worlds we have mentioned proceed those forces which penetrate into our lives. Here we have to point out that in a previous epoch human beings were primarily dependent upon influences from the physical world, primarily so constituted as to receive impulses out of the physical world. This lies behind us as the Graeco-Roman epoch. During this epoch Christ worked on earth in a physical body. Since the human being was then primarily constituted to receive the influence of forces existing in the physical world, Christ had to appear on the physical plane.

At present we live in an epoch in which the focus is on developing thinking, in which man receives his impulses out of the world of thought, the astral world. Even external history demonstrates this. We can scarcely refer to philosophers of the pre-Grecian era; at most, to a preparatory stage of thinking. Hence the history of philosophy begins with *Thales*.[40] Only after the Graeco-Roman epoch does scientific thinking appear. Intellectual thinking develops for the first time about the sixteenth century. This explains the great progress in the sciences, which exclude all emotion from the activity of thought. And science is so specially beloved in our day because in it thought is not permeated with emotions. Our science is void of feeling, and seeks its well-being in the utter absence of sentiments. Woe betide someone who experiences any feeling in connection with a laboratory experiment! This is characteristic of our epoch, which brings the human being into contact primarily with the astral plane.

The next age, following our own, will already be more spiritual. There the emotions will play a role even in connection with science. If anyone then wishes to sit an examination for admission to some scientific study, it will be necessary for him to be able to sense the light that exists behind everything, the spiritual world which brings everything into existence. The test of scientific work will then consist in whether a person can develop sufficient emotion; otherwise he will fail the examination. Even though the candidate may have any amount of knowledge, he will not be able to pass the examination if he does not have the right sentiments. This certainly sounds very odd but it will be true, nonetheless, that the laboratory table will be raised to the level of an altar where the real test will consist in whether, in the electrolysis of water into oxygen and hydrogen, for instance, a person develops feelings corresponding with what the gods feel when this occurs. The human being will then receive his impulses from an intimate connection with the lower devachan.

And then will come the age that is to be the last before the next great earth catastrophe. This will be the age when man will be connected with the higher world in his will impulses, when morality will be dominant on the earth. Then neither external ability nor the intellect nor the feelings will hold the first rank, but impulses of will. Not man's skill but his moral quality will be the decisive thing. Thus humanity will have reached the epoch of morality, during which man will be in a special relationship with the world of higher devachan.

It is a fact that in the course of evolution ever greater powers of love will awaken in the human being, out of which he may draw his knowledge, his impulses and his activities.

At an earlier period, when Christ came down to the earth in a physical body, human beings could not have perceived Him otherwise than in a physical body. In our age the forces are actually awaking through which we will not see Christ in His physical body, but in an etheric form which will exist on the astral plane. Even in our century, from the 1930s on, and increasingly up to the middle of the century, a great number of human beings will behold the Christ as an etheric form. This will constitute the great advance on that earlier epoch, when human beings were not yet ripe for beholding Him in this way. This is what is meant by the saying that Christ will appear in the clouds; He will appear as an etheric form on the astral plane.

But it must be emphasized that He can be seen in this epoch only in the etheric body. Anyone who believes that Christ will appear again in a physical body loses sight of the progress made by human powers. It is a mistake to suppose that such an event as the appearance of Christ can recur in the same manner as that in which it has already taken place.

The next event, then, is that human beings will see Christ on the astral plane in etheric form, and those who are then living on the physical plane, and who have absorbed the teachings of spiritual science, will see Him. Those who are no longer living, but who have prepared themselves through spiritual-scientific work will see Him, nonetheless, in etheric raiment between their death and rebirth. But there will be human beings also who are not yet ready to see Him in the etheric body. Those who have scorned spiritual science will not be able to see Him, but will have to wait till the following incarnation, when they may devote themselves to spiritual knowledge and so be able to prepare themselves to understand this manifestation. It will then no longer depend upon whether someone has actually studied spiritual science or not while living on the physical plane, but to those who have not, the appearance of the Christ will be a rebuke and a torment, whereas those who strove to attain a knowledge of the spirit in the preceding incarnation will understand what they behold.

Then will come an epoch when still higher powers will

awaken in human beings. This will be the epoch when the Christ will manifest Himself in a still loftier manner: in an astral form in the lower world of devachan. And in the final epoch, that of moral impulse of will, the human beings who have passed through the other stages will behold the Christ in His glory, as the form of the greatest 'Ego', as the spiritualized Ego-Self, as the great Teacher of human evolution in the higher devachan.

Thus things evolve as follows: in the Graeco-Roman epoch Christ appeared on the physical plane; in our epoch He will appear as an etheric form on the astral plane; in the next epoch as an astral form on the plane of lower devachan; and in the epoch of morality as the very essence and embodiment of the Ego.

We may now ask ourselves for what purpose spiritual science exists. It is so that there may be a sufficient number of human beings who will be prepared when these events take place. And now already spiritual science is working to enable human beings to enter in the right way into connection with the higher worlds, so that they may enter rightly into the etheric-astral, into the aesthetic-devachanic, into the moral-devachanic. In our epoch it is the spiritual-scientific movement whose special aim is to enable the human being in his moral impulses to develop a right relationship with the Christ.

The next three millennia will be devoted to making visible the appearance of the Christ in the etheric. Only to those whose feelings are wholly materialistic will this be unattainable. A person may think materialistically when he admits the validity of matter alone and denies the existence of everything spiritual, or also through the fact that he draws the spiritual down to a material level. A person is materialistic if he admits the existence of the spiritual only when clothed in matter. Even some theosophists are materialists. These

believe that humanity is doomed to the necessity of beholding Christ again in a physical body. One does not escape from
being a materialist through being a theosophist, but through
comprehending that the higher worlds exist even when we
cannot see them in sense manifestation, but must develop
ourselves to the stage when we can behold them.

If we allow all this to pass through our minds, we may say
that Christ is the true moral impulse permeating humanity
with moral power. The Christ impulse is power and life, the
moral power which permeates us. But this moral power must
be understood. Precisely in our own epoch it is necessary for
Christ to be proclaimed. For this reason anthroposophy has
the mission also of proclaiming the Christ in His etheric form.

Before Christ appeared on earth and passed through the
Mystery of Golgotha, the teaching of Christ had already been
prepared in advance. The physical Christ had also already
been proclaimed. It was primarily Jeshu ben Pandira who
was the forerunner and herald, a hundred years before
Christ. He also had the name *Jesus*, and, in contrast to Christ
Jesus, he was called Jesus ben Pandira, son of Pandira. This
man lived about a hundred years before the Christian era
began. One does not need to be a clairvoyant in order to
know this, for it is to be found in rabbinical writings, and this
fact has often been the occasion for confusing him with Christ
Jesus. Jeshu ben Pandira was at first stoned and then hanged
from the beam of a cross while Jesus of Nazareth was actually
crucified.

Who was this Jeshu ben Pandira? He is a great individuality who, since the time of Buddha—that is, about 600
BC—has been incarnated once in nearly every century in
order to help humanity advance. To understand him, we must
go back to examine the nature of the Buddha.

We know, of course, that Buddha lived as a prince in the
Sakya family five and a half centuries before the beginning of

our Christian era. The individuality who became the Buddha at that time had not been a Buddha before. Buddha, that prince who gave humanity the doctrine of compassion, had not been born in that age as Buddha. For 'Buddha' does not signify an individuality but is a rank of honour. This Buddha was born as a bodhisattva and was elevated to the level of Buddha in the twenty-ninth year of his life, while he sat absorbed in meditation under the bodhi tree and brought down from the spiritual heights into the physical world the doctrine of compassion. A bodhisattva he had previously been—that is, in his previous incarnations—and then he became a Buddha. But in consequence the position of bodhisattva—that is, of a teacher of humanity in physical form—thereby became vacant, and had to be filled again. As the bodhisattva who had incarnated at that time ascended in the twenty-ninth year of his life to be Buddha, the rank of the bodhisattva was at once transferred to another individuality. Thus we must speak of a successor to the bodhisattva who had now risen to the rank of Buddha. The successor to the Gautama-Buddha-bodhisattva was that individuality who incarnated a hundred years before Christ as Jeshu ben Pandira, as a herald of Christ in the physical body.

He is now the bodhisattva of humanity until he in his turn advances to the rank of Buddha in 3,000 years from now. In other words, he will require exactly 5,000 years to rise from a bodhisattva to a Buddha. He who has been incarnated nearly every century since that time, is now incarnated at present too, and will be the real herald of the Christ in etheric raiment, just as he prophesied the physical appearance of the Christ.

Many of us will ourselves experience people during the 1930s—and more and more later in the century—who will behold the Christ in etheric raiment.

Spiritual science exists to prepare for this, and everyone

who works at the task of spiritual science shares in this preparation.

The manner in which humanity is taught by its leaders, but especially by a bodhisattva who is to become the Maitreya Buddha, changes greatly from epoch to epoch.

Spiritual science could not have been taught in the Graeco-Roman epoch as it is taught today; this would not have been understood by anyone at that time. In that period, the Christ being had to make manifest in physically visible form the goal of evolution, and only thus could He then work.

Spiritual research spreads this teaching increasingly among human beings, and they will come to understand the Christ impulse more and more, until the Christ Himself enters into them. Today it is possible by means of the physically uttered word, in concepts and ideas, by means of thinking, to make the goal understandable and to influence human souls for the good, in order to fire them with enthusiasm for aesthetic and moral ideals. But the speech of today will be superseded in later periods of time by forces capable of mightier stimulation than is possible at present through speech alone. Then will speech, the word, release powers conveying feelings of the heart from soul to soul, from master to pupil, from the bodhisattva to all those who do not turn away from him. It will then be possible for speech to be the direct bearer of aesthetic feelings. But the dawn of a new epoch is needed for this. In our time it would not be possible even for the bodhisattva himself to exert such influences through the larynx as will then be possible.

And during the final period of time, before the great War of All against All, the situation will be such that, as speech is at present the bearer of thoughts and conceptions and as it will later be the bearer of emotions, so will it then carry the moral element, moral impulses, transmitting these from soul to soul. At present the word cannot exert a direct moral influence. Such words can by no means be produced by our larynx as it is today. But such a spiritual power will one day exist. Words will be spoken through which the human being receives moral strength. Three thousand years after our present time, the bodhisattva we have spoken of will become the Buddha, and his teaching will then cause will impulses to stream directly into humanity. He will be the one whom the ancients foresaw: the Buddha Maitreya, a bringer of Good.

He has the mission of preparing humanity in advance so that it may understand the true Christ impulse. His mission is to direct man's gaze more and more to what he can love, increasingly to enable what is disseminated as theory to flow into a moral channel, so that at length all that we can possess in the form of thoughts shall stream into moral life. And, whereas it is still entirely possible today for a person to be very able intellectually but be immoral, we are approaching a time when it will be impossible for anyone to be at the same time intellectually shrewd and immoral. It will be impossible for mental shrewdness and immorality to go hand in hand.

This is to be understood in the following way. Those who have kept themselves apart and have opposed the course of evolution will be the ones who will then battle together, all against all. Even those who today develop the highest intelligence will gain nothing from their cleverness unless they develop further in feeling and morality. The highest intelligence is, indeed, developed in our epoch. It has reached its climax. But someone who has developed intelligence today and who neglects the possibilities of further evolution, will destroy himself by his own intelligence. This will then be like an inner fire consuming him, devouring him, making him so small and feeble that he will become stupid and unable to achieve anything—a fire that will annihilate him in the epoch when moral impulses have reached their climax. Whereas a person can be very dangerous today by means of his immoral shrewdness, he will then be without power to harm. Instead of this power, the soul will then possess ever-increasing moral powers—indeed, moral powers such as a contemporary person cannot in the least conceive. The highest power and morality are needed to receive the Christ impulse into ourselves so that it becomes power and life in us.

Thus we see that spiritual science has the task in the present stage of the evolution of humanity of planting the seeds for its future evolution. Of course, we must also take into account in spiritual science what has to be considered in regard to the whole of creation—that is, that errors may occur. But even one who cannot as yet enter into higher worlds can carefully test these things and see whether they have the ring of truth: the details must be consistent. Test what is proclaimed, all the individual data which are brought together regarding human evolution, the distinct phases of Christ's appearance, and the like, and you will see that things mutually confirm one another. This is the evidence of truth available even to someone who does not yet see into higher worlds. One can be quite assured: for those who are willing to test things, the doctrine of Christ reappearing in the spirit will prove to be the only true one.

Jeshu ben Pandira and the Christ Impulse

2. Leipzig, 5 November 1911

Since we spoke yesterday of the differentiation of the soul life of the human being into three parts—the realm of concepts, or of thought, the realm of emotions, and the realm of will impulses—it should be interesting to us now to raise the question: How can self-discipline, the nurturing of soul life, set to work in an appropriate way to develop and cultivate these three aspects of the soul? Here we shall begin with our life of will, our will impulses, and ask ourselves what characteristics we must specially cultivate if we wish to work in a beneficial way on our will life?

The most beneficial influence on our will is exerted by a life wholly directed towards comprehending karma. We might also say a soul life which strives to develop, as its primary characteristic, serenity and acceptance of our destiny. And what better way can one find of developing this acceptance, this calmness of soul in the presence of one's destiny, than by making karma an actual content in one's life?

What do we mean by this? It means that when our own sorrow or the sorrow of another comes upon us, when we experience joy or the heaviest blow of fate, we shall really be fully aware that, in a certain higher sense—not just theoretically but in a living way—we ourselves have given the occasion for this painful blow of fate. This means developing a mood in which we accept an experience of joy with gratitude, but are also clearly aware, especially in regard to joy, that we must not lose ourselves entirely, since this is perilous.

If we desire to progress in our development, we can conceive joy in the following way. For the most part, joy is something which points to a future destiny, not to one already past. In human life joy is usually something one has not deserved through previous actions. When we investigate karma by occult means, we always discover that in most cases joy has not been earned, and we should accept it gratefully as sent to us by the gods, as a gift of the gods, and to say to ourselves: The joy which comes to meet us today ought to kindle in us the will to work in such a way as to take into ourselves the forces streaming to us through this joy, and to apply these usefully. We must look upon joy as a sort of prepayment on account for the future.

In the case of pain, on the other hand, we have usually merited this, and we always find the cause in our present life or in former lives. And we must then realize with the utmost clarity that we have often failed to conduct ourselves in our outward life in accordance with this karmic mood. When faced with pain we are not able always to conduct ourselves in outward life in a way that appears to accept our destiny. We do not generally have an insight into such a thing at once—into the law of destiny. But even though we are not able to conduct ourselves outwardly in such a way, yet the important thing is that we do this inwardly.

And even if we have not conducted ourselves outwardly in accordance with this karmic mood, yet we should say to ourselves in the depths of our souls that we ourselves have been the cause of all such things. Suppose, for instance, that someone strikes us, that he beats us with a stick. In such a case it is usual for a person to ask: 'Who is it that strikes me?' No one says in such a case: 'It is I that beat myself.' Only in the rarest cases do people say that it is really they who are punishing themselves. And yet it is true that we ourselves lifted the stick against another person in days gone by. Yes, it is you yourself who raises the stick. When we have to get rid of a hindrance, this is karma. It is karma when others hold something against us. It is we ourselves who cause something to happen to us as recompense for something we have done. And thus we come to a right attitude toward our life, to a broadening of our self, when we say: 'Everything that befalls us comes from ourselves. Our own action is fulfilled outwardly even when it seems as if someone else performed it.'

If we develop such a way of viewing things, then our serenity, our acceptance of our karma in all occurrences, strengthens our will. We grow stronger in facing life with serenity, never weaker. Through anger and impatience we become weak. In the face of every occurrence we are strong when we are serene. In contrast we become continually weaker in will through moroseness and unnatural rebellion against destiny.

Of course, we must take a broad view of what we consider as destiny. We must conceive this destiny of ours in such a way that we say to ourselves, for instance, that the development of precisely one power or another at a certain period of one's life belongs also to a person's karma. And this is precisely where mistakes are often made in the education of children. Here karma links up with the problem of education, for education is destiny, the karma of the human being in youth.

We weaken the will of someone when we expect him to learn something, to do something for which his capacities are not yet adequate. In educating one must come to see clearly in advance what is suitable for each stage of life in accordance with the universal karma of humanity, so that the right thing may be done. Doing the wrong thing is rebelling against destiny, against its laws, and is connected with enormous weakening of the will. It is not possible to discuss here how a weakening of the will is associated with all premature awakening of the sensual appetites and passions. It is the prematurely awakened appetites, instincts and passions which are especially subject to this law. For making premature use of the bodily organs is *contrary* to destiny. All that is directly against the karma of humanity, all actions opposing the existing provisions of nature, are associated with a weakening of the will.

Since any true fundamental principles of education have long been lacking, there are many people in the world now who did not pass through their youth in the right way. If humanity does not undertake to base what is *most important of all*, the education of the young, on the principles of spiritual science, a race will arise with ever weaker wills—and not merely in an outward sense. This takes a deep hold of the life of the human being. Ask a number of people how they came into their present occupations. You may be sure that most of them will answer: 'Well, we don't know; we have in some way been pushed into this situation.' This feeling that one has been pushed into something, has been driven into it, this feeling of discontent, is also a sign of weakness of will.

Now, when this weakness of will is brought about in the manner described, still other results follow from this for the human soul, especially when the weakness of will is evoked in such a way that states of anxiety, of fear, of despair are produced at a youthful age. It will be increasingly necessary for human beings to have a fundamental understanding of higher laws in order to overcome states of despair, for despair is exactly what can be expected when we do not proceed in accordance with knowledge of the spirit.

A monistic and materialistic world view can only sustain people's strength of will through two generations. Materialism can satisfy just two generations: the one that founded the conception and the pupils who have received it from the founders. This is the peculiarity of the monistic and materialistic world view: the one who works in the laboratory or the workshop and who founded the view, whose powers are fully occupied and activated by what he is building up in his mind, experiences an inner satisfaction. But one who merely associates himself with these theories, who takes over a materialism ready-made, will not be able to achieve this inner satisfaction; and then despair will work back upon the culture of the will, and evoke weakness of will. Weakening of the will, human beings lacking energy, will be the results of this world view.

The second of the three aspects of the supersensible life we mentioned yesterday is that of the emotions. What affects the emotions favourably?

If we take the utmost pains to acquire an attentive attitude of mind, a marked attentiveness to the events in our surroundings—do not imagine that this attentiveness is very generally and strongly developed by people—this can be of great value to us. I have often had cause to mention a single example. In a certain country, teachers' examinations were once altered, and for this reason all the school teachers had to sit their examinations again. The examiner had to test both old and young teachers. The young ones could be tested on the basis of what they had learned in teachers' colleges. But how should he test the old teachers? He decided to ask them only about the subjects which they had themselves been teaching year after year in their own classes, and the result showed that very many of them had no notion of the very subjects they themselves had been teaching!

Attentiveness, the habit of following with vital interest the things that occur in one's environment, is most beneficial in the cultivation of the emotions especially.

Now the emotions, like everything else in the soul, are connected in a certain way with the will; and when we influence our emotional life unfavourably, we may thus indirectly influence our will impulses. We nurture our emotions favourably when we place ourselves under the law of karma in relation to our anger and passions, when we hold fast to karma. And this we find in what occurs in our environment. We find it, for example, when anyone does the opposite of what we had expected. We may then say to ourselves: 'All right; that is simply what he is doing!' But we may also become angry and violent, and this is a sign of weakness of will.

Outbursts of violent temper hinder the right development of the emotions and also the will, and also have a far more extensive influence, as we will soon see. Now anger is something that a person does not by any means have under his control. Only gradually can he learn to dispense with anger. One must have patience with oneself. To anyone who believes he can achieve this in the twinkling of an eye I must repeat the story of a teacher who was very keen to rid his pupils of anger. When faced with the fact that, after all his efforts, a boy still became angry, he himself became so angry that he threw the ink bottle at the child's head. A person who permits himself to do such a thing must ponder karma for many, many weeks.

What this signifies will become clear to us if we take this occasion to look a little more deeply into the life of the human soul. There are two poles in our soul life: the life of will on the one hand and that of thoughts, of conceptions, on the other. The emotions, the feelings of the heart, are in the middle. Now we know that the life of man alternates between sleeping and waking; and while the human being is awake, his life of thoughts and conceptions is especially active. For the fact that the will is not very wide awake can become clear to anyone who observes closely how a will impulse comes about. We must first have a thought, a concept; only then does the will thrust upward from the depths of the soul. The thought evokes the will impulse. When the human being is awake, he is awake in thought, not in will.

But occult science teaches us that when we sleep everything is reversed. Then the will is awake and very active, and thought is inactive. We cannot know this in a normal state of consciousness, for the simple reason that we know things only by means of thoughts and these are asleep. In this state we do not observe that our will is active. But if we attain clairvoyance and arrive at the world of imaginative representations, we then observe that the will awakes the moment thinking falls asleep. And the will slips into the pictures we thus perceive and awakens these. The pictures are then woven out of will. Thus thoughts are then asleep but the will is awake.

This awakening in our will is connected with our whole human nature in a manner entirely different from our thinking. Depending on whether a person works or does not work, is well or ill, is serene or hot-tempered, the will becomes healthy or unhealthy. And the health or unhealthiness of our will works in the night upon our life-condition, right into the physical body. Very much depends upon whether one develops a mood of serenity during the day, acceptance of destiny, and thus prepares one's will so that this will may be said to develop a pleasant warmth, a feeling of well-being; or whether, on the other hand, one develops anger. This unhealthiness of the will streams into the body during the state of sleep at night and is the cause of numerous illnesses, whose causes are sought for but not found because the resulting physical illnesses appear only after the lapse of years or even decades. Only one who surveys great stretches of time can see in this way the connection between conditions of the soul and of the body. Even for the sake of bodily health, therefore, the will must be disciplined.

We can also influence our emotions through serenity and

acceptance of our karma so that they work beneficially upon our bodily organization. On the other hand, this organization is most injured through apathy, lack of interest in what is occurring around us. Such apathy is becoming more and more widespread, it is the reason why so few people take an interest in spiritual things. It may be supposed that objective reasons lead to the adoption of a materialistic view of life. But actually such objective reasons for a materialistic view of life do not really exist. No, it is apathy; no one can be a materialist without being apathetic. It is a lack of attention to our surroundings. Anyone who observes his environment with alert interest is met everywhere by things that only spiritual knowledge can explain. But apathy deadens the emotions and leads to weakness of will.

Furthermore, special significance attaches to the characteristic called obstinacy—the attitude of mind that insists inflexibly upon one thing or another. Unhealthy emotions can also bring about obstinacy. These things are often like the serpent that bites his own tail. All that we have mentioned may be caused by obstinacy. Even people who go through life very inattentively may be very obstinate. People who are altogether weak-willed are sometimes discovered to persist obstinately in something when we had not expected it, and weakness of will becomes constantly more marked if we do not strive to overcome obstinacy. It is precisely in persons with weak wills that we find this quality of obstinacy. On the other hand, when we endeavour to avoid becoming obstinate we shall see that in every instance we have improved our emotions and strengthened our wills. Every time that we actually are goaded by an impulse to be obstinate but refuse to yield to it, we become stronger for facing life. We shall notice the benefits if we proceed systematically against this fault; through struggling to overcome obstinacy we attain inner satisfaction. Healthy cultivation of emotions specially depends upon our struggling in every way to overcome obstinacy, apathy, lack of interest. In other words, interest and attentiveness in relation to the environment foster both the feelings and the will. Apathy and obstinacy have the opposite effect.

For a sound emotional life, we have the fine word *sensibility*. Having sensibility means that something creative and purposeful occurs to one. Children ought to play in such a way that the imagination is stimulated, that the spontaneous activity of their souls is stimulated, so that they have to reflect about their play. They ought not to arrange building blocks according to prescribed patterns: this merely develops pedantry, not creative imagination and sensibility. We are developing creative imagination when we let children do all sorts of things in sand, when we take them into the woods and let them form little baskets out of burs, and then stimulate them to make other things of burs stuck together. Things which draw on a certain inventive talent nourish sensibility and creative imagination. Strange as it may seem, such cultivation of sensibility brings serenity of soul, inner harmony, and contentment.

Moreover, when we go for a walk with a child, it is good to leave him free to do whatever he will, provided he does not behave too badly. And when the child does anything we should show our pleasure, our participation and interest; we should not be unresponsive or lacking in interest in what the child produces out of his own inner nature. Even when instructing a child, we should connect what we teach him with the forms and processes of nature. When children reach an older stage, we should not then occupy them with riddles or puzzles taken from newspapers; this leads only to pedantry. On the contrary, observation of nature offers us the opposite of what newspapers generally offer for the cultivation of emotions. A serene heart and a harmonious life of feeling determines not only mental health but also bodily health, even though long stretches of time may intervene between cause and effect.

We come now to the third aspect of supersensible life, to thinking. We nurture and sharpen this especially by developing characteristics which seem to have nothing whatever to do with thinking, with concepts. The best method of developing good thinking is by complete absorption and insight, not so much through logical exercises but by observing one thing and another, using processes in nature for this purpose in order to penetrate into hidden mysteries. Through absorption in problems of nature and of humanity, through the endeavour to understand complex personalities, through the intensifying of attentiveness, we grow wise. Absorption means striving to unravel something by thinking, by conceiving. We shall be able to see that such mental absorption has a wonderfully good effect in later life.

The following example is taken from life. A little boy showed his mother remarkable aspects of his observation, which were associated with extraordinary devotion and capacity for insight. He said: 'You know, when I walk on the streets and see people and animals, it seems as if I had to enter into the people and the animals. I met a poor woman, and I entered into her, and this was terribly painful to me, very distressing.' (The child had not seen any sort of poverty at home.) 'And then I entered into a horse and then into a pig.' He described this in detail, and was stimulated to an extraordinary degree of compassion, to special deeds of pity, through feeling union with the life of others. Whence does this come, this expansion of one's understanding for other beings? If we think the matter over in this case, we are led back into a preceding incarnation, when the person in question had cultivated absorption in things, in the secrets of things, as we have described.

But we do not have to wait until the next incarnation for the results which follow our cultivation of devotion to and absorption in things. These manifest themselves even in a single life. When we are induced in earliest youth to develop all of this, we shall develop in later life a clear, transparent thinking, whereas otherwise we develop scrappy, illogical thinking. It is a fact that truly spiritual principles can advance us in our life.

During recent decades there have been few truly spiritual principles underlying education, almost none at all. And now we are experiencing the results. There is an extraordinary amount of wrong thinking in our day. One can suffer the pains of martyrdom from experiencing the terribly illogical ways of the world. Anyone who has acquired a certain clairvoyance does not simply feel that one thing is correct and another incorrect, but he suffers actual pain when confronted by illogical thinking; and a sense of well-being in connection with clear, transparent thinking. This signifies that he has acquired a feeling for such things, and this enables him to distinguish clearly. And this brings far truer differentiations when one has actually reached this stage. It gives a far truer discrimination between truth and untruth. This seems incredible, but it is true. When something erroneous is said in the presence of a clairvoyant person, the pain which rises in him shows him that this is illogical, erroneous. Illogical thinking is extraordinarily widespread; at no time has illogical thinking been so widespread as in our own time, in spite of the fact that people pride themselves so much on their logical thinking. The following is an example that may well seem somewhat crass, but is typical of the habit of experiencing things without interest or thought.

I was once travelling from Rostock to Berlin. Into my compartment entered two people, a gentleman and a lady. I sat in one corner and wished only to observe. The gentleman was very soon behaving strangely, though he was otherwise probably a well-educated person. He lay down, sprang up again in five minutes; then again he groaned pitiably. Since the lady thought he was ill, she was seized by pity, and very soon a conversation between them was in full flow. She told him that she had clearly noticed he was ill, and that she knew what it meant to be ill, for she was ill also. She said she had a basket with her in which she had everything that was effective in curing her. She said: 'I can cure anything, for I have the remedy for everything. And just think what a misfortune has befallen me! I have come from deep inside Russia all the way here to the Baltic Sea, in order to recuperate and to do something for my ailment, and, just as I arrive, I find that I have left at home one of my important remedies. Now I must turn back at once, and my hope of convalescence has been in vain.'

The gentleman then narrated his sufferings, and she gave him a remedy for each of his illnesses, and he promised to do everything she said, making notes about all. I think there were eleven different prescriptions. She then began to enumerate all of her illnesses one by one; and he began to show his knowledge of what would cure them: that for one ailment she could be helped in a certain sanatorium, and for another in another sanatorium. She, in turn, wrote down all the addresses and was only worried that the pharmacies might be closed for Sunday when she arrived in Berlin. These two people never for one moment noticed the strange contradiction of each knowing only what might help the other one, but knowing no means of help for themselves. Thus these two educated people were able to bathe in a sea of nonsense.

Such things must be clearly seen when we demand that self-knowledge shall give insight. We must require self-knowledge to develop our coherent thinking, but especially absorption in and devotion to the matter in hand. All these things work together in the soul. Scrappy thinking has the inevitable result, even though this takes a long time to appear, of making a person morose, sullen, hypochondriacal about everything; and frequently we do not know where the causes of this are to be found. Insufficient cultivation of concentration and insight makes one sullen, morose, hypochondriacal. What is so absolutely essential to thinking seems at first sight to have nothing to do with it. All obstinacy, all self-seeking, have a destructive effect upon thinking. All characteristics connected with obstinacy and selfishness—such as ambition, vanity—all these things that seem to tend in a very different direction make our thinking unsound, and act unfavourably upon our mood of soul. We must seek, therefore, to overcome obstinacy, self-seeking, egoism; and cultivate, on the contrary, a certain absorption in and devotion to things, and a certain self-sacrificing attitude toward other beings. Absorption, devotion and a self-sacrificing attitude in regard to the most insignificant objects and occurrences have a favourable effect upon thinking and upon one's mood. In truth, self-seeking and egoism bring their own punishment because the self-seeking person becomes more and more discontented, complains more and more that he comes off badly. When anyone feels this way about himself, he ought to acknowledge the law of karma and ask himself, when he is discontented: 'What self-seeking has brought this discontent upon me?'

Thus we can describe how we may develop and how we may injure the three aspects of soul life, and this is extraordinarily important. We see, therefore, that spiritual science lays deep hold upon our life, for true observation of spiritual principles may lead us to self-education, and this is of the most vital importance, and will become of ever-increasing significance. The time in man's evolution has passed when human beings were led by the gods from above, from the higher worlds. In ever-increasing measure, human beings will have to do things for themselves, without being directed and led.

With regard to what the Masters have taught about working our way upward to Christ, who will appear in this very century on the astral plane, greater understanding of what this advance means for humanity can be achieved only when the human being learns increasingly to find his own direction, provide his own impulses. Just as we explained to you yesterday that human beings gradually work their way upward to Christ, so must we gradually perfect in freedom our thinking, feeling, and will impulses. And this can be achieved only through self-mastery, self-observation. Just as in earlier times, in ancient clairvoyance, the gods gave man impulses from above, so will man determine his own way in later times through newly developing clairvoyance. This is why anthroposophy appears precisely in our time, so that mankind may learn to develop soul characteristics in the right way. In this way man learns to meet what the future will bring. Only in this way can we understand what must one day come about: that those who are both clever *and* immoral will be cast out and rendered harmless.

The characteristics I have spoken of are important for every human being. But they are especially important to those determined to strive in a particular way to attain characteristics, speedily and rationally, which will become more and more necessary for humanity. For this reason it is the leaders of mankind who strive to achieve this development in very special measure in themselves, because highest attainments can be reached only by means of the highest attributes.

This evolution is carried through to the highest degree of all by that individuality who once ascended to the rank of a bodhisattva, when the preceding bodhisattva became a Buddha, and who has, since then, been incarnated once in nearly every century; who lived as Jeshu ben Pandira, herald of the Christ, a hundred years before Christ. Five thousand years are needed for his ascent to the rank of a Buddha, and this Buddha will then be the Maitreya Buddha. He will be a Bringer of Good, because (as can be seen by those who are sufficiently clairvoyant) he succeeds through the most intense self-discipline in developing to the utmost powers manifesting in magical moral forces which enable him to impart heart forces and moral impulses to human souls through the word itself. We cannot as yet develop on the physical plane any words capable of doing this. Even the Maitreya Buddha could not do this at present—could not develop such magical words. Today only *thoughts* can be directly imparted by means of words.

How is he preparing himself? By developing to the highest possible degree those qualities which are called good. The bodhisattva develops in the highest degree what we may describe as devotion, serenity in the presence of destiny, attentiveness to all occurrences in one's surroundings, devotion to all living beings, and insight. And although many incarnations will be needed for the future Buddha, yet he devotes himself during his incarnations primarily to giving attention to what will come about. What he now does is relatively little, since he is utterly devoted to preparing for his future mission.

This mission will be achieved through a special law pertaining to this bodhisattva alone. This law we shall understand if we take account of the possibility that a complete revolution in the soul's life may occur at a certain age.

The greatest of such transformations that ever occurred took place at the baptism by John. What occurred there was that the ego of Jesus, in the thirtieth year of his life, abandoned the flesh; and another ego entered: the Christ Ego, leader of the sun beings.

A like transformation will be experienced by the future Maitreya Buddha. But he experiences such a revolution in his incarnations quite differently. The bodhisattva patterns his life on that of Christ, and those who are initiated know that he manifests in every incarnation very special characteristics. It will always be noted that, in the period between his thirtieth and thirty-third years a mighty revolution occurs in his life. There will then be an interchange of souls, though not in so mighty a manner as in the case of Christ. The 'ego' which has until then given life to the body passes out at that time, and the bodhisattva becomes, in a fundamental sense, altogether a different person from what he has been hitherto, even though the ego does not cease and is not replaced by another, as was true of the Christ.

This is what all occultists call attention to: that he cannot be recognized before this time, before this transformation. Up to this time—although he will be absorbed intensely in all things—his mission will not be especially conspicuous; and even though the revolution is certain to occur, no one can ever say what will then happen to him. The earlier period of youth is always utterly unlike that into which he is transformed between his thirtieth and thirty-third years.

Thus does he prepare for a great event in which the old ego passes out and another ego then enters. And this may be such an individuality as Moses, Abraham or Elijah. This ego will then be active for a certain time in this body; thus can take place what must take place in order to prepare the Maitreya Buddha. For the rest of his life he lives with this ego which enters at that moment.

What then occurs is like a complete transformation. Indeed, what is needed for the recognition of the bodhisattva can then occur. And when he appears after 3,000 years, elevated to the rank of Maitreya Buddha, his 'ego' will remain in him but will be permeated inwardly by still another individuality. And this will occur in his thirty-third year, in the year in which, in the case of Christ, the Mystery of Golgotha occurred. And then will he come forth as teacher of the Good, as a great teacher who will prepare the true teaching of Christ and the true wisdom of Christ in a manner entirely different from what is possible today.

Spiritual science must prepare for what will one day take place upon our earth.

Now anyone in our time can cultivate those characteristics which are injurious to the emotional life, such as apathy, etc. But this results in a laxity in the emotions, a laxity in the inner soul life, and such a person will no longer be able to carry out his task in life, will no longer be able to fulfil it. For this reason everyone may consider it a special blessing if he can acquire for himself a knowledge of what is to occur in the future. Whoever has the opportunity today to devote himself to spirit knowledge, enjoys a karmic gift of grace.

For having a knowledge of these things gives a foundation for security, devotion, and peace in our souls, for serenity, confidence and hope in meeting what faces us in the coming millennia of the evolution of humanity. All who can know these things should consider this a special good fortune, something which evokes the highest powers of the human being, which can enkindle everything in his soul that seems at the point of being extinguished or is in a state of disharmony, or approaching destruction. Enthusiasm, fire, rapture become also health and happiness in outer life.

He who earnestly acquaints himself with these things, who can develop the necessary absorption in these things, will surely experience the happiness and inner harmony they can bring him. And, if anyone in our Society does not yet find this manifest in himself, he should for once accept such knowledge and say:

If I have not yet felt this, the fault lies in me. It is my duty to steep myself in the mysteries one may hear today. It is my duty to feel that, as a human being, I am one link in a chain which has to stretch from the beginning to the end of evolution, in which are linked together all human beings, individualities, bodhisattvas, Buddhas, Christ. I must say to myself: 'To feel that I am a link in it is to be conscious of my true worth as a human being. This I must sense; this I must feel.'

The Christ Impulse as Living Reality

1. Munich, 18 November 1911

Anthroposophically orientated spiritual science is based on occult science, as we have often emphasized, which brings us knowledge of the forces underlying the various epochs, and also enables us to understand what is at work in the cultural periods of our own epoch. So we must speak of these inner forces of our own time, whenever and wherever we meet, in order to understand the tasks of spiritual science in relation to what is at work beneath the surface of life, and so that occult research can help us direct our lives in harmony with the great goals of mankind.

In order to speak about contemporary occult trends it would be a good thing to start from the point where deep, occult research can lead us to what is also taking place in the supersensible world in our time. By way of introduction we must also take into account what we have right in front of us at present, though we can only give a general sketch of it and not go into any details. Many things can be spoken of without embarrassment only in anthroposophical gatherings, for ours is a time of dogmatism and abstraction. The strange thing is that this basic characteristic is not recognized in exoteric life, and people generally believe that their thoughts and actions are free of dogma, when in fact they are extremely dogmatic. They think they are taking their lead from reality, although they are really lost in the wildest abstractions. Therefore it is worthwhile bringing the realities of anthroposophically orientated spiritual science to the attention of wider circles, to open up the possibility for an understanding of our epoch, though it will probably be a long time before the outside world wants to develop a deeper understanding for these things. We do not see how tied up in dogmas and abstractions our civilization is, until we stop looking at it from the abstract point of view and begin seeing it in a really living way. One then finds a trend of thought whose chief characteristic consists in the laying down of ready-made dogmas that enlightened people are required to accept, whilst imagining they are being genuinely discriminating. Something of the sort is evident in the so-called monistic movement, though it is not justified in calling itself monistic. It gets its chief dogmas from modern natural science, in fact that particular branch of it which, strictly speaking, likes acquiring knowledge through purely external methods. If this natural science were to limit itself to its own field of activity, it could do important work; instead of this it leads to the formation of a new religion. People take the facts of materialistic natural science and turn them into abstract dogmas. And anyone who is of the opinion that he is right because he is convinced of these dogmas himself, believes that the others have lagged a long way behind. Such people completely ignore the rich tapestry of human individuality, and strive only to cram their heads with external dogmas, and to regard the conclusions drawn from abstractions as the most important thing. This leads to the formation of cliques and sects whose adherents cling to expert opinions, principles and dogmas which they then advocate as *the* important thing.

All that comprises the anthroposophically orientated spiritual movement represents the opposite of this. This movement does not set out to follow a number of doctrines but to place the worth of the human individual in the foreground.

Anthroposophically orientated spiritual science leads to social life based on mutual trust between people. Human beings should and will come together who have trust in one another. And in joint tasks one ought to say: You are the right person, not because you adhere to this or the other principle, but because you can achieve this or that and do not disturb other people in the course of your work. Nothing could be worse than the bad modern habit of sectarianism taking hold of anthroposophical life. It is not only when you are in full agreement with your neighbour that you should listen to him; even if you are not, you should still maintain freedom and flexibility for yourself and for him, and, with this recognition of individualities, work educationally in the anthroposophical movement. Our time has very little understanding for this sort of thing. It aims at generalities. What seems right to one can make others think him a fool. In the anthroposophical movement we must make a clean sweep of that. If this attitude were not prevalent in the wider, materialistic world, people would hasten of their own accord to understand human individuals in our own way, and then a scientific spirituality would soon appear that would be bound to lead to a world conception of a spiritual kind. But people are rigid with dogmas and therefore cannot attain this.

If you examine the principles upheld in monistic gatherings, you would soon see that none of these principles and dogmas are based on the outlook and results of present-day science but on those of fifteen to twenty years ago. Thus, for instance, a distinguished personality in modern scientific circles said at a recent scientific meeting in Koenigsberg: 'Facts of physics are all tending in a certain direction. People always used to speak of ether as being something present in matter and all around us, and it was taken for granted without taking the other known material sciences into account. But this idea has gradually met with justified doubt, and therefore we must now ask what physicists should assume to be there in place of the ether.' His answer was: purely mathematical constructions, Hertz' and Maxwell's equations, conceptual formulae. According to these, light does not spread through space by means of ether vibrations, but, assuming them not to be there, it overcomes non-material, vacuum-space in a way formulated through the equations referred to, so that according to this the transmission of light appears to be bound to concepts and ideas. It could quite easily happen that anyone who pointed to such hypotheses of the most up-to-date science in a monistic meeting could be mistaken for a mad theosophist, making the absurd proposition that thoughts are the bearers of light. Yet Max Planck[41] of Berlin, a respected authority on natural science, declared this to be his scientific opinion. If, therefore, the monists wanted to make progress in science, they would also have to accept this expert opinion. As this is not the case, a monistic religion will only be possible if its supporters believe they have a scientific basis, but do not know that their assumptions have long been superseded. People who think in a monistic way are only sustained by so-called intellectual research and its underlying world conception, or the biassed dogmas arising out of this. The anthroposophically orientated theosophist, in contrast, turns to facts that cannot deprive anyone of freedom or lead to the formation of sects, and so each individual can remain free.

An important aspect of the anthroposophically orientated spiritual movement is that it gives an impulse for self-education in a way that is hardly equalled at the present time. We must understand what we ourselves are as a movement, and realize that this movement is based on foundations that can only be found within this movement and nowhere else.

Life itself can show us this. There are many people who think we ought to take what anthroposophically orientated spiritual science has to offer and present it in philosophical terms, in the style of official science, to make spiritual science more acceptable to the representatives and followers of officialdom. But that cannot be done, because it is impossible to make compromises between the occult stream of spiritual science and any other movement that arises from the characteristic outlook of our times, like the monistic one, for instance—that is, one that has a completely different basis. To bring about compromises between the two, even if only in form, is impossible. It is much more a matter of aiming at introducing a new impulse into the culture of our times. The others cannot even understand or explain their own basic facts, nor gain any objective distance to them because they lack the courage to draw the conclusions arising from these facts. On closer examination we find incomplete thought processes in every sectarian movement, including scientific circles, and spiritual science must see these for what they are, for we know that a half truth or a quarter truth is worse than a total fallacy because it deceives the outside world, which is not competent to judge. The anthroposophist must enter the very nerve of the spiritual movement in order to understand the external, materialistic trend because the latter sometimes works with facts that are tending in the direction of spiritual truth, but are not fully developed.

If medical science has serious intentions of researching into the human body, it cannot ignore the sphere, the concepts and the results of occult investigation. The psychoanalysis of Sigmund Freud[42] in Vienna, which enjoys a large and growing interest, gives us an instructive example of the difficulties arising in this sphere. It began by investigating the life of the soul in both the physically and the mentally ill, in an attempt to discover certain psychic causes there, in the long-forgotten early years, for example, because there was a definite feeling that what is still there in the unconscious has its lasting effect on later life too. An ingenious doctor of this school, Dr Breuer,[43] tried to put patients into a condition of hypnosis, and then let them make a kind of confession, so that he could probe into the depths of their souls. You all know that it is a great relief to talk about what is oppressing you. People were often cured by these hypnotic confessions, or they were well on the way to it. Even without hypnosis Freud often achieved the same results by means of well-chosen questions. Apart from this he discovered that happenings of a largely unconscious kind are revealed in dream life, and out of this a kind of dream interpretation arose in the school of psychoanalysis. It would be wrong to suggest that this could provide a good opportunity to strike a compromise between spiritual science and such research because, despite the quarter truth contained in it, one would soon become aware that it leads to the wildest errors and that it would, in fact, be preferable to keep to purely materialistic interpretations. Spiritual science, when properly understood, has to reject such things. The point is that these ideas about the soul's dream life and the resulting theory are steeped in coarse, sense-bound thinking, and it is therefore not possible to turn it into a spiritual truth. In order to do that one needs the spiritual foundations that spiritual science has to offer, otherwise one gropes around in obscure hypotheses and theories and explains them in a materialistic way. And that is the way things have turned out in the Freudian school. They certainly got as far as the symbolism of dreams, but wove into them ideas of the materialistic age, whilst Schubert's[44] and Volkelt's[45] ideas began to go in the right direction but could not be further developed. People came to regard dreams as symbolic of sexual life, because our time is incapable of realizing that this area is the lowest revelation of innumerable worlds that rise far above our world in spiritual significance. By so doing they are turning it into something that gives an irresponsible flavour to a whole field of investigation, and, in consequence, brings about the most serious errors. Therefore the only thing that spiritual science can say about the Freudian school is that it has to reject its research on the grounds that it is superficial. If it would first of all thoroughly acquaint itself with spiritual investigation, these truths would produce quite different results. You can therefore begin to see that our age is an intellectual age, an age of dogma, that drives people into a wild chaos of instincts and passions and is satisfied with what is merely intellectual and abstract.

In the example of the Freudian school therefore, we see an area of soul life being shown in a wrong light and dragged down by the worst kind of materialism. It tries to relate everything to sex, a procedure, one could say, that arose out of the scientists' own personal inclination, only they are not conscious of it, and which is dilettante into the bargain.

We must feel how necessary it is that spiritual investigation rejects half and quarter truths and only adopts those it can defend with its own principles, for we realize that spiritual science can give people strength to work out of themselves. It is important to stress that my first books did not grow out of theosophy, yet outsiders find it strange that I nevertheless became a theosophist later on. That is a short-sighted, narrow-minded view, however. It is characteristic of these books that despite their strictly scientific attitude they do not have dealings with what is regarded as official science, or assume the style that believes itself capable of making general definitions.

Spiritual science should draw abundant life from the foundations of occultism, make no compromises and show a courage that is lacking in other domains. Whoever refuses to make any compromises of this kind, acquires a reputation for being inadequate in the eyes of those people who always want one to give way, but do not do so themselves. Spiritual science, in contrast, stands in the world as a spiritual movement firmly established on its own foundations; its members must always be conscious of this fact, and see this as a vital element. It sometimes happens that people interested in specific research come into spiritual science, but where spiritual science and spiritual investigations are concerned it is not a case of specific interests. Each individual can follow these up for himself, and he should not expect spiritual science to follow after him. Spiritual science must penetrate into our whole culture and have the courage to carry out its task rigorously and consistently in an age that is justifiably called intellectual.

But do not let us imagine that this intellectuality ought to merge in the same way with spiritual life, for we have to take our start from facts that are reached by clairvoyant means. We find, then, that the life of the soul has three basic elements. There is, firstly, the life of concepts, intellectuality, which initially only comes to expression in perception. When we consider intellectuality by itself, we notice that it is bound in the widest sense to the material world from which man abstracts his mental images. These images themselves, however, are supersensible. From the very connection between the life of mental imagery and the life of perception we see that the former is [not] connected with the physical plane. If we involve ourselves in difficult thoughts and think to such an extent that we get tired, then we sleep well, provided that only the life of thought and not the life of feeling was engaged in the activity. Therefore we can grasp the statement that the life of thought is a supersensible process, and is connected with the next element, the astral world. It is from the astral plane that those forces come that awaken and sustain the life of thought in the human soul.

The second element consists of the waves of feeling that pass through our soul, such as pleasure and displeasure, joy and pain, sorrow, love, dislike, and so on. The flow of thought and feeling is intimately connected with our ego, and these feelings can rob us of our sleep because their emotional unrest prevents us entering the astral plane. We can understand therefore that this astral plane brings us into connection with lower devachan, which does not accept our emotions if they are impure; in other words, that part of the astral world that is lower devachan rejects them.

Morality and will impulses are the third element. The person who can look back on good deeds when reviewing his day can experience a moment of bliss before falling asleep. He enjoys a condition of which he can say: If only it were possible to prolong it, to enjoy the enlivening power of it, so that it could take hold of one's whole soul life as a fructifying force! This enables us to understand what occult investigations tell us, that will impulses point us to higher devachan, where they are accepted only if they issue from a pure will and accord with this spiritual world. Thus our life of mental images and concepts, our intellectuality, is closely connected with the astral world, our life of feeling with lower devachan and our life of will with higher devachan.

In addition to these we have our life of sense perception on the physical plane. These four elements develop at a different rate in human incarnations during the various cultural epochs.

When we consider the occult background, we see how the life of perception comes to the fore in the Graeco-Roman era, how the Greek and the Roman were completely attuned to the physical world that they esteemed so highly. Our time, the fifth cultural epoch, is that of thinking, of intellectuality. This is why the abstract sciences are flourishing. The coming sixth age will retain intellectual life, in the same way as we in the fifth have retained the life of perception, and will in addition express itself in the feeling life of the soul. The environment will affect people so that it causes them pleasure and displeasure, joy and pain, sympathy and antipathy, to a degree that as yet can only be felt by the occultist who is capable of overcoming mere intellect, and understanding certain aspects of life with real feeling, without lengthy logical reasoning. The occultist feels displeasure at illogical things, joy and peace of soul at logical things. If he defends something that he immediately sees to be right, he has to prove it nowadays with a lengthy argument, in order to be understood. The occultist feels pain especially vividly when he reads the newspaper, because it is particularly in the daily papers that one frequently finds illogicality incarnate. You have to read them, nevertheless—being selective if possible—in order to keep in touch with the outside world. You should not, however, be selective in the way the professor of Chinese was, who told his colleague one day, in a great state of agitation: I have just this moment discovered—it was the year 1870–71—that Germany has been at war with France for half a year, because I only read the Chinese newspapers!

In the last post-Atlantean epoch, the seventh era, the sense for morality will develop, that is, the sense for will impulses. Remarkable progress will come about through this. Occult investigations, even those of the present-day, show us that someone can be very clever and intellectual without being moral. Nowadays intellectuality and morality exist alongside each other. Little by little, however, the curious fact will emerge that a person's immorality will kill off his cleverness, so that in the far future an immoral person will actually be stupid or will have to become so. A moral era is coming in which the morality of our whole soul life and the intellectuality of those later times will become one.

Although man has within his soul all the four elements we have mentioned, sense perception predominated over all others in the Graeco-Roman era, and intellectuality is added to this to a greater degree in the present; in the penultimate era, the sixth period, emotion will predominate, and in the seventh, the last cultural epoch, it will be morality—and in a way we can only dream of today. We cannot even imagine what it will be like as Socrates could, who considered that virtue could be both taught and learnt. All this, however, will become reality by the seventh epoch, for tendencies already clearly perceptible in occultism foretell this.

Intellectuality, then, is the chief spiritual characteristic of our age, but there is a difference between the way it comes to expression in the materialistic thinking of the world and in spiritual science. Man is connected through his intellect with the astral plane, but he will only be conscious of this—and he will only make the right use of it—when he has developed clairvoyance. This will begin in an ever-increasing number of human beings in the course of the twentieth century. Progress will only be made in this direction when people not only develop a heightened intellect for themselves but also raise it up into the astral world. The human being who has advanced to intellectual clairvoyance in this way, can and will approach the etherically visible Christ more and more clearly in the course of the next three thousand years. In bygone times, however, when man was mainly connected with the physical plane, Christ could only appear in physical incarnation. In the present age of the intellect He can appear only in etheric form. Spiritual science wishes to prepare mankind for this in such a way that it acquires a proper understanding and makes proper use of the clairvoyant faculties that are slowly appearing and will, in the course of natural evolution, come to be used for spiritual vision later on. And this will ensure that in the second half of our intellectual age the Christ will be seen clairvoyantly in His etheric form.

The age of feeling will develop the soul further in a different respect, enabling it to enter the lower devachanic world in a conscious way. Christ will appear as a form of light in the lower devachanic world to a number of human beings, revealing Himself through sound; and from His astral body of light He will fill their receptive souls with the Word that was active in astral form in the beginning, as is expressed by John in the opening words of his Gospel.

In the age of morality a number of human beings will perceive the Christ revealing Himself from higher devachan in His true Ego that surpasses all human egos in inconceivable greatness, and with such splendour that it can bestow on man the highest possible moral impulses. Such is the connection between the impulses of the different cultural epochs and the soul of man. From higher and ever higher worlds will come the forces that flow into man and become active within him. Perception in the physical world is wonderful indeed; even more wonderful is the intellect when it attains predominance and forms a connection with the astral world, and even greater still are the feelings and morality that are connected with the devachanic world.

Thinking it through logically you will realize the logic in this evolution, because life everywhere confirms it. The anthroposophist goes to meet such evolution, not only in broad sweeps and universal truths but also in the individual details of human development. In the aberrations of the world around us, the striving towards intellectual dogma is very prominent, but for spiritual knowledge the intellect has to become spiritualized so that it can understand the more advanced results of occult investigation. We can see this clearly from the fact that in the Graeco-Roman era, through the Mystery of Golgotha, we are presented in physical form with what then developed further so as to lead humanity upwards through its effect on the human soul. It is necessary above all that man learns to understand what this Christ impulse signifies for our world. It has to be stressed that this Christ impulse is a living reality streaming into mankind, and that Christ did not give the world a doctrine or a theory but the *impulse* for new life. Let us take a serious look at this.

Since the Saturn stage, throughout the stages of Sun and Moon, man has developed his physical, etheric and astral bodies. The ego could only appear on earth in bodies that were sufficiently prepared for it, and then develop further under the nurturing influence of the Christ impulse, because Christ is the same macrocosmically as our ego is to us microcosmically. The four principles of the macrocosm are connected in manifold ways with our four lower principles, including the most important of these, the ego. In our present cultural epoch, higher human principles can already be glimpsed in our development. Life spirit, spirit self and spirit man will be developed in us out of the higher spirit worlds through macrocosmic principles. Not through the fourth macrocosmic principle, however, but through the help of beings that have no macrocosmic significance of their own but only microcosmic significance. These will work as teachers among mankind, since they have themselves advanced by one or more principles beyond man himself. Christ, in contrast, is a macrocosmic being at the fourth stage of His macrocosmic development, just as man is at the fourth stage microcosmically.

So you should keep macrocosmic and microcosmic principles apart, but be clear about the fact that the four first macrocosmic principles of course include all the higher macrocosmic principles. Thus the microcosmic beings work as teachers and seek to carry mankind forward through their teaching, whereas Christ, working as a macrocosmic reality, is not a teacher like the other teachers of humanity, for He united Himself with the earth as a reality, as power, as very life.

The loftiest teachers of the successive epochs are the so-called bodhisattvas who already in the pre-Christian era pointed to Christ in His full reality of being; again in the Christian era they point to Him as a power who is now united with the earth. Thus the bodhisattvas work both before and after Christ's physical life on earth. He, who was born as the son of a king in India 550 years before Christ, lived and taught for twenty-nine years as a bodhisattva, and then ascended to the rank of Buddha; thereafter he was never again to appear on the earth in a body of flesh, but from then onwards he worked from the spiritual world. When this bodhisattva became Buddha he was succeeded in that very moment by the new boddhisattva whose mission it is to lead mankind to an understanding of the Christ impulse. This came to pass before the appearance of Christ on the earth, for around 105 BC there lived in Palestine a man still to this day defamed in rabbinical literature, Jeshu ben Pandira, and he was this new bodhisattva. Jesus of Nazareth is an essentially different being, in that when He reached the age of thirty He became the bearer of Christ at the Jordan baptism by John.

It was Jeshu ben Pandira from whom the Essene[46] teachings were mainly derived. One of his pupils bore the name of Matthew, and he too pointed towards the Mystery of Golgotha. Jeshu ben Pandira was stoned by his enemies and his corpse was hung on a cross as a further mark of contempt. His existence can be established without the help of occult research for plenty is said about him in rabbinical literature, although the information is either misleading or deliberately falsified. He bore within him the individuality of the new bodhisattva and was the successor of Gautama Buddha. The name of his pupil Matthew passed over to later pupils; and there was a Gospel known by that name in existence already since the time of the first Matthew, in the form of a description of rituals contained in the ancient mystery-scripts. In the life of Christ Jesus the essential content of these mysteries became reality on the physical plane. What were previously only pictures from the mysteries, seeds as it were of subsequent happenings, now became reality. Thus the Christ Mystery had already been known prophetically, had indeed been enacted in the ceremonies of the ancient mysteries, before it became, once and once only, an actual event on the physical plane.

The bodhisattva who once lived as Jeshu ben Pandira comes down to the earth again and again in a human body and will continue to do so in order to fulfil the rest of his task and particular mission which cannot yet be completed. Although its consummation can already be foreseen by clairvoyance, no larynx exists that is capable of producing the sounds of the speech that will be uttered when this bodhi-sattva rises to the rank of Buddha. In agreement with oriental occultism, therefore, it can be said: Five thousand years after Gautama Buddha, that is to say, towards the end of the next three thousand years, the bodhisattva who is his successor will become Buddha. But as it is his mission to prepare human beings for the epoch above all connected with the development of true morality, when in future he becomes Buddha his spoken words will contain the magic power of goodness. For thousands of years, therefore, oriental tradi-tion has predicted: Maitreya Buddha, the Buddha who is to come, will be a bringer of goodness through the word. He will then be able to teach human beings the real nature of the Christ impulse, and in that age the Buddha stream and the Christ stream will flow into one. Only thus can the Christ Mystery be truly understood.

The Christ Impulse as Living Reality

2. Munich, 20 November 1911

So mighty and all-pervading was the impulse poured into the evolution of mankind by the Christ that its waves surge onwards into future epochs. In the fourth epoch of post-Atlantean civilization this impulse was manifested in the incarnation of Christ in a human, physical body. And we are now approaching an epoch when the impulse will manifest in such a way that human beings behold the Christ on the astral plane in an etheric form.

Yesterday[47] we heard of human beings who in still later epochs will be able to behold Him in even higher forms in the aesthetic and moral spheres. But when we speak in this way of the Christ impulse we are concerned with ideas which will be resolutely opposed, above all by the churches of Christendom. Great and incisive measures have been and are necessary in the onward progress of human evolution in order to promote increasing understanding of the Christ impulse. Hitherto, indeed, such understanding has been lacking. And anyone who considers modern theology will realize not only the futility of the attitude maintained by opponents of Christianity, but also by those who claim to be its steadfast adherents. The theosophical movement in the West should have become that stream of spiritual life which draws on true and genuine sources to awaken understanding for Christianity in the modern age, but such endeavours met with strong opposition.

It is important to understand the real sources of Christianity, but owing to lack of time they cannot all be mentioned today. We shall speak only of those which have been accessible to mankind since the thirteenth century.

Since the thirteenth century the movement connected with the name of Christian Rosenkreutz has been an integral part of the spiritual life of mankind. Spiritual measures of a very definite kind were necessary in the thirteenth century to enable the influence connected with this name to become part of the spiritual life of the modern age. At the time when the spiritual world was entirely shut off from human vision, a council of twelve wise men came together. All the spiritual knowledge then existing, of the world and its secrets, was gathered from their separate different spheres into this council. By means of certain occult processes, the wisdom that had passed over from Atlantis to the holy rishis had been transmitted to seven of these twelve men. In four others lived the wisdom of the sacred mysteries of the Indian, Persian, Egyptian and Graeco-Roman epochs respectively. And what had so far unfolded as characteristic of the fifth post-Atlantean epoch constituted the wisdom of the twelfth. The whole scope of spiritual life was thus accessible to these twelve.

Now it was known at that time that a certain individuality who had been a contemporary of the Mystery of Golgotha was to be born again as a child. Meanwhile, through a number of incarnations, this individuality had unfolded a power of deep and fervent piety, devotion and love. The council of the twelve wise men took this child into their care soon after he was born; shut off from the outside, exoteric world, he came under no influence save theirs; they cared for all his bodily needs and were also his teachers. The manner of the child's development was altogether unique; the profound spirituality he bore within him as the fruit of many incarnations came to expression, too, in his outer, bodily form. He was a weak and sickly child, but his body became marvellously transparent. He grew up and developed in such a way that a radiant, shining spirit indwelt a body that had become transparent. Through a profoundly wise form of education, all the wisdom from the ages preceding and during post-Atlantean times which the twelve wise men were able to impart, rayed into his soul. Through deeper soul-forces, not through the intellect, the treasures of all this wisdom united in the soul of this child. He then fell into a strange condition. For a certain period of time he ceased to take nourishment; all external functions of life were as though paralysed, and the whole of the wisdom received by the child rayed back to the twelve. Each of them received back what he had originally given, but now in a different form. And those twelve wise men felt that now, for the first time, the twelve great religions and world conceptions had been united into one interconnected whole. And henceforward what we call rosicrucian Christianity lived in these twelve men.

The child lived only for a short time longer. In the external world we give the name Christian Rosenkreutz to this individuality. But it was not until the fourteenth century that he was known by this name. In the fourteenth century he was born again and lived then for more than a hundred years. Even when he was not incarnated in the flesh, he worked through his etheric body, always with the purpose of influencing the development of Christianity in its true form as the synthesis of all the great religions and systems of thought in the world. And he has worked on into our time, either as a human being or from his etheric body, inspiring all that was done in the West to establish a synthesis of the great religions. His influence today is increasing all the time. Many a person of whom we do not expect it, is a pupil chosen by Christian Rosenkreutz. Nowadays it is already possible to speak of a sign by means of which Christian Rosenkreutz calls one whom he has chosen. Many people can discover this sign in their life; it may express itself in a thousand ways, but these different manifestations all lead back to a typical form which may be described as follows.

Someone may, for example, be chosen in the following way. A person embarks upon some undertaking; he spares no effort to make it successful and forges straight towards his goal. While he is ruthlessly making his way in the world (he may be a thorough materialist), he suddenly hears a voice saying: 'Stop what you propose to do!' And he will be aware that this was no physical voice. But now suppose that he refrains from pursuing his project. Then he will be able to realize that if he had continued ruthlessly towards his goal, this would certainly have led to his death.

These are the two essential aspects: firstly that he knows with certainty that the warning came from the spiritual world; and secondly, that he knows death would have come to him had he persisted in his undertaking. One who is to become a pupil is shown that he has been saved, moreover, by a warning proceeding from a world which, to begin with, he dwells outside of. So far as earthly circumstances are concerned, death has already come to him and his further life is to be regarded as a gift. And when the person in question realizes this he will be led to the resolve to work in a spiritual movement. If the resolve is taken, this means that he has been chosen. This is how Christian Rosenkreutz begins to gather his pupils around him, and many human beings, if they were sufficiently alert, would be conscious of such an event in their life.

The human beings of whom it can be said that they were, or will be, united in this way with Christian Rosenkreutz, are those who should be the pioneers of a deeper understanding of esoteric Christianity. This stream of spiritual life connected with Christian Rosenkreutz provides the highest means for enabling the Christ impulse to be understood in our time. The beginning was already made long, long ago—a hundred years before the Mystery of Golgotha, through Jeshu ben Pandira, whose essential mission it was to make preparation for the coming of Christ. He had a pupil, Matthew, whose name subsequently passed over to his successor living at the time of Jesus of Nazareth. The greatest deed accomplished by Jeshu ben Pandira was to originate and prepare the Gospel according to St. Matthew. The content of this Gospel derives from a ritual of initiation, and passages such as that concerning the temptation, and others, too, originate from the ancient mysteries. All these processes in the evolution of humanity were to be enacted on the physical plane too. This was written down in outline by the pupil of Jeshu ben Pandira.

Jeshu ben Pandira was not spared from the hard fate he himself predicted; he was stoned, and his corpse was suspended from a cross. The original chronicle was preserved in the hands of a few of his adherents, in deep secrecy. We can best follow what happened to it later on when the great Church father, Jerome[48] himself says that he had received the document of the Matthew Gospel from a Christian sect. The original record was held at that time in the secret keeping of a small circle and through certain circumstances came into the hands of Jerome. He was charged by his bishop with the task of translating it. Jerome himself narrates this; but he says at the same time that because of the form and manner of the transcription, it should not pass into outside hands. He wanted to translate it in such a way that its secrets would remain secret—and he says, furthermore, that he himself does not understand it. The nature of what thus came into existence was such that one person could express it in one way and another in a different way in secular language. And this is how it has come down to posterity. In reality, therefore, the world does not yet possess the Gospels in their true form. There is every reason and justification then for spiritual research today, in shedding new light upon the Gospels, to go back to the Akashic Record, because there and there only are they to be found in their original form.

Let there be no mistake about it. Christianity in its true form has yet to be separated from the dross. One sign among many others indicates how necessary this is: in the year 1873 in France a count was taken of true, genuine catholics. They amounted to one third; the other two-thirds proved no longer to be adherents in the real sense—and these two-thirds were certainly not people who never feel the need of religion! People's religious longings do incline towards the Christ; but the true sources of Christianity must be rediscovered. And it is to this end that the stream of spiritual life emanating from Jeshu ben Pandira flows into the other stream which, at the beginning of the thirteenth century, is connected with the name of Christian Rosenkreutz.

It is also necessary for us to know that one of the characteristics of the incarnations of the bodhisattva is that in his youth he cannot be recognized as such. Between his thirtieth and thirty-third year a great revolution takes place so that this individuality is fundamentally transformed. For example a Moses or Abraham individuality can take possession of a bodhisattva individuality at this time of his life.

About 3,000 years after our present time this bodhisattva will become the Maitreya Buddha. And then his influence will flow from the spiritual world into the hearts of human beings as a magical, moral power. In this way the two streams work together, the stream of the Maitreya Buddha and the western stream connected with Christian Rosenkreutz.

Faith, Love, Hope. The Third Revelation to Mankind

1. Nuremberg, 2 December 1911

This evening and tomorrow evening we are going to attempt a coherent study of the being of man, and of his connection with occult aspects underlying our present time and the near future.

From various indications I have given here you will have grasped that today we are, to some extent, facing a new revelation, a new annunciation to mankind. If we keep in mind the recent periods of man's evolution, it may well be that we shall best understand what is approaching if we connect it with two other important revelations. In doing so we shall be considering, it is true, only what has been revealed to mankind in times relatively near to our own.

These three revelations—the one now to come and the two others—may be best understood when compared with the early development of a child. Observing the child rightly, we find that on first coming into the world it has to be protected and cared for by those around it; it has no means of expressing what is going on within it or of formulating in thought what affects its soul. To begin with the child cannot speak, cannot think; everything must be done for it by those who have received it in their midst. Then it starts to speak. Those who watch it attentively—this is mentioned in my book *The Education of the Child*—will know that first it imitates what it hears; but that in the early days of talking it has no understanding which can be attributed to thinking. What the child says does not arise out of thought, but the other way round. It learns to think by talking; learns gradually to apprehend in clear thought what previously it was prompted to say out of the obscure depths of feeling.

Thus we have three successive periods in the child's development—a first period when it can neither speak nor think, a second when it can speak but not yet think, and a third when it becomes conscious of the thought-content in what it says. With these three stages in the child's development we may compare what mankind has gone through—and has still to go through—since about 1,500 years before the Christian era.

The first revelation of which we can speak, as coming to mankind during the present cycle of time, is the revelation proceeding from Sinai in the form of the Ten Commandments. Anyone going more deeply into the significance of what was revealed to mankind in these commandments will find great cause for wonder. The fact is, however, that people take these spiritual treasures so much for granted that little thought is given to them. But those who reflect upon their significance have to confess how remarkable it is that in these Ten Commandments something is given which has spread through the world as law; something which in its fundamental character still holds good today and forms the basis of the law in all countries, in so far as, during the last 1,000 years, they have gradually embraced modern civilization. Something all-embracing, grand, universal, is revealed to mankind, as if to say that there is a primal Being in the spiritual world whose image is here on earth—the ego. This Being can so infuse His own power into the human ego, so pour Himself into it, that man can follow the norms, the laws, given in the Ten Commandments.

The second revelation came about through the Mystery of Golgotha. What can we say about this Mystery? What can be said was indicated yesterday in the public lecture, 'From

Jesus to Christ'. It was shown there how we have to trace back all physically embodied human beings to the original human couple on earth. And as we can understand man's bodily nature only as descending through the generations from this couple, so in order rightly to understand our ego's greatest gift that must root itself more and more deeply into our ego during earthly existence, we must trace it back to the Mystery of Golgotha.

It need not here concern us that in this connection the old Hebrew tradition has a different conception from that of modern science. If we trace back mankind's blood-relationship, its bodily relation, to that original human couple, Adam and Eve, who once lived on earth as archetypal individuals, as the primal forebears of mankind, and if we must therefore say that the blood flowing in people's veins goes back to that human pair, we can ask: Where must we look for the origin of the most precious gift bestowed on our soul, that holiest, most valuable gift, which accomplishes in the soul never-ending marvels and makes itself known to our consciousness as something higher than the ordinary ego within us? For the answer we must turn to what arose from the grave on Golgotha. In every human soul that has experienced an inner awakening there lives on what then arose, just as the blood of Adam and Eve continues to live in the body of every human being.

We have to see a kind of fountain-head, a primal fatherhood, in the risen Christ—the spiritual Adam who enters the souls of those who have experienced an awakening, bringing them, for the first time, to the fullness of their ego, to what gives life to their ego in the right way. Thus, just as the life of Adam's body lives on in the physical bodies of all human beings, what arose from the grave on Golgotha flows in like manner through the souls of those who find the path to it. That is the second revelation given to mankind; we are able to learn what came about through the Mystery of Golgotha.

If in the Ten Commandments man has received guidance from without, this guidance may be compared to what happens to the child before it can either speak or think. What is done for the child by its environment is comparable to what the old Jewish law achieved for all mankind which until then, as it were, lacked the power of speaking and thinking. People have now learnt to speak however—or, rather, have learnt something that may be compared with a child's learning to speak: they have gained knowledge of the Mystery of Golgotha through the Gospels. And the way in which they first understood the Gospels may be compared with how a child learns to speak. Through the Gospels there has come to human souls and human hearts some degree of understanding for the Mystery of Golgotha, which has found its way into human feelings and perceptions, and into the soul-forces arising in us when, for example, we allow the deeply significant, intuitive scenes and pictures drawn from the Gospels by great painters to work upon us. It is the same with traditional pictures—pictures of the adoration of the Child by the Shepherds or by the Wise Men from the East; of the flight into Egypt and so on. All this leads back in the end to the Gospels; it has reached man's understanding in such a way that he may be said to have learnt to speak, in his own fashion, about the Mystery of Golgotha.

Viewed in this way we are now moving towards the third period, which may be compared with how the child learns the thought-content in its own speech and can become conscious of it. We are approaching the revelation which should give us the full content, the thought-content, of the Gospels—all they contain of soul and spirit. For at present the Gospels are no better understood than the child understands what it says before it can think. In the context of world history people are meant to learn through spiritual science to reflect upon the thoughts in the Gospels; to let the whole deep spiritual content of the Gospels work upon them for the first time. This is connected with a further great event which human beings can feel approaching, and which they will experience before the end of this twentieth century. This event can be brought before our souls in somewhat the following way. If we return to the nature of the Mystery of Golgotha, we realize that those elements of the Christ which rose from the grave of Golgotha have remained with the earth, so that they can directly affect every human soul, and can in each soul awaken the ego to a higher stage of existence. Speaking thus of the Mystery of Golgotha we may say: Christ then became the Spirit of the earth and since that time has remained so. In our day, however, a change in Christ's relation to man is coming, an important change connected with what all of you have come to know something about—the new revelation to man of the Christ.

This revelation can also be characterized in another way. For this indeed we must turn to what happens when a person goes through the gate of death. (This is something that could not be described in books, but must now be spoken of.) When a person has passed through the gate of death, has experienced the backward survey over his previous earthly life and come to the point when his etheric body is laid aside and the time has come for his kamaloka, he first meets two figures. Usually only one is mentioned, but to complete the picture— and this is a reality for every true occultist—we must say that before his kamaloka a person is confronted by two figures. What I am now telling you holds good, it is true, only for people of the West and for those who, during the last 1,000 years have been connected with western culture. A person after death is confronted by two figures. One of these is Moses—the person knows quite clearly that it is Moses who stands before him, holding up the tables of the law. In the Middle Ages they spoke of Moses 'with his stern law'. And in his soul the person is keenly aware of how far in his inmost being he has transgressed against this law. The other figure is 'the cherubim with the flaming sword', who pronounces judgment on these transgressions. That is an experience a person has after death. Thus, in accordance with our spiritual science, it can be said that there is a kind of settlement of our karmic account by these two figures—Moses with the stern law and the cherubim with the flaming sword.

In our time, however, a change is approaching, an important change: Christ is becoming Lord of Karma for all those who, after death, experience what has just been described. Christ is taking up the office of judge. Let us look more closely into this fact. From the world-conception of spiritual science we all know that a karmic account is kept of our life; that there is a certain balancing between the deeds on the credit side of the account—the sensible deeds, the fine deeds, those that are good—and, on the other side, the bad, ugly, lying deeds and thoughts.

Now it is important that in the further course of a person's earthly life he should himself adjust the balance of this karmic account. But this living out of the result of his good and splendid deeds, or those that are bad, can be done in many different ways. The particular adjustment in our future life is not always determined according to the same pattern. Suppose someone has done a bad action; he must compensate for it by doing a good one. This good action, however, can be achieved in two ways, and it may require the same effort on the man's part to do good only to a few people as to benefit a considerable number. To ensure that in future, when we have found our way to Christ, our karmic account will be balanced—made part of the cosmic order—in such a way that the settlement will benefit as many people as possible—that will be the concern of Him who in our time is becoming Lord of Karma—it will be the concern of the Christ.

This taking over by Christ of the judging of human deeds is a result of His direct intervention in human destiny. This intervention is not in a physical body, but on behalf of those people on earth who will increasingly acquire the capacity of perceiving Him. There will be people, for instance, who, while carrying out some deed, suddenly become aware— there will be more and more cases of this from now on, during the next 3,000 years—of an urge to step back from what they are doing, because of a remarkable vision. They will perceive in a dreamlike way what appears to be an action of their own; yet they will not be able to remember having done it.

Those who are not prepared for such a thing to happen in the course of their evolution will look upon it merely as imagination run wild or as a pathological condition of the soul. Those, however, who are sufficiently prepared through the new revelation coming in our time to mankind by means of spiritual science—that is, through this third revelation during the latest cycle of mankind—will realize that all this points to the growing of new human faculties enabling people to see into the spiritual world. They will also realize that this picture appearing to their soul is a forewarning of the karmic deed that must be brought about—either in this life on earth or in a later one—to compensate for what they have done.

In short, people will gradually achieve, through their own efforts, the faculty for beholding a vision of the karmic adjustment, the compensating deed, which must come about in future. From this fact it can be seen that in our time, too, we should say, as did John the Baptist by the Jordan: Change your state of soul, for the time is coming when new faculties will awake in human beings.

But this form of karmic perception will arise in such a way that here and there the figure of the etheric Christ will be directly visible—the actual Christ as He is living in the astral world—not in the physical body, but visible to the newly awakened human faculties. He will manifest on earth, as counsellor and protector of those who need advice, help or solace in the loneliness of their lives.

The time is coming when human beings who feel depressed and miserable for one or other reason will increasingly find the help of their fellows less important and valuable. This is because the force of individuality, of individual life, will count for more and more, while the power of one man to work helpfully upon the soul of another, which held good in the past, will constantly tend to diminish. In its stead the great Counsellor will appear, in etheric form.

The best advice we can receive for the future is, therefore, to make our souls strong and full of energy, so that with increased strength, the further we advance into the future, whether in this incarnation—and certainly this applies to young people of today—or in the next, we may realize that newly-awakened faculties give us knowledge of the great Counsellor who is becoming at the same time the judge of human karma; knowledge, that is, of Christ in His new form. For those people who have already prepared themselves here for the Christ event of the twentieth century, it will make no difference whether they are in the physical body when this event becomes a widespread experience, or have passed through the gate of death. Those who have passed on will still have the right understanding of the Christ event and the right connection with it, but not those who have thoughtlessly passed by this third great annunciation to mankind given through spiritual science. For we must prepare for the Christ event here on earth while in the physical body. Those who go through the gate of death without even glancing at spiritual science during their present incarnation, will have to wait until their next before gaining a right understanding of the

Christ event. The fact of the matter is that those who on the physical plane have never heard of the Christ event are unable to come to an understanding of it between death and rebirth. They, too, must wait until they can prepare for it on their return to the physical plane.

Thus mankind now faces the mighty event referred to—Christ takes upon himself the office of judge and intervenes in an etheric body, directly from the astral world, in the evolution of mankind, becoming visible in various places among human beings.

It is characteristic of human evolution, however, that old human attributes not closely connected with spiritual evolution gradually lose significance. When we consider human evolution since the Atlantean catastrophe we can say: Among the great distinctions and differences prepared during the Atlantean age, present-day human beings have become accustomed to those of race. We can still speak in a certain sense of an old Indian race, of an old Persian race, of an Egyptian or a Graeco-Latin one, and even of something in our own time corresponding to a fifth race. But the concept of race in relation to human evolution is ceasing to have a right meaning. Something that held good in earlier times will no longer do so in the sixth cultural epoch which is to follow our own—namely, that it was essential to have some geographical centre from which to spread the culture of the epoch. The important thing is the spreading of spiritual science among human beings without distinction of race, nation or family. In the sixth cultural epoch those who have accepted spiritual science will come from every race, and will found, all over the globe, a new culture no longer based on the concept of race—which will have lost its significance. In short, what is important in the world of maya, the external world of space and location, vanishes away; we must learn to recognize this in the further development of our spiritual-scientific movement.

At the beginning this was not understood. Therefore, we see how, when we read Olcott's book *The Buddhist Catechism*,[49] which is otherwise so useful, we have the impression that races always go on like so many wheels. But for the coming time such concepts are losing their significance. Everything subject to limitations of space will lose significance. Hence anyone who thoroughly understands the meaning of human evolution understands also that the coming appearance of Christ during the next 3,000 years does not entail Christ being confined to a body bound by space, nor limited to a certain territory. Neither will His appearance be limited by an inability to appear in more than one place at a time. His help will be forthcoming at the same moment here, there, and everywhere. And as a spiritual being is not subject to the laws of space, anyone who can be helped by Christ's direct presence is able to receive that help at one end of the earth just as well as another person at the opposite end. Only those unwilling to recognize the progress of mankind towards spirituality, and what gradually transforms all the most important events into the spiritual, can declare that the Christ being is limited to a physical body.

We have now described the facts concerning the third revelation and how this revelation is already in process of throwing new light on the Gospels. The Gospels are the language, and, in relation to them, anthroposophy is the thought-content. As language is related to a child's full consciousness, so are the Gospels related to the new revelation that comes directly from the spiritual world—related, in effect, to what spiritual science is to become for mankind. We must be aware that we have in fact a certain task to fulfil, a task of understanding, when we come—first out of the soul's unconscious depths, and then ever more clearly—to discern our connection with anthroposophy.

We must look upon it, in a sense, as a mark of distinction

bestowed by the world-spirit, as a sign of grace on the part of the creative, guiding spirit of the world, when today our heart urges us towards this new annunciation, this third revelation, added to those proclaimed from Sinai and then from the Jordan. To learn to know man in his entire being is the task given in this new annunciation—to perceive ever more deeply that the body we are principally conscious of is enclosed in other members of man's being, which are important for our whole life.

It is necessary for our friends to learn about these matters from the most various points of view. Today we will begin by first saying a few words about man's inner being. You know that if we start from the actual centre of his being, from his ego, we come next to the sheath to which we give the more or less abstract name of astral body. Proceeding further out-wards we find the so-called etheric body, and still further outside, the physical body. From a real experience of life, however, we can also speak about the human sheaths in another way. Today we will take directly from life what can, it is true, be learnt only from occult conception, but can be understood through unprejudiced observation.

Many of those whom the so-called scientific world-view has made arrogant and overbearing, now say: 'The ages of faith are long past; they were fit for mankind in their stage of childhood but mankind has now progressed to knowledge. Today people must have knowledge of everything and should no longer merely believe.' Now that may sound all very well, but does not rest on genuine understanding. We must ask more questions about such matters than merely whether in the course of human evolution knowledge has been gained through ordinary science. This other question must also be asked. Does faith, as such, mean anything for mankind? May it not be part of a man's very nature to believe?

Naturally, it might be possible that people should want, for some reason, to dispense with faith, to put it behind them. But just as one can get away with playing fast and loose with one's health without any obvious harm for a while, it might very well be—and is actually so—that people come to look upon faith merely as a well-worn gift granted to their fathers in the past. This is just as if for a time they were recklessly to abuse their health, thereby using up the forces they once possessed. When a person regards faith in that way, however, he is still—where the life-forces of his soul are concerned—living on the old gift of faith handed down to him through tradition. It is not for man to decide whether to lay aside faith or not; faith is a question of life-giving forces in his soul. The important point is not whether we believe or not, but that the forces expressed in the word 'faith' are necessary to the soul. For the soul incapable of faith becomes withered, dried-up as the desert.

There were once people who, without any knowledge of natural science, were much cleverer than those who nowadays promote a scientific world-view. They did not say what people imagine they would have said: 'I believe what I do not know.' They said: 'I believe what I know for certain.' Knowledge is only the foundation of faith. We should know in order to take increasing possession of those forces which are forces of faith in the human soul. In our soul we must have what enables us to look towards a supersensible world, makes it possible for us to turn all our thoughts and conceptions in that direction.

If we do not possess forces such as are expressed in the word 'faith', something in us goes to waste; we wither as do the leaves in autumn. For a while this may not seem to matter—then things begin to go wrong. Were people really to lose all faith, they would soon see what it means for evolution. By losing the forces of faith they would be incapacitated for finding their way about in life; their very existence would be undermined by fear, care and anxiety. To put it briefly, it is through the forces of faith alone that we can receive the life which should well up to invigorate the soul. This is because, imperceptible at first for ordinary consciousness, there lies in the hidden depths of our being something in which our true ego is embedded. This something, which immediately makes itself felt if we fail to bring it fresh life, is the human bodily sheath where the forces of faith are active. We may term it the faith-soul, or—as I prefer—the faith-body. It has hitherto been given the more abstract name of astral body. The most important forces of the astral body are those of faith, so the term astral body and the term faith-body are equally justified.

A second force that is also to be found in the hidden depths of our being is the force expressed by the word 'love'. Love is not only something linking people together; it is also needed by them as individuals. When someone is incapable of developing the force of love he, too, becomes dried-up and withered in his inner being. We have merely to picture to ourselves someone who is actually so great an egoist that he is unable to love. Even where the case is less extreme, it is sad to see people who find it difficult to love, who pass through an incarnation without engendering in themselves the living warmth that only arises when we can love at least something on earth.

Such people are a distressing sight, as in their dull, prosaic way they go through the world. For love is a living force that stimulates something deep in our being, keeping it awake and alive—an even deeper force than faith. And just as we are cradled in a body of faith, which from another aspect can be called the astral body, so are we cradled also in a body of love, or, as we call it in spiritual science, the etheric body, the body of life-forces. For the chief forces working in us from the etheric body, out of the depths of our being, are those expressed in a person's capacity for loving at every stage of his existence. If a person could completely empty his being of the force of love—but that indeed is impossible even for the greatest egoist, thanks be to God, for even in egoistical striving there is still some element of love. Even someone who is unable to love anything else can often begin, if he is sufficiently avaricious, to love money, at least substituting for charitable love another love—albeit one arising from egoism. But if, as I was saying, there were no love at all in a person, the bodily sheath which should be sustained by love-forces would shrivel, and the person, empty of love, would actually perish; he would really meet with physical death.

This shrivelling of the forces of love can also be called a shrivelling of the forces of the etheric body; for the etheric body is the same as the body of love. Thus at the very centre of a human being we have his essential kernel, the ego, surrounded by its sheaths; first the body of faith, and then round it the body of love.

If we go further, we come to another set of forces we all need in life, and if we do not, or cannot, have them at all—well, that is very distinctly to be seen in our external nature. For the forces we need as life-giving, vitalizing forces are those of hope, of confidence in the future. As far as the physical world is concerned, people cannot take a single step in life without hope. They certainly make strange excuses, sometimes, if they are unwilling to acknowledge that human beings need to know something of what happens between death and rebirth. They say: 'Why do we need to know that, when we don't even know what will happen to us tomorrow? So why are we supposed to know what takes place between death and a new birth?' But do we actually know nothing about the following day? We may have no knowledge of what is important for the details of our supersensible life, or, to state it more bluntly, whether or not we shall be physically alive. We do, however, know one thing—that if we are physically alive the next day there will be morning, midday, evening, just as there are today. If today as a carpenter I have made a table, it will still be there tomorrow; if I am a shoe-maker, someone will be able to put on tomorrow what I have made today; and if I have sown seeds I know that next year they will come up. We know about the future just as much as we need to know. Life would be impossible in the physical world were not future events to be preceded in this rhythmical way by hope. Would anyone make a table today without being sure it would not be destroyed in the night; would anyone sow seeds if he had no idea what would become of them?

It is precisely in outer physical life that we need hope, for everything is upheld by hope and without it nothing can be done. The forces of hope, therefore, are connected with the last bodily sheath of our being, with our physical body. What the forces of faith are for our astral body, and the love-forces for the etheric, the forces of hope are for the physical body. Thus someone who is unable to hope, someone always despondent about what he supposes the future may bring, will go through the world with this clearly visible in his physical appearance. Nothing makes for deep wrinkles, those dead-ening forces in the physical body, sooner than lack of hope.

The inmost kernel of our being may be said to be sheathed in our faith-body or astral body, in our body of love or etheric body, and in our hope-body or physical body; and we com-prehend the true significance of our physical body only when we bear in mind that, in reality, it is not sustained by external physical forces of attraction and repulsion—that is a mate-rialistic idea—but has in it what, according to our concepts, we know as forces of hope. Our physical body is built up by hope, not by forces of attraction and repulsion. This itself can show us that the new spiritual-scientific revelation gives us what is right, what we need.

By revealing the all-embracing laws of karma and reincarnation, spiritual science gives us something which permeates us with spiritual hope, just as does our awareness on the physical plane that the sun will rise tomorrow and that seeds will eventually grow into plants. It shows, if we understand karma, that our physical body, which will perish into dust when we have gone through the gate of death, can be rebuilt for a new life through the forces imbuing us with hope. Spiritual science fills people with the strongest forces of hope. Were this spiritual science, this new revelation for the present time, to be rejected, people would naturally still return to earth in future, for life on earth would not cease on account of people's ignorance of its laws. Human beings would incarnate again; but there would be something very strange about these incarnations. Human beings would gradually become a race with bodies wrinkled and shrivelled all over, earthly bodies which would finally be so crippled that people would be entirely incapacitated. To put it briefly, in future incarnations a condition of dying away, of withering up, would assail mankind if our human consciousness, and from there the hidden depths of our being right down into the physical body, were not given fresh life through the power of hope.

This power of hope arises through the certainty of knowledge gained from the laws of karma and reincarnation. Already there is a tendency in human beings to produce withering bodies, which in future would become increasingly rickety even in the very bones. Marrow will be brought to the bones, forces of life to the nerves, by this new revelation, whose value will not reside merely in theories but in its life-giving forces—above all in those of hope.

Faith, love, hope, constitute three stages in the essential being of man; they are necessary for health and for life as a whole, for without them we cannot exist. Just as work cannot be done in a dark room until it is lit, it is equally impossible for a human being to survive in his fourfold nature if his three sheaths are not permeated, warmed through, and strengthened by faith, love, and hope. For faith, love, hope are the basic forces in our astral body, our etheric body, and our physical body. And from this alone you can judge how the new revelation makes its entry into the world, permeating the old language with thought-content. Are not these three wonderful words urged upon us in the Gospel revelation, these words of wisdom that ring through the ages—faith, love, hope? But little has been understood of their whole connection with human life, so little that only in certain places has their right sequence been observed. It is true that faith, love, hope are sometimes put in this correct order; but the significance of the words is so little appreciated that we often hear faith, hope, love, which is incorrect; for you cannot say astral body, physical body, etheric body, if you would give them their right sequence. That would be putting things higgledy-piggledy, as a child will sometimes do before it understands the thought-content of what is said. It is the same with everything relating to the second revelation. It is permeated with thought; and we have striven to permeate with thought our explanation of the Gospels. For what have these Gospels meant for people up to now? They have been something with which to fortify mankind and to fill them with great and powerful perceptions, something to inspire people to enter into the depth of heart and feeling in the Mystery of Golgotha. But now consider the simple fact that people have only just begun really to reflect upon the Gospels! And in doing so they have straightaway found contradictions upon which spiritual science alone can help to throw light. Thus it is only now that people will begin to let the thought-content of the Gospels, given them in a language of supersensible worlds, work upon their souls. In this connection we have pointed out what is so essential and of such consequence for our age: the new appearance of the Christ in an etheric body, for His reappearance in a physical body is ruled out by the whole character of our times.

Thus we have shown that the Christ, in contrast as it were to the suffering Christ on Golgotha, is appearing now as Christ triumphant, Christ the Judge, and Lord of Karma. This has been foreshadowed by those who have painted Him as the Christ of the Last Judgment. Whether painted or described in words, something is there represented which at the appointed time will come to pass.

In truth, this begins in the twentieth century and will hold good until the end of the earth. It is in our twentieth century that this judgment, this ordering of karma, begins; and we have seen how infinitely important it is for our age that this revelation should come to people so that even concepts such as faith, love, hope, can be truly valued for the first time.

John the Baptist said: Change your mood of soul, the Kingdom of Heaven is at hand. That is, take to yourselves the human ego that need not diminish itself in order to approach the spiritual world. This points clearly to the important fact that with the event of Palestine the time came for the supersensible to pour light into the ego of man, so that the heavens were able to descend into his ego. Previously, the ego could come to people only by sinking into their unconscious. Those who interpret everything materialistically say that the Christ, reckoning with the weaknesses, errors and prejudices of His contemporaries, even foretold, like the credulous people of His time, that either a thousand-year kingdom world come about or that a great catastrophe would befall the earth. Neither of these events however, they say, came about.

There was indeed a catastrophe, but perceptible only to the spirit. The credulous and superstitious, who believe

Christ to have foretold how He would literally descend from the clouds, interpreted His meaning in a materialistic way. Today, also, there are people who interpret materialistically what is to be grasped only in spirit, and when nothing happens in a material sense they judge the matter in just the same way as was done in the case of the thousand-year kingdom. How many indeed we find today who, speaking almost pityingly of those things, say that Christ was simply influenced by the beliefs of His time and looked for the impending descent to earth of the Kingdom of Heaven. That was a weakness on Christ's part, they say, and then it was seen— and remarked upon even by distinguished theologians—that the Kingdom of Heaven has not come down to earth.

It may be that people will meet our new revelation, too, in such a way that after a time, when the enhancement of human faculties is in full swing, they will say, 'Well, nothing has come of all these predictions of yours', not realizing that they just cannot see what is there. Thus do events repeat themselves. Anthroposophy is intended to gather together a large number of people, in preparation of the fulfilment of what those with a right knowledge say: that during this century the new revelation and new supersensible facts are appearing in human evolution. These will then continue to unfold, becoming ever more significant throughout the next 3,000 years, until important new revelations are once more vouchsafed to mankind.

Faith, Love, Hope. The Third Revelation to Mankind

2. Nuremberg, 3 December 1911

Yesterday we tried to gain a conception of the importance in human life of what may be termed the supersensible revelation of our age. We indicated that this was to be regarded as the third revelation in the most recent cycle of mankind, and should, in a certain sense, be seen in sequence to the Sinai revelation and the revelation at the time of the Mystery of Golgotha. We ought not to look upon this feature of our age as something affecting us merely theoretically or scientifically; as anthroposophists we must rise to an ever fuller realization that we are neglecting something essential in our evolution if we hold aloof from all that is being revealed to us now and will be revealed in the future. It is quite fitting that the external world should at first pass this by, or even treat it as sheer fantasy; and quite natural also that many people should initially pay no attention to the harmful consequences of disregarding these things. But anthroposophists should be clear that the souls in human bodies today, irrespective of what they absorb at present, are working their way towards a quite particular future. What I shall have to say concerns every soul, for it is part of the whole trend of change in our time.

The souls incarnated today have only recently advanced to that stage of genuine ego-consciousness which has been in preparation during the course of evolution ever since the ancient Atlantean period. But for the people of those ancient days, up to the time when the Mystery of Golgotha intimated a great transformation, this ego-consciousness was gradually freeing itself from a consciousness of which modern people no longer have any real knowledge. People of today generally distinguish only between our ordinary condition of being awake and the state of sleep, when consciousness is in complete abeyance. Between these states they recognize also the intermediate one of dreaming, but from the present-day perspective they can regard it only as a kind of aberration, a departure from the normal. Through dream-pictures certain events from the depths of soul-life rise into consciousness; but in ordinary dreaming they emerge in such an obscure form that the dreamer is scarcely ever able properly to interpret their very real bearing on deep supersensible processes in his life of soul.

In order to grasp one characteristic feature of this intermediate, dreaming state—a state well understood in earlier times—let us take an ordinary dream which a modern scientific investigator of dreams, able to interpret it only superficially and in a materialistic way, has made into a regular riddle. A highly significant dream! You see, I am taking my example from the science of dreams, which—as I have mentioned before—has today been given a place, little understood though it is, among sciences such as chemistry and physics. The following dream, a characteristic one, has been recorded. I might easily have taken my example from similar unpublished dreams; but I would like to deal with one which raises certain problems for present-day commentators, who have no key to such matters.

The case is as follows. A married couple had a much beloved son, who was the apple of their eye. One day he fell ill, and his condition worsened in a few hours so quickly that at the end of this one day he passed through the gate of death. Thus to all outward appearance this couple's son was abruptly snatched from them, and the son himself torn from a life full of promise. The parents naturally mourned their son. During the months following there was a great deal in the dreams of both husband and wife to remind them of him. But, quite a long time—many, many months—after his death, there came a night when his father and mother had exactly the same dream. They dreamed that their son appeared to them saying he had been buried alive, having only been in a trance, and that they merely had to look into the matter to be convinced that this was true.

The parents told each other what they had dreamed on the same night, and such was their attitude to life that they immediately asked the authorities for permission to have their son's body disinterred. The request was refused, giving the parents further cause for grieving.

Now the researcher who gave his account of the dream, and could think of it only in a materialistic way, was faced with great difficulties. He finally explained it in a remarkable way which is bound to seem very contrived to anyone reading it. He said: We can only assume that one parent had the dream, and the other, hearing it when awake, got the idea that he (or she) had dreamt it also. To present-day consciousness this interpretation at first seems fairly obvious, but it doesn't go very deep. I have expressly mentioned that for anyone well-versed in dream-experiences there is nothing unusual in several people having the same dream at the same time.

Let us try now to look into this dream-experience from the point of view of spiritual science. The results of spiritual investigation show how a person who has gone through the gate of death lives on as an individuality in the world of spirit. We know, too, that there are definite connections between every thing and every being in the world, and that this is evident in the link that unites those who have departed with people still on earth, when the latter lovingly concentrate thoughts on their dead. There is no question of there not being a connection between those on the physical plane and those who have left it for the supersensible world. There is always a connection when those left on the physical plane turn their thoughts to the dead—a connection that may continue even when their thoughts are directed elsewhere. But the point is that human beings, organized as they are now for life on the physical plane, are unable to become conscious of these bonds when awake. Having no knowledge of a thing, however, does not justify denying its existence; that would be a very superficial conclusion. On that basis, those now sitting in this room and not seeing Nuremberg could easily prove there is no such place. So we must be clear that it is only because of their present-day organization that people know nothing of their connection with the dead; it exists all the same.

However, knowledge of what is going on in the depths of the soul can occasionally be conjured up into consciousness, and this happens in dreams. It is one thing we have to reckon with when considering dream-experiences. Another thing is the knowledge that passing through death is not the sudden leap imagined by those knowing nothing about it; it is a gradual transition. What occupies a soul here on earth does not vanish in a moment when we die. What we love, we continue to love after our death. But there is no possibility of satisfying a feeling which depends for its satisfaction on a physical body. The wishes and desires of the soul, its joys, sorrows, the particular tendencies it has during incarnation in a physical body—these naturally continue even when we have passed through the gate of death. We can therefore understand how strong was the feeling in that young man, meeting death quite unprepared, that he would like to be still on earth, and how keen was his longing to be in a physical body. This desire, working as a force in the soul, lasted for a long, long time during his kamaloka.

Now vividly picture to yourselves the parents, with their thoughts engrossed by this beloved dead son. Even in sleep the connecting links were there. Just at the moment when both father and mother began to dream, the son, in accordance with the state of his soul, had a particularly keen desire that we may perhaps clothe in these words: 'Oh! If only I were still on earth in a physical body.' This thought on the part of the dead son sank deep into his parents' souls, but they had no special faculty for understanding what lay behind the dream. Thus the imprint of the thought on their life of soul was transformed into familiar images. If they could have clearly perceived what the son was pouring into their souls, their interpretation would have been: 'Our son is longing just now for a physical body.' In fact the dream-image clothed itself in words they understood—'He has been buried alive!'—which hid the truth from them.

Thus, in dream-pictures of this kind we should not look for an exact replica of spiritual reality; we must expect the actual objective occurrence to be veiled in accordance with the dreamer's degree of understanding. Today it is the peculiar feature of the dream-world that—if we are unable to go into these matters more deeply—we can no longer regard its pictures as faithful images of what underlies them. We are obliged to say that something always lives in our soul behind the dream-image, and this image can be regarded only as a still greater illusion than the external world we see when we are awake.

It is only in our time that dreams are appearing to people in this guise; strictly speaking only since the events in Palestine, when ego-consciousness took on the form it has now. Before then, the images appeared while people were in a state different from either waking or sleeping—a third state, more like the one prevailing in the supersensible world. Human beings lived with the dead in spirit far more than is possible nowadays. There is no need to look back many centuries before the Christian era to realize that countless numbers of people were then able to say: 'The dead are certainly not dead; they are living in the supersensible world. I can perceive what they are feeling and seeing, what they now actually are. This holds good also for other beings in the supersensible world; those, for instance, whom we know as the hierarchies.'

Thus, for human beings in certain states between waking and sleeping, these were experiences of which only the last degenerate echoes linger on in dreams. Hence it was very significant for people to feel this disappearance of something they once possessed. In that transitional epoch of human evolution, when the great events were taking place in Palestine, there was indeed cause for saying: 'Change your mood of soul; quite different times are coming for mankind.' And among the changes was this—that the old possibility of seeing into the spiritual world, of personally experiencing how matters stood with the dead and with all other spiritual beings, was going to pass away.

The history of those olden days offers ample evidence of this living with the dead—notably in the religious veneration arising everywhere in the form of ancestor-worship. This was founded on belief in the reality and activity of those who had died. And whereas it continued almost everywhere during the transitional period, peoples' experience was this, though perhaps not put clearly into words: 'Formerly our souls could rise to the world we call that of the spirit, and we were able to dwell among higher beings and with the dead. But now our dead leave us in quite another sense; they disappear from our consciousness and the old vivid contact is no more.'

We come here to something exceptionally difficult to grasp, but the intelligent mind, the intelligent soul, can learn to do so. It was the early Christians who felt most vividly the loss of direct psychic contact with the dead, and it was this that made their worship of God so full of meaning, so infinitely deep and holy. They compensated for what was lost by the reverent feeling they brought to their religious ceremonies; when, for instance, they sacrificed at the graves of their dead or celebrated the Mass, or observed any other religious rite. In fact, it was during this period of transition, when consciousness of the dead was seen to be waning, that altars took the shape of coffins. Thus it was with this kind of feeling for human mortal remains—different from that of the ancient Egyptians—that the service of God, the service of the spirit, was reverently performed. As I have said, this is something not easy to understand. We need, however, only observe the form of an altar, and allow our hearts to respond to this gradual change in man's whole outlook, and feeling and understanding will then arise for the change and its consequences.

We see, therefore, that slowly, gradually, the present state of the human soul came about. From indications given yesterday it can be gathered that what has thus come into being will again be succeeded by a different state, for which people are already developing faculties. The example I gave you yesterday of how a person will see, in a kind of dream picture, his future karmic compensation for some deed, means the re-awakening of faculties that will lead the soul once more to spiritual worlds. In relation to earthly evolution as a whole, the intermediate state when the soul is cut off from the supersensible world, will prove to be comparatively short. It had to come about for man to be able to acquire the strongest possible forces for his freedom. But something else of which I have spoken was bound up with the whole progress of human evolution—that only in this way were people able to acquire a feeling of the ego within them; to have, that is, the right ego-consciousness. The farther we advance into the future, the more firmly will this ego-consciousness establish itself within us, continually increasing in significance. In other words, the force and self-sufficiency of human individuality will be increasingly accentuated, so that it becomes necessary for people to find in themselves their own means of support and self-reliance.

Thus we see that the ego-consciousness people have today does not go back as far as is usually imagined. Only a few incarnations ago, people had no ego-feeling such as is characteristic of them today. And as the ego-feeling is intimately connected with memory, we need not be surprised that many people should not have begun, as yet, to look back on their previous incarnations. Because of the undeveloped state of this feeling for their ego during early childhood, people do not even remember what happened to them then; so it seems quite understandable that, for the same reasons, they are as yet unable to remember their earlier incarnations. But now we have come to the point when man has developed a feeling for his ego, and the forces are unfolding which will make it necessary in our coming incarnations to remember those who have gone before. The days are drawing near when people will feel bound to admit: 'We have strange glimpses into the past, when we were on the earth before but living in another bodily form. We look back and have to say that we have already been on earth.' And among the faculties appearing more and more in human beings will be one which arouses the feeling of looking back to one's own earlier incarnations.

Just think how in human souls now on earth the inner force is already arising which will enable them, in their next incarnations, to look back and to recognize themselves. But for those who have not become familiar with the idea of reincarnation this looking back will be a veritable torment. Ignorance of the mysteries of repeated earthly lives will be actually painful for these human beings; forces in them are striving to rise and bear witness to earlier times, but this cannot happen because all knowledge of these forces is rejected. Not to learn of the truths now being advanced by spiritual science does not just mean neglecting mere theories; but means preparing a torment for oneself in future incarnations. In these times of transition, accordingly, something is happening; the slow preparation for it can also be gathered from our second Mystery Play, *The Soul's Probation*, where the characters' former incarnations are portrayed—incarnations that occurred just a few centuries earlier. This preparation is already taking place; and now, thanks to the wisdom of cosmic guidance, human beings will be given positive opportunities for making themselves familiar with the truths of the Mysteries.

At present comparatively few people find their way to spiritual science; their number is modest compared with that of the rest of mankind. It may be said that interest in anthroposophy is not yet very widespread. But, in our age, the law of reincarnation is such that those now going through the world apathetically, ignoring what experience can tell about the need for exploring the riddles of life, will incarnate again in a relatively short time, and thus have ample opportunity then for absorbing the truths of spiritual science. That is how things stand. So that when perhaps we see around us people we esteem, people we love, who will have nothing to do with anthroposophy, are even hostile towards it, we ought not to take it too much to heart. It is perfectly true, and should be realized by anthroposophists, that refusing to examine spiritual science, or anthroposophy, means preparing a life of torment for future incarnations on earth. That is true, and should not be treated lightly. On the other hand, those who see friends and acquaintances they care for showing no inclination towards anthroposophy can say: 'If I become a good anthroposophist myself, I shall find an early opportunity, with the forces remaining to me after death, to prove helpful to these souls'—provided the living link we have spoken of exists. And because the interval between death and rebirth is becoming shorter, these souls, too, will have the opportunity of absorbing the Mystery-truths that must be absorbed if torment is to be avoided in peoples' coming incarnations. All is not yet lost.

We have therefore to look upon anthroposophy as a real power; but on the other hand must not be unduly grieved or pessimistic about the matter. It would be mistaken optimism to say: 'If that is how things are, I need not accept the truths of spiritual science till my next incarnation'. If everyone were to say that there would be too few opportunities for effective aid to be given through subsequent incarnations. Even if those wishing for anthroposophy can now receive its truths from a few people only, the situation will be different for the countless hosts of those who, in a comparatively short time, will be eagerly turning to anthroposophy. A countless number of anthroposophists will then be needed to make these truths known, either here on the physical plane, or—if they are not incarnated—from higher planes.

That is one thing we must learn from the whole character of the great change now taking place. The other is that all this has to be experienced by the ego so that it should rely increasingly upon itself, becoming more and more independent. The self-reliance of the ego must come for all souls; but it will mean disaster for those who make no effort to learn about the great spiritual truths, for increasing individualism will be felt by them as isolation. On the other hand, those who have made themselves familiar with the deep mysteries of the spiritual world will thereby find a way to forge ever stronger spiritual bonds between souls. Old bonds will be loosened, new ones formed. All this is imminent, but it will only gradually come about.

We are living at present in the fifth post-Atlantean period, which will be followed by a sixth and then by a seventh, when a catastrophe will come upon us, just as one came between the Atlantean and post-Atlantean periods. When I gave lectures on the Apocalypse here in Nuremberg, you heard a description of this coming catastrophe, of how it will resemble and how differ from the one in old Atlantis.

If we observe life around us, we might express the particular feature of our age in the following way. The most active element in human beings today is their intellectualism, their intellectual conception of the world. We are living altogether in an age of intellectualism. It has been brought about through quite special circumstances, and we shall come to understand these if we look back to the time before our present fifth post-Atlantean cultural epoch, the Graeco-Roman, as it is called. That was a remarkable period when human beings had not reached their present state of detachment from natural phenomena and their knowledge of the world. But at the same time it was the epoch in which the ego dawned. The Christ event had also to happen in that epoch, because it was then that the ego dawned in a special way.

What then is our present experience? It is not just of the ego's dawning; we now experience how one of our bodily sheaths casts a kind of reflection upon the soul. The sheath to which we yesterday gave the name of 'faith-body' casts its reflection on to the human soul, in this fifth epoch. Thus it is a feature of present-day man that he has something in his soul which is, as it were, a reflection of the astral body's faith-nature. In the sixth post-Atlantean epoch there will be a reflection within man of the love-nature of the etheric body, and in the seventh, before the great catastrophe, the reflection of the hope-nature of the physical body.

For those who have heard lectures I have recently been

giving in various places, I would note that these gradual developments have been described from a different point of view both in Munich and in Stuttgart; the theme, however, is always the same. What I am now describing in connection with the three great human forces, faith, love, hope, was there represented in direct relation to the elements in a person's soul-life, but it is all the same thing. I have done this intentionally, so that anthroposophists may grow accustomed to get the gist of a matter without strict adherence to particular words. When we realize that things can be described from many different angles, we shall no longer pin so much faith on specific words but focus our efforts on the matter itself, knowing that any description amounts only to an approximation of the truth. This insistence on someone's original words is the last thing that can help us get to the heart of a matter. The one helpful means is to harmonize what has been said in successive lectures, just as we learn about a tree by studying it not from one direction only but from many different aspects.

At present, then, it is essentially the force of faith of the astral body which, shining into the soul, is characteristic of our time. Someone might say: 'That is rather strange. You are telling us now that the ruling force of the age is faith. We might admit this is the case for those who hold to old beliefs, but today so many people are too mature for that, and they look down on such old beliefs as belonging to the childish stage of human evolution.' It may well be that people who say they are monists believe they do not believe, but actually they are more ready to do so than those calling themselves believers. For though monists are not conscious of it, all that we see in the various forms of monism is belief of the blindest kind, believed by the monists to be knowledge. We cannot describe their doings at all without mentioning belief. And, apart from the belief of those who believe they do not believe, we find that, strictly speaking, an endless amount of what is most important today depends upon the reflection the astral body throws into the soul, thereby giving it the character of ardent faith. We have only to call to mind lives of the great figures of our age. Richard Wagner's, for example, and how even as an artist he was aspiring all his life to a certain intensity of faith; it is fascinating to watch this in the development of his personality. Everywhere we look today, the light and shadow of our time can be interpreted as the reflection of faith in what we may call man's ego-soul.

Our age will be followed by one upon which the need for love will cast its light. What can also be called Christian love will manifest in a very different form in the sixth cultural epoch. Slowly we draw nearer to that epoch; and by making those in the anthroposophical movement familiar with the mysteries of the cosmos, with the nature of various individualities both on the physical plane and on the higher planes, we try to kindle love for everything that exists. This is not done so much by *talking* of love, as by feeling what can kindle love in the soul. Thus we prepare for the sixth epoch by means of anthroposophy. Through anthroposophy the forces of love are specially aroused in the whole human soul; and what we need for gradually acquiring a true understanding of the Mystery of Golgotha is prepared. For although the Mystery of Golgotha came to pass, and although the Gospels have evoked something which yesterday was likened to how children learn to speak, the deepest lesson—the mission of earthly love in its connection with the Mystery of Golgotha—has not yet been grasped. Full understanding of this will be possible only in the sixth post-Atlantean cultural epoch, when people grow to realize more and more that the foundations for it are actually within them; and out of their innermost being, in other words out of love, do what should be done. Then the guidance of the Commandments will have been outlived and the stage reached that is described in Goethe's words: 'Duty is when one loves the commands one gives to oneself.' When forces waken in our souls which impel us to do what we should through love alone, we then discover in ourselves something that must gradually become widespread in the sixth cultural epoch. Then quite special forces, of the etheric body too, will make themselves known to humankind.

To understand what will increasingly come about in this way, we have to consider it from two angles. One aspect is related to something that has certainly not come yet and is only dreamt of by the most advanced in spirit: a quite particular relationship to morals, ethics and the understanding, intellectuality. Today a person may be quite a rascal, yet at the same time intelligent and clever. He may even use his very cleverness to further his knavery. People do not yet have to combine their intelligence with an equal degree of morality. To all that we have been anticipating for the future this must be added—that as we advance, it will no longer be possible for these two qualities of the human soul to be kept apart, or to exist in unequal measure. A person who, according to the reckoning of his previous incarnation, has become particularly intelligent without being moral, will in his new incarnation possess only a stunted intelligence. Thus, to have equal amounts of intelligence and morality in future incarnations he will be obliged, as a consequence of universal cosmic law, to enter his new incarnation with an intelligence that is crippled, so that immorality and stupidity coincide. For immorality has a crippling effect upon intelligence. In other words, we are approaching the age when morality and what has now been described for the sixth post-Atlantean epoch as the etheric body's love forces shining into the ego-soul, point essentially to the harmonizing of intelligence and morality. That is the one aspect to be considered.

The other aspect is this—that it is solely through harmony of this kind, between morality and intelligence, that the whole depth of the Mystery of Golgotha is to be grasped. This will come about through the individuality who, before Christ Jesus came to earth, prepared man for that Mystery; and in his successive incarnations he will develop ever greater powers as teacher of the greatest of all earthly events. This individuality, whom in his rank as bodhisatva we call the successor of Gautama Buddha, was incarnated in the individual living about a hundred years before Christ under the name of Jeshu ben Pandira. Among his many students was one who had at that time already, in a certain sense, written down a prophetic version of the Matthew Gospel, and this, after the Mystery of Golgotha had been fulfilled, needed only to be given a new form.

There have been, and will continue to be, frequent incarnations of the individuality who appeared as Jeshu ben Pandira, until he rises from the rank of bodhisattva to that of Buddha. According to our reckoning of time this will be in about 3,000 years, when a sufficient number of people will possess the faculties we have spoken of, and when, in the course of a remarkable incarnation of the individual who was once Jeshu ben Pandira, this great teacher of mankind will have become able to act as interpreter of the Mystery of Golgotha in a very different way from what is possible today. It is true that even today a seer into the supersensible worlds can gain some idea of what is to happen then; but the ordinary earthly organization of man cannot yet provide a physical body capable of doing what that teacher will be able to do approximately 3,000 years hence. There is, as yet, no human language through which verbal teaching could exert the magical effects that will spring from the words of that great teacher of humanity. His words will flow directly to human hearts, into their souls, like a healing medicine;

nothing in those words will be merely theoretical. At the same time the teaching will contain, to an extent far greater than it is possible to conceive today, a magical moral force carrying to hearts and souls a full conviction of the eternal, deeply significant brotherhood of intellect and morality.

This great teacher, who will be able to give to a mankind that is ripe for it the profoundest instruction on the nature of the Mystery of Golgotha, will fulfil what Oriental prophets have always said—that the true successor of Buddha would be the greatest teacher of the good for all mankind. For that reason he has been called in oriental tradition the Maitreya Buddha. His task will be to enlighten human beings about the Mystery of Golgotha, and for this he will draw ideas and words of the deepest significance from the very language he will use. No human language today can evoke any conception of it. His words will directly, magically imprint into human souls the nature of the Mystery of Golgotha. So in this way too we are approaching what we may call the future moral age of man; in a certain sense we could describe it as a coming Golden Age.

Even today, however, when we speak out of anthroposophy, we point in full consciousness to what is destined to come about—how the Christ will gradually reveal Himself to ever higher powers in human beings, and how the teachers, who up to now have taught only particular peoples and individuals, will become interpreters of the great Christ event for all who are willing to listen. And we can point out how the dawning of the age of love also provides conditions needed for this age of morality.

Then will come the last epoch, during which human souls will receive the reflection of what we call hope; when, strengthened through the force flowing from the Mystery of Golgotha and from the age of morality, human beings will take forces of hope into themselves. This is the most important gift they need in order to face the next catastrophe and to begin new life, just as the post-Atlantean age brought new life to birth.

When in the final post-Atlantean epoch our external culture, with its tendency to logic and calculation, comes to a climax, bringing no feeling of satisfaction but leaving those who may not have developed the spiritual within them to face their culture in utter desolation—then out of spirituality the seed of hope will be sown, and in the next period of human evolution this will grow to maturity. If the spirit is denied all possibility of imparting to human souls what it can give, and what the anthroposophical movement has the will to convey, this external culture might for a short while be able to hold its own. Ultimately, however, people would ask themselves what they had gained and say: 'We have high-tech equipment—undreamt of by our ancestors—to transmit our thoughts all over the earth, yet what good does it do us? The most trivial, unproductive thoughts are sent hither and thither, and human ingenuity has to be strained to the utmost to enable us to transport from some far distant region, by means of all kinds of perfected appliances, something for us to eat; or to travel at high speeds round the globe. But in our heads there is nothing worth sending from place to place, for our thoughts are cheerless; moreover, since we have had our present means of communication, they have become even more cheerless than when they were conveyed in the old snail-like fashion.'

In short, despair and desolation are all that our external civilization can spread over the earth. But, in the last cultural epoch, souls who have taken up the spiritual in life will have become enriched though standing amongst the ruins of external cultural life. Their surety that this acceptance of the spiritual has not been in vain will be the strong force of hope within them—hope that after a great catastrophe a new age will come for human beings, when there will appear in external life, in a new culture, what has already been prepared spiritually within the soul.

Thus, if we permeate our whole being with spiritual science, we advance step by step, in full consciousness, from our age of faith, through the age of love and that of hope, to what we can see approaching us as the highest, truest, most beautiful goals of humanity.

Cosmic Ego and Human Ego. Supersensible Microcosmic Beings. The Nature of Christ

Munich, 9 January 1912

This evening we need to talk further about the nature of Christ Jesus. It is necessary because this theme is so much under discussion at present, particularly in theosophical circles, and because there is a very real need to reach complete clarity on much that is said about it.

Many may regard the issue we will examine today as rather odd, yet it is a very important one. We will start from human evolution. We know of course that evolution progresses by means of humanity passing through certain cyclical epochs. And we have often spoken of the five cultural epochs up to and including our own time, which followed the great catastrophe that transformed life on the ancient continent we call Atlantis into our life on the newer continents. We speak of the first, the ancient Indian epoch; the second, the great cultural epoch of ancient Persia; the third, the Egyptian-Chaldean-Babylonian culture; the fourth, the Graeco-Roman—which a broader view of things considers did not really fade away until some time between the eighth and twelfth post-Christian centuries AD; and then of our present, fifth post-Altantean cultural epoch, which began in 1413.

Now human souls—all those who sit here of course included—have passed through various incarnations in these succeeding cultural epochs up to the present time: some incarnating more frequently, others passing through relatively fewer incarnations. These souls have acquired this or that characteristic from their experiences, according to the nature of each of these epochs, and carried it with them from earlier into later incarnations. In other words they manifest as souls at this or that stage of development according to what they experienced in various previous cultural epochs.

Now we can further say that on the whole—and this is only a general rule—only a particular member or aspect of man's nature is evolved and developed in each cultural epoch. In our own epoch people are chiefly called upon to develop what in our movement we term the consciousness soul, by allowing to work upon them everything which our epoch can give them. During the Graeco-Roman period, in contrast, the mind or rational soul mainly evolved, while in the Egyptian-Chaldean-Babylonian period it was the sentient soul. In ancient Persian civilization the sentient or astral body developed, and in ancient India what we call the etheric or life body. These various parts of man's being have been developed in each individual soul, or will be, as it passes in one, or more often several, incarnations through each of these cultural epochs. In the sixth post-Atlantean cultural epoch that follows our present one, what we term spirit self will chiefly be developed, or manas as people are used to calling it in theosophical literature; and in the last, the seventh post-Atlantean cultural epoch, what we call life spirit will evolve, termed budhi in theosophical circles. Spirit man or atma will in a certain sense only unfold in a far-distant future following a further catastrophe.

At present therefore, and in the near future, we are in the midst of developing what is called the consciousness soul, by living through the everyday conditions of our culture, of what surrounds us.

But we know that all this evolution of the separate members we distinguish within the soul is intimately related to something else—to the gradual incorporation of the human ego in human nature, which is the whole task and aim of

earthly evolution. Thus we have as it were two inter-
penetrating streams of evolution: there is the Earth evolution
we are passing through following Saturn, Sun and Moon
evolution; and then, as earthly humanity we have the particular task of developing this fourth member of human nature,
of adding this ego to the other principal members of human
nature: to the physical, etheric and astral bodies. We have to
distinguish between these two: between the larger span of the
overall stream of evolution related to the great embodiments
of our earth planet itself, and that smaller-scale stream of
evolution which I described previously as occurring within
the comparatively short span of the post-Atlantean period.

No one who has understood what has been said will be able
to ask: 'But how can it be that on Old Sun man had already
developed the etheric or life body, and that then a special
development of this same body is said to have taken place
during the ancient Indian epoch?' Those who have rightly
understood will not ask such a question, for the facts are
these: the human etheric or life body was implanted in us on
Old Sun, and so we arrived at the stage of Earth evolution in
possession of an etheric body. But it can then be refined and
further developed, can be worked upon by subsequent soul-
members which human beings evolve. In other words, man
receives his etheric or life body at a particular, fairly
advanced stage when he incarnates in an ancient Indian
body; but during this post-Atlantean period he works upon it
with the ego and everything he has acquired so far, makes it
finer-structured. So what develops and evolves in our post-
Atlantean cultural epoch is essentially a refining, a finer
working into the various members of human nature.

If you now examine all of evolution and consider what has
been said, the fourth post-Atlantean epoch, the Graeco-
Roman, will appear to you as of quite particular importance.
For it is there that a greater degree of refining must occur

within the mind or rational soul. But up to that time the ego, which belongs to the greater evolutionary stream, has undergone an especially high degree of development. We can say that, up to the fourth post-Atlantean epoch, up to Graeco-Roman times, this human ego has evolved to a certain stage; and now it must penetrate the mind or rational soul, and in our time the consciousness soul.

Now in a certain sense there is an intimate relationship between the human ego and man's three soul-members, the sentient soul, the mind or rational soul, and the consciousness soul. It is in these three soul-members of our being that the inner life of the human ego chiefly dwells. And in our fifth post-Atlantean cultural epoch in particular, it will live most inwardly in the consciousness soul, because it is there that the pure ego can express itself unhindered by the other bodies. In our present time we are indeed living in an epoch in which this ego is most called upon to develop, to build upon its own foundations.

And if we then cast our gaze forwards into the future, and say that in the next, the sixth cultural epoch, man will evolve the spirit self or manas, we recognize that this spirit self is really already a step beyond the sphere of the ego. Basically we would be unable to evolve this spirit self in the future through our own powers, but are dependent on the help flowing towards us from higher beings. We have reached a stage in the evolution of our ego where we can only rely on our own powers to evolve as far as the consciousness soul. But this evolution will not be complete unless we anticipate and in a certain sense prefigure the more advanced stage that will only fully come about on Jupiter, that will only attain its complete, inherently human evolution on the next embodi-ment of our planet. Up until the end of Earth evolution man is meant to develop his ego. He has had an opportunity to carry out this development within the sentient, mind and consciousness soul. But the real spirit self will only become human property, our real possession, on Jupiter. On Jupiter we will have the same kind of relationship to the spirit self as we do here on Earth to the ego. In other words, if we develop spirit self already during the Earth cycle, we cannot yet have the same relationship to it as we do to the ego. Of our ego we say: 'We are that, that is what we truly are.' But when, in the next epoch, the sixth post-Atlantean, the spirit self comes to expression, we will not be able to refer to this spirit self as our 'self', but will say: 'Our ego has evolved to a certain stage where our spirit self can shine in as though from higher worlds, like a kind of angel being that is other than what we are, can shine in upon us and take possession of us.' That is how our spirit self will appear to us. And only on Jupiter will it appear in such a way that it becomes our own true being, like our ego. In such a way does human evolution advance.

Thus in the next, the sixth post-Atlantean cultural epoch, we will feel as though drawn to what shines in upon us. We will not refer to our spirit self as though it were within us, but will say: 'I participate in a being who shines in upon me from higher worlds, that leads and guides me, that has come to be my leader and guide through the grace of higher beings!' That aspect of our being that will only become our real possession on Jupiter we will experience as a kind of guiding light shining down upon and into us from higher worlds. And it will later be the same with the life spirit or budhi, and with spirit man and so forth. Thus a time will come when we speak differently of ourselves than we do now. How do we speak of ourselves when we refer to ourselves in spiritual-scientific terms? We say: 'I have three bodies, physical, etheric and astral. Within these I have my ego, as real earthly possession, developing within these three bodies. These three bodies are as it were my lower nature. I have grown beyond them, and look down to this my lower nature, seeing in what my ego has become my true being for the present, which increasingly is to grow, to develop more and more.'

In future we will have to speak differently. We will say: 'I do not just have my lower nature and my ego, but I have a higher nature which I look up to as something that is part of me in the same way as the bodily sheaths I received in the past.' In other words we will in future feel ourselves placed midway between our lower and higher nature. We already know our lower nature; in the future we will come to know our higher nature as something above us in the same way we now experience our lower nature below us. So we can say that during earthly evolution we grow from our fourth to our fifth, sixth and seventh aspect. But the fifth, sixth and seventh aspects will not become our direct possession during actual Earth evolution, but will be something we only gradually attain to. This is how we should really view things.

A time will come when we experience that although it was our earthly mission to develop our ego, we nevertheless have a kind of prophetic anticipation of our evolution on Jupiter. The evolutionary path we undergo during the Earth cycle, by means of which we permeate ourselves with a human ego nature, refining the lower aspects of our being up until now, and in future developing higher aspects—is something that other, more advanced beings whom we call angels or angeloi have already previously undergone in former embodiments of our planet, on Moon, Sun and Saturn. For them too there was formerly a kind of fourth aspect or member that they evolved. And then in the second half of a particular planetary embodiment they prefigured what would fully unfold in them in the future, on Earth, in the same way that we will prefigure what is to come about on Jupiter. At that time they did not fully incorporate it into themselves as their possession, but related to it as something which they looked up to.

If we look back firstly to Old Moon evolution, we must

speak of beings who, just like we human beings during Earth evolution, should have attained to the seventh aspect of their being—yet, like us too, not in the sense of making it their full possession, but of looking up to it. When we speak of luciferic beings, we are talking of those who during Old Moon evolution remained at the stage a human being would remain at who, during Earth evolution, does not develop his fifth, sixth or seventh aspects, who refuses to do so, perhaps stopping at the fourth, or fifth. These beings did not evolve fully in other words, and now stand at many diverse stages of development. Thus we can say that human beings passed over from Old Moon evolution to Earth evolution in such a way that they brought with them a normal path of evolution. Those human beings who concluded their evolution brought a normal evolutionary path with them: their physical, etheric and astral bodies. And their real task on Earth is to develop the ego. Other beings, higher than man, were meant to develop on Old Moon what in them corresponds to the human ego. But they would only have been able to develop this Moon ego fully by prefiguring *all* that would have been their fifth, sixth and seventh aspects, the fifth of which they would need to bring to full completion during Earth evolution. They should have prefigured these aspects as far as the seventh. They did manage just about to evolve the fifth or sixth—did not get stuck at the fourth as such therefore—but nevertheless were not able fully to develop it because they failed to prefigure the fifth, sixth *and* seventh aspects, remaining stuck instead at the fifth or sixth.

So we can distinguish two sorts of such Moon beings: those firstly who managed to evolve their fifth aspect, as we humans would if we evolved the spirit self in the sixth post-Atlantean epoch, and then stopped short and failed to develop the sixth and seventh aspects. We can examine this kind of luciferic beings who evolved their fifth aspect; and then examine the other kind of luciferic moon beings who evolved their sixth aspect but not their seventh. Both kinds existed at the beginning of Earth evolution, when man was preparing to develop his ego. So what was the situation for these beings at the beginning of Earth evolution? There were beings present who were hungrily waiting to develop their sixth aspect during Earth evolution—luciferic beings who had only managed to evolve as far as their fifth aspect on the Moon and wished to develop their sixth on Earth. And there were also beings of the second kind present, who had evolved their sixth aspect on the Moon, and now wished to develop their seventh on Earth. That was what they expected from Earth evolution. And this was when man, with three aspects so far evolved, made the transition to Earth in order to evolve his fourth.

So we can distinguish man, waiting to evolve his ego, then the luciferic beings waiting to evolve their sixth, and those waiting to evolve their seventh aspects. We will disregard the luciferic beings who wished to evolve their fifth aspect, who also existed.

This gives us three kinds of microcosmic Earth beings, three kinds of beings who had arrived in the arena of Earth evolution. Of these three only one could attain a physical body on Earth; for the conditions Earth provides, by means of its whole earthly circumstances, for physically incarnate bodily evolution, can only be provided for a fourth human aspect. Only a being that wished to evolve its fourth aspect as ego was able to gain a physical body. The other beings, wishing to develop a sixth and seventh aspect, could not have such a body. For there was no possibility within Earth conditions that would have enabled beings entering Earth evolution—who were so unsuited to this Earth evolution—to acquire a physical body directly. There was no possibility for them to get such a physical body by direct means. So what

must they do? They had to say: 'We cannot find direct access
to a physical human body consisting of flesh and bones, for
such bodies are only available to human beings who wish to
develop an ego. Instead we must resort to a kind of surrogate
physical body; we must find human beings who are the most
highly evolved, who, let us say, have evolved their fourth
aspect. We must crawl into them, and our being must work
within them in such a way that it can develop its sixth or
seventh aspect.'

This meant that among the ordinary people of ancient
times there were those possessed by higher beings of a luciferic kind—who were naturally more advanced than the
human being since they were trying to evolve their sixth or
seventh aspect while man was still at the stage of evolving
his fourth. Such higher, luciferic beings therefore went
about in earthly human bodies. These were the leaders of
earthly mankind for they knew, understood and were able
to do far more than other human beings. We hear tell of
these beings in ancient stories and legends, in which they
appear as the great founders of cities, great leaders of
nations and so forth. These were not just ordinary human
beings but people possessed by higher beings of a luciferic
kind, possessed in the best sense of the word. We can only
rightly understand human Earth evolution when we take
account of such things.

Particularly the lower beings of this kind continually strive
to advance their evolution in one human body after another,
since they themselves cannot acquire a body. Luciferic beings
have always had a longing to continue their evolution within
other, human, beings by possessing them—and they are still
doing this today. Lucifer and his hosts are at work in the
human soul. We are the arena of luciferic evolution. Whereas
we human beings simply take an earthly physical body to
evolve, these luciferic beings take *us* and evolve within us.

And that is our temptation—the fact that luciferic beings are at work within us.

In the meantime, though, these luciferic spirits have evolved just as we have. Many a spirit of this kind who, let us say, was on the verge of developing a sixth aspect at the time man entered the Atlantean period, has now reached the stage—remembering that Earth evolution is abnormal for such a spirit—of developing a seventh aspect. He achieves this by taking possession of a human being once more, perhaps spending a number of years using all that this human being can experience as he furthers his own development. This does not do injury to human nature. For the fact that we can bring the consciousness soul to expression at this time means that a luciferic spirit who is in the process of evolving his seventh aspect can possess us. What happens when a high luciferic spirit possesses someone? The person becomes a genius! But one who, because he is a human being possessed and overshadowed by a higher being, is impractical in ordinary daily life; yet has a radical new and decisive influence in some field or other.

One really ought not to speak about such a luciferic spirit as though he were something hateful. He develops like a parasite within the human being, but in such a way that the person possessed and subject to his influence manifests genius, inspiration. Thus the luciferic spirits are absolutely necessary. And people of genius in the world are those in whom, at least for a few years, a luciferic being is hard at work. If that were not the case then Edouard Schuré[50] would not have been able to portray Lucifer as a sympathetic being. Lucifer is closely connected with the world's great cultural advances, and it is narrow-minded of traditional Christianity to see in this being nothing more than a wicked devil. This is gross philistinism. In *Faust* we read: 'Nature is sin, spirit the devil: between them they nurture doubt, their malformed child.'[51] Certainly, it suits the limited horizons of traditional Christianity to regard Lucifer as the devil and to hate him; but a knowledge of human evolution tells us that the luciferic principle is at work in geniuses. The science of the spirit needs to look these things in the face and recognize that we would have no impetus in progressing to our fifth and sixth aspects if these spirits did not move us forwards. We do indeed owe this forward propulsion to the luciferic spirits, through the fact that they are striving for their own evolution and this means we can grow beyond our own limited human ego, as is somewhat flippantly said of poets, geniuses and artists.

Thus we look up to the luciferic spirits as leaders of mankind in a certain sense. We must free ourselves from the narrow, orthodox Christian conception that Lucifer is merely a devil to be hated. We must recognize the liberating influence of the luciferic principle, that has also been ordained by benevolent gods; for this is what lifts us beyond ourselves in the course of earthly evolution, so that we can prophetically anticipate something that we will not truly own until the time of Jupiter and so forth. During Earth evolution, therefore, reciprocal influence is exerted upon one another by microcosmic beings who were present at the beginning of this evolution. Thus we can say that in developing our own ego we are led further by beings higher than man, who have already evolved their fifth aspect and are now developing their sixth or even their seventh aspect, while we are still at work on our fourth.

These luciferic beings are thus microcosmic beings higher than man. And now let us turn aside from these spirit beings whom we regard as luciferic, and come to examine the nature of Christ.

The Christ is radically different from other beings who participate in earthly evolution. He is a being of a quite different order. He is not a being who, like the luciferic spirits, remained behind during Moon evolution, but one who, prefiguring Moon evolution, remained behind at a still earlier stage, during Old Sun evolution already; and remained behind through a certain assured wisdom far exceeding that of human beings. We cannot view this being in the same way as the other beings we have referred to as microcosmic ones. Such microcosmic beings are those who have been connected with Earth evolution from its beginnings. The Christ was not directly connected with Earth evolution but with Sun evolution. He was a macrocosmic being from the beginning of Earth evolution onwards, in other words one who is involved in quite different evolutionary conditions from those to which microcosmic beings are exposed. And His evolutionary conditions were specific to Him. They were such that this macrocosmic Christ being had evolved the macrocosmic fourth principle outside earthly conditions, the macrocosmic Ego. For his evolution, for Christ evolution, it was normal to bring to perfection a macrocosmic Ego outside of earthly conditions, and then to descend to earth. Thus for the evolution of the Christ being it was normal—as he descended from the macrocosm down to our earth—to bring with Him the great impulse of the macrocosmic Ego, so that the microcosmic ego, the human ego, could take up this impulse and evolve further. For Christ it was normal to have developed the macrocosmic Ego impulse—not the microcosmic ego—as far as human beings had developed the microcosmic ego on earth. Thus the Christ being is a being similar in a certain sense to man, except that man is microcosmic and has brought his four principles to microcosmic expression, his ego also as microcosmic earth-ego, while the Christ manifests a cosmic Ego. But his evolution had progressed in a way that meant He had grown very great and significant through the full development of this Ego that He brought down to earth. And He did not yet have the fifth and sixth macrocosmic principles, for He will develop these so that He can give them to man on Jupiter and Venus.

The Christ is therefore a being of fourfold nature—up to and including His macrocosmic Ego—as man is at the microcosmic level. And just as man has the mission to evolve his ego during Earth, in order to receive, so did the Christ have the mission of evolving His Ego in order to give. When He descended to earth everything in His being was directed at bringing His fourth principle to expression in as perfect a form as possible. Now every microcosmic principle has an inner relationship with the corresponding macrocosmic one. The fourth macrocosmic principle in Christ corresponds to the fourth microcosmic principle in man, and the fifth in Christ will correspond to man's spirit self.

Thus Christ began His earthly course by bringing down to man from the macrocosm what he needed to develop in the microcosm; but He brought it as macrocosmic principle. He entered into earthly evolution in such a way that He did not possess a fifth, sixth and seventh principle—just as man did not.

The Christ is a being who has evolved macrocosmically as far as the fourth principle, and who during the course of Earth undertakes the evolution of His fourth principle through bestowing everything that man needs to develop his ego.

A complete overview therefore shows us that there were three types of being at the beginning of Earth evolution: human beings who were to receive their fully developed fourth principle on earth; a class of luciferic beings who were to evolve their sixth principle; and another class who were to evolve their seventh. The fact that these latter beings were to develop their sixth and seventh principles means that, in this respect, they stand higher than man. But they also stand higher than Christ in this respect, for Christ is at the stage of bringing His fourth principle to expression on the earth in devotion to mankind. The Christ will not be the one who, let us say, stimulates human beings to bring something to expression other than the actual ego, the inmost being of man—to reach higher and higher levels. It is the luciferic spirits who will do this, who will in a certain sense lead human beings beyond themselves.

An external view of things could therefore lead one to say: 'In that case the Christ is actually lower than luciferic spirits, for He comes to earth with something that is closely related to man's fourth principle.' It is true that He does not try to lead man beyond himself, but only deeper into his own soul nature. He strives to bring man's individual being of soul increasingly into itself, into its own. The luciferic beings have developed the fourth, fifth, sixth principle, and therefore are in a certain sense higher than Christ. In practical terms this will in future come to expression in the fact that, by taking up the Christ principle into human nature, this nature will grow more and more profound, will take up more and more light and love within itself, so that human nature will necessarily experience light and love as its deepest, ultimate possession. The gift of the continual, ever-ongoing Christ impulse will be the endlessly deepening inwardness of the human soul. And when Christ comes, as has been described in various lectures, His only effect will be in deepening human souls. The other spirits, who have higher principles than the Christ—although only of microcosmic nature—will in a certain sense lead man beyond himself. Christ, on the other hand, will make people more inward, but also more humble. The luciferic spirits will lead man beyond himself and make him clever, bright, a genius—but also give him a certain haughtiness, will teach him that he can become superhuman already during Earth evolution. Therefore everything that will in future lead man to something as it were beyond himself, that will make him proud of his own human nature—here on earth already—will be a luciferic influence. From Christ will come, in contrast, all that deepens us, that in relation to our inner life will deepen us in a way which is only possible through the full development of the fourth principle.

People who take an external view of things will say: Christ is really lower than luciferic beings, for He only develops the fourth principle, while they develop higher ones. Yet there is a difference: these other beings develop the higher principles as though parasitically grafted on to human nature, while the Christ develops the fourth principle by fully empowering, permeating and penetrating human nature with it. Just as the flesh and blood of Jesus of Nazareth was once empowered, permeated and penetrated by the fourth macrocosmic principle, so will the bodies of those be permeated with the fourth macrocosmic principle who take Christ up into themselves. And in the same way that the fourth macrocosmic principle is the gift of Christ, the sixth and seventh principles will be the gift of luciferic spirits. In future a time will come—which is already beginning to dawn—when people lacking in wisdom will say: 'Yes, when we read the Gospels or let work upon us what Christ gave humanity, we see that His teaching does not in the least attain to that height at which other spiritual beings stand who are connected with man.' It is true that such beings are in a certain sense higher than man, but they cannot permeate the whole human being, only his reason, his intellectual genius!

A time will come when people elevate the most powerful and important of these luciferic spirits—who will try to lead man beyond himself—to a position of great honour and distinction, regarding him as a great leader of mankind. They will state: 'Of course, what Christ was able to give was really only a transitionary stage!' There are already people who say: 'Who needs the teachings of the Gospels? We've already moved beyond them.' As I have said, people will look to a spirit of outstanding brilliance who will take possession of the flesh and blood of a human being and permeate it with his genius; and they will say: 'He is greater than Christ; for Christ was in reality nothing more than the one who enabled us to develop the fourth principle, while this spirit enables us to get as far as the seventh principle during Earth evolution!'

Thus the Christ Spirit and the spirit of this other being will confront one another: the Christ Spirit from whom people will be able to hope to receive the mighty macrocosmic impulse of their fourth principle; and the luciferic spirit, who will in a certain sense try to lead them beyond it.

People would do well to stand firm and tell themselves that all they should take from luciferic spirits is what they can look up to in the same way they look down on their lower nature. But inasmuch as people come to think that Christ can only offer the fourth principle, while other spirits provide the sixth and seventh, they will come to worship and elevate the Antichrist.

Thus will the Antichrist gain ascendancy over Christ in the future. And we will be able to make no objection to this with our outward reason and insight. For it will be possible to point to many things in which the Antichrist demonstrates greater intellect and genius than the deepest human Christ principle increasingly flowing into the soul. Christ brings us the fourth macrocosmic principle which, because it is macrocosmic, is infinitely more important than all microcosmic principles. It is stronger than them, although it is related to the human ego, stronger than everything else that can be attained in the course of Earth evolution. But because it is 'merely' the fourth principle, people will say that what Christ brings is lower than the fifth, sixth, seventh principles that come from luciferic spirits, and in particular is lower than what comes from the Antichrist.

It is important that people pursuing the science of the spirit gain insight into this. Already, in respect of the teachings of Copernicus—which, as it were, showed us the earth in movement, tore it away from the fixity in which it had formerly been placed and set it orbiting the sun, showing how the earth is a speck of dust in the cosmos—people say: 'How can the Christian idea survive in the face of that!' People engineer a contradiction between the Christian idea and this science by saying that in former times one could look up to the Cross of Golgotha and to Christ, for then it seemed the earth was a chosen place in the cosmos, and the other planets looked small and as though there for earth's purposes. At that time, one can say, man regarded the earth as worthy of bearing the Cross of Golgotha! But when Copernican teachings took off, people started saying rather sarcastically that since the other planetary bodies are at least of equal significance with the earth, Christ must have wandered from one to the other. Since the other planets are mostly much larger than the earth, it is, they said, rather strange that this God-man completed His work of redemption on our little world! A Nordic scholar actually said this.[52] He said that the Christ drama appeared to him like performing a large-scale, star-studded production in a village hall instead of a grand theatre. He thought it was ridiculous not to have the greatest drama of the world performed on a large planet!

An odd way of thinking indeed! And one can reply that the Christ legend itself has made it clear that one ought not to say such idiotic things, for it starts in a poor barn rather than some noble, wealthy place. This is as much as to say that one should not make the kind of objection that the Nordic scholar came out with. What people often do not consider is how inconsistent they are with their very clever ideas. This idea simply does not hold up in the face of the great, simple truth that is already contained in Christian legend. And if this Christian legend places the birth of Jesus in a poor barn rather than a palace, it seems natural that the earth, rather than the largest planets, should be chosen as the place to bear the Cross. The whole way, in fact, in which Christian teachings describe what Christ had to bring mankind, anticipates those great teachings which the science of the spirit should nowadays give us once more. When we let the Gospels work upon us, we can find there the deepest spiritual-scientific truths, as we have often seen. But *how* is this great wisdom contained in the Gospels? It strikes me that if those people who do not have a single spark of the Christ impulse in them are to elevate themselves to an understanding of what is written in the Gospels, they must more or less turn their brains upside down, even develop a certain quality of genius. That normal consciousness does not suffice is clear from the fact that so few people have any understanding at all for a spiritual-scientific interpretation of the Gospels. Through luciferic powers, by developing genius, one can only gain a purely external understanding of the Gospels. But how do their truths appear to us in the actual form they are given? We encounter them as if they pour forth unstinted, like ripest goodness, from what we call the being of Christ—without effort, without any strain—and speak directly to hearts that allow themselves to be imbued with the Christ impulse, illuminating and warming the soul through and through.

The manner in which these greatest gifts of wisdom come to man is the opposite of the manner in which intellectual cleverness works. These truths pour forth fully-formed from the fourth macrocosmic principle in Christ Jesus, in a direct, elemental, original way so that they can pass directly to human beings. Yes, pains have been taken to ensure that human cleverness, all luciferic sharp-wittedness in human

206 ESOTERIC CHRISTIANITY

evolution, will expend much effort in trying to interpret these words of Christ, and only very gradually work through to their simplicity and grandeur, to their fundamental nature. And as with Christ's words so also with His deeds.

If we describe a fact such as the Resurrection with the means that spiritual science provides, what strange fact do we encounter? A very important German theosophist, Troxler,[53] stated in the 1820s already that one could see how human reason was increasingly imbued with the luciferic principle. He said that human reason was wholly luciferic in all its efforts to grasp things. In general it is hard to explain deeper theosophical wisdom. Those of you who were at my lecture cycle in Prague[54] will remember that I referred to Troxler at the time in order to show that he already knew something which can now be taught about the human etheric or life body. He stated, as I said, that human intellect is imbued with luciferic forces.

If, without recourse to these luciferic forces, we now try to grasp the Resurrection through our good, theosophical powers, we have to say that something significant occurred at the Jordan baptism, that the macrocosmic Christ being, who subsequently lived on the earth for three years, penetrated the three bodily sheaths of the St. Luke Jesus, and these then passed through the Mystery of Golgotha with the Christ being. Christ Jesus' course of development during these three years was naturally different from that of other human beings. How can we use the principles of spiritual science to grasp the essence of the Resurrection? What actually occurred?

Jesus of Nazareth stood by the river Jordan. His ego separated from the physical, etheric and astral bodies, and the macrocosmic Christ being descended, took possession of these three bodies and then lived until 3 April of the year 33, as we can discover. But this was life of a different kind. For, beginning already before the baptism, this life of Christ in the body of Jesus of Nazareth was a slow dying process. With every advancing stage during these three years, one can say that something of the bodily sheaths of Jesus of Nazareth died. Gradually these sheaths died away, so that after three years the whole body of Jesus of Nazareth was close to being a corpse, and was only held together by the power of the macrocosmic Christ being. You should not imagine that this body in which Christ lived was, say a year and a half after the Jordan baptism, the same as any other body. An ordinary human soul would have immediately felt this body falling away from it, for it could only be held together by the mighty macrocosmic Christ being. This was a continual, slow death, over three years. And this body had reached the verge of dissolution when the Mystery of Golgotha occurred. And then all that was necessary was for those men—as it is related—to come to treat the body with their strange spices, creating a chemical union between these particular, special substances and the body of Jesus of Nazareth, in whom the macrocosmic Christ being had lived for three years, and then lower it into the grave. Very little was needed for this body to fall to dust in the grave and for the Christ spirit to clothe itself, one can say, in an etheric body condensing into visibility. Thus the risen Christ was wrapped in an etheric body condensed into visibility. He went about in this way and appeared to those to whom He was able to appear. He was not visible to all, since it was really only a condensed etheric body that he bore after resurrection. What had been placed in the grave crumbled into dust. And the most recent occult researches confirm that an earthquake did indeed occur. It was striking for me to find a suggestion in the Gospel of St. Matthew that an earthquake had occurred, after discovering this fact through occult research. The earth opened, the dust of the corpse fell into the chasm and united with the whole substance of the earth. The violent trembling caused by the earthquake shook and scattered the cloths as described in the St. John Gospel. It is wonderfully described in the St. John Gospel. This is the occult way of grasping the Resurrection, which does not need to conflict with what the Gospels say. I have often pointed out that Mary Magdalene did not recognize the Christ when He met her. How could she not recognize someone whom she had seen only a few days before, especially when this was such an important individuality as Christ Jesus? When it is related that Mary Magdalene did not recognize Him, it must be because she encountered Him in a different form. She only recognizes Him when she hears Him speak, as it were. Then she becomes aware of Him.

And all details in the Gospels become comprehensible to us from an occult perspective.

Yet someone might object that the Risen One, when He appeared to the disciples, urged Thomas to touch His wounds. One might therefore think that these wounds were still there and that Christ had come to the disciples in the same body that had crumbled into dust. No! Just imagine that someone has a wound: the etheric body contracts more tightly at that point, forms a kind of scar. And in this particularly contracted etheric body, from which the constituents of the new etheric body were drawn with which the Christ being clothed Himself, were especially dense places—so that Thomas too could sense that this was a reality.

This Gospel passage is particularly wonderful from an occult perspective. It in no way contradicts the fact that we have here an etheric body condensed to visibility through the power of Christ, paving the way for the Emmaus scene. This is described in the Gospel not as an ordinary intake of nourishment, but as a dissolution of food directly through the etheric body, through Christ's power, without involvement of the physical body.

All these things can nowadays be understood by following the esoteric principles of spiritual science. The Gospels can in a certain sense be taken literally—apart from passages that have been badly translated. It is wonderful how every small detail comes into focus and can be understood; and those who see this can, on noticing some contradiction, say to themselves: 'I'm still not clever enough to understand this!' They feel less 'clever' than modern theologians who say they cannot understand the Resurrection as described in the Gospels! But by grasping the fundamental aspect of things, we can indeed understand it.

What impression does all this make on human intellect and reason? Well, it has the effect that people say: 'If I am to believe in the Resurrection then I must erase all that I have so far attained through logic and reason. I cannot do that. So the Resurrection must be demolished instead.' The reason that speaks like this is imbued with luciferic character, which cannot grasp these things. It will increasingly come to reject the great fundamental words and facts of former times, and those surrounding the Mystery of Golgotha. But the science of the spirit will be called upon to grasp these things right down to their smallest details. It will not reject what can extend beyond the fourth macrocosmic principle as fifth, sixth and seventh principles; but nevertheless it will see in the former the greatest impulse that has been given to Earth evolution.

But from this you can see that understanding the Christ-aspect of earth evolution is not completely straightforward, since the objection is in a certain sense justified that particular spirits, luciferic spirits lead us onwards towards other—but only microcosmic—principles. I have previously expressed this by saying that the Christ is a kind of centre, a focal point, where being works through deed, through what it is itself. Surrounding Christ there sit the twelve bodhisattvas of the world who are illumined by what radiates from Christ, and who elevate it, through working upon it with their wisdom firstly, to higher principles. But from the fourth principle there also radiates everything that illumines these higher principles, inasmuch as these evolve during Earth. A great deal of error in regard to the uniqueness of Christ is caused by the fact that people are unclear that Christ represents not just the fourth principle, but the fourth *macrocosmic* principle; and that though higher principles can be developed, these are only microcosmic principles developed by beings who did not complete their evolution on Old Moon. Nevertheless, in their own way they stand higher than man, for they evolved during Moon evolution what people on Earth still need to evolve.

If we wish to understand the true place of the Christ principle within Earth evolution, and be clear why in future the Antichrist will in many respects be set higher than Christ Himself, we need to elevate ourselves to an understanding of such things as have here been described. The Antichrist may appear cleverer perhaps, may seem to possess greater intellectual brilliance than Christ, and will gain a powerful following. But the science of the spirit should prepare itself to withstand the deception that has been characterized here. Above all, a sure anchorage in good spiritual-scientific principles will be needed, to avoid being deceived in this realm. The task and mission of the esotericism that has developed in the West since the thirteenth century, and which we have often referred to, was above all to elaborate and clearly reveal what can be said in this respect about Christ. Those who stand firm on the solid ground of this esotericism will recognize more and more clearly the central place of Christ for Earth evolution. And increasingly people will come, in contrast to all the supposed reincarnations of Christ on earth, to recognize this simple fact: just as a pair of scales can only be supported at one focal point, not two or more, so must Earth evolution have a central, fundamental impulse. Those who assume that Christ incarnates several times, make the same mistake as someone who thinks that scales must be supported at two points in order to function properly. It doesn't work! And a being that walked the earth in several incarnations would not be Christ. This is what every trained occultist will come to see in relation to the nature of Christ. A simple comparison can always illumine the uniqueness of the nature of Christ, and in that sense too, the Gospels and the science of the spirit are in complete harmony.

The Dawn of Occultism in the Modern Age

1. Kassel, 27 January 1912

Today's lecture will be historical in character, and the day after tomorrow I shall speak of matters which will give us deeper insight into the impulses contained in the thinking, willing and actions of rosicrucianism. We can only understand the work of rosicrucianism as it is today when we realize that it was never a model laid down once and for all but assumes a different form in every century. This is because rosicrucianism must always adapt itself to the conditions of the times. It is quite obvious to us that the fundamental impulses of spiritual science must increasingly find their way into the culture of the present age; but we know, too, that this is difficult in our present western culture. Spiritual science cannot make different human beings of us from one day to the next, because our karma has placed us in western culture. Our task is not as simple as that of representatives of communities based upon race or the tenets of a particular religion. For our fundamental principle must be that we are not rooted in the soil of a specific creed but regard the different systems of religion as forms and variations of the one, universal life. It is the seed of spiritual truth in all religions for which spiritual science must seek. As a Westerner, the anthroposophist may very easily be misunderstood, above all by the different religious confessions and schools of thought in the world.

If we rightly understand our task as scientists of the spirit we must hold fast to the principle of historical development, realizing that spiritual science is an integral part of this development. Each one of you here has been incarnated in every epoch of culture—indeed more than once. What is the purpose of these reincarnations? Why must the human being pass through all these different schoolings in succeeding periods of culture and civilization? It was this question which brought Lessing[55] to avow his belief in the idea of reincarnation. Lessing thought to himself: Human beings have lived through all the earlier periods of culture and they must return again and again in order to learn new things and to be able to connect the old with the new. There must be a purpose in the fact that we pass through different incarnations, and the purpose is that in each of them the human being shall add new experiences to the old.

As you have often heard, there are great differences between the successive epochs of culture. Today we shall speak in greater detail of an extremely important period, the thirteenth century. Human beings in incarnation at that time lived through an experience which had not fallen to the lot of others. What I am now about to say is known to all who have reached a certain high level of spiritual life and who are now again in incarnation.

In the thirteenth century spiritual darkness fell for a time upon all human beings, even the most enlightened, and also upon the initiates. Whatever knowledge of the spiritual worlds existed in the thirteenth century came from tradition or from those who in still earlier times had been initiates and were able to call up memories of what they had then experienced. But for a brief space of time it was impossible even for these people to have direct vision of the spiritual world. Darkness had to fall for this short period to prepare for the intellectual culture which was to be characteristic of our modern age. The important point is that we have this kind of culture today in the fifth post-Atlantean epoch. Culture in the Greek epoch was quite different. Instead of the modern, intellectual kind of thinking, direct perception was then the dominant faculty; the human being was one, as it were, with what he saw and heard, even with what he thought. He did not cogitate and reason as he does today, which is right and correct, for this is the task of the fifth post-Atlantean epoch.

In the thirteenth century it was necessary for especially suitable personalities to be singled out for initiation, and the initiation itself could only take place after that brief period of darkness had come to an end. The name of the place in Europe where these events that I shall now describe took place cannot yet be made known, but before very long this too will be possible.

We shall speak today of the dawn of occultism in the modern age. Twelve men were living at the time of the darkness, twelve men of deep spirituality, who came together in order to further the progress of humanity. None of them possessed the power of direct vision of the spiritual world, but they were able to bring to life within them memories of what they had experienced through earlier initiation. And by the dispensation of the karma of mankind, the legacy of the ancient culture of Atlantis was embodied in seven of these twelve men. In my book *An Outline of Esoteric Science* it is stated that the seven wise teachers of the ancient, holy Indian civilization bore within them the surviving wisdom of Atlantis. These seven men were incarnated again in the thirteenth century and formed part of the twelve; it was they who were able to look back to the seven streams of the ancient Atlantean wisdom and to their further course. The task assigned to each of the seven was to make one of the seven streams of wisdom fruitful both for the culture of the thirteenth century and for that of our modern age. These seven individualities were joined by four others; unlike the first seven, these other four were not able to look back to times of the primeval past; they looked back to what mankind had acquired from occult truths during the four epochs of post-Atlantean culture. The first of the four looked back to the period of ancient India, the second to that of ancient Persia, the third to that of Egyptian-Chaldean and Babylonian-Assyrian culture, and the fourth to that of the Graeco-Roman age. These four joined the seven in the council of the wise men in the thirteenth century; the twelfth had fewest memories; he was the most intellectual of the twelve and it was his task to cultivate and foster the external sciences. These twelve individualities did not live on only in the sphere of western occultism, but could also be 'incorporated' as it were in people who possessed some genuine knowledge of occultism. Goethe's poem *The Mysteries*[56] gives a certain indication of this.

Thus there were twelve outstanding individualities, joined by a thirteenth who, after the period of darkness had come to an end, was to be chosen for the kind of initiation necessary in western culture. The circumstances are very mysterious, and I can only give you the following information in the form of a narrative. To me it is objective truth, but you yourselves can put it to the test by gathering together what has been said by anthroposophical spiritual science during the last few years, in addition to what you know of history since the thirteenth century.

It was known to the council of twelve wise men that a child was to be born who had lived in Palestine at the time of Christ and had been present when the Mystery of Golgotha had taken place. This individuality had strong heart forces and a power of deep, inward love which circumstances had since helped him to unfold. An individuality of extraordinary spirituality was incarnated in this child. It was necessary in this case for a process to be enacted which will never be repeated in the same form. What I shall tell you does not describe a typical initiation but an altogether exceptional happening. It was necessary for this child to be removed from the environment into which he was born and to be placed in the care of the twelve at a certain place in Europe. But it was not the external measures adopted by the twelve wise men that are of essential importance; what is important is the fact that the child grew up with the twelve around him, and because of this, their wisdom was able to stream into him. One of the twelve, for example, possessed Mars wisdom and therewith a definite quality of soul—a mood of soul tempered by this Mars wisdom. The forces of Mars culture endowed his soul with the faculty, among others, of presenting occult sciences with a fiery enthusiasm and ardour. Similar planetary influences were also at work in other faculties distributed among the twelve. The influences pouring from the twelve wise men worked in such mutual accord that the soul of the child was harmoniously formed. And so the child grew up under the unceasing care of the twelve. Then, at a certain time, when the child had grown into a young man of about twenty, he was able to give expression to something that was a kind of reflection of the twelve streams of wisdom—but in a form altogether new, new even to the twelve wise men. The metamorphosis was accompanied by violent organic changes. Even physically the child had been quite unlike other human beings; he was often very ill and his body became transparent, as though filled with light. Then there came a time when for some days the soul departed altogether from the body. The young man lay as if dead ... And when the soul returned it was as though the twelve streams of wisdom were born anew, so that the twelve wise men, also, could learn something quite new from the youth. He was now able to speak of quite new experiences. There had come to him, through the Mystery of Golgotha, an experience similar to that of Paul on the road to Damascus.

Thereby it was possible for all the twelve world conceptions, religious and scientific—and fundamentally there are only twelve—to be amalgamated into one comprehensive whole, which could do justice to them all. Of what was taught we shall speak the day after tomorrow. It remains now to be said that the young man died very soon afterwards. His life on earth had been brief. His mission has been to create this synthesis of the twelve streams of wisdom in the sphere of thought and to bring forth the new impulse which he could then bequeath to the twelve men who were to carry it further. A great and significant impetus was thus given. The name of this individuality from whom this impulse originated was Christian Rosenkreutz.[57] He was born again in the fourteenth century and this earthly life lasted for more than a hundred years. In this new earthly life he brought to outward fruition all that he had lived through in the brief space of time of his previous life. He travelled all over the West and over practically the whole of the then known world in order to receive anew the wisdom which in his former life had quickened in him the new impulse—the impulse which, as a kind of essence, was to filter into the culture of the times.

This new impulse also came to expression in the exoteric world. The inspiration of the being of whom we have spoken, worked, for example, in Lessing. It is not, of course, possible to give outward proof of this, but Lessing's whole mode and manner of thinking is such that the rosicrucian impulse it contains is perceptible to one versed in these matters. Again in the nineteenth century—an age so ill-adapted for the ideas of karma, reincarnation and the like—this impulse worked exoterically. It is an interesting fact that towards the end of the forties of the nineteenth century a certain scientific body offered a reward for the best philosophical treatise on the subject of the immortality of the soul: the one that was awarded the prize was by Widenmann,[58] who accepted the principle that the soul has many earthly lives. Naturally this essay does not speak of reincarnation in the way spiritual science now does; but it is interesting that such a treatise should have appeared at that time and have been awarded the prize. And other contemporary psychologists also acknowledged their belief in repeated earth lives. The thread of belief in reincarnation and karma was never entirely broken. Moreover the early writings of the founder of the Theosophical Society, the great H.P. Blavatsky,[59] are explicable only when we recognize the rosicrucian inspiration underlying them.

Now it is of the greatest importance for us to know that whenever the rosicrucian inspiration is given, in each century, the bearer of the inspiration is never outwardly named. His identity is known only to the very highest initiates. Today, for example, it is only permissible to speak of happenings of a hundred years ago; for this is the period of time which must elapse before they may be spoken of openly. The temptation to pay fanatical veneration to authority vested in some personality—which is the worst thing of all—would be too great. This danger is too near at hand. Silence is a necessary precaution not only against the wiles of ambition and pride, which it might be possible to resist, but above all because of the occult, astral attacks which would be directed all the time against such an individual. Hence the rule that these things may not be spoken of until a hundred years have elapsed. Such studies must help us to realize that rosicrucianism is at the very heart of historical development, at the focal point of evolution.

By a simple comparison let me explain to you what is meant by this. Think of a pair of scales. There must be only one focal point or fulcrum, for if there were two, no weighing would be possible. One such fulcrum is also necessary in the process of historical evolution. Eastern world conceptions do not admit this, nor do they recognize historical evolution in this sense; and the same applies to Schopenhauer.[60] But it is the task of Western humanity to acknowledge the course of history—and it is the mission of rosicrucianism to promote a kind of thinking which admits the reality of a fulcrum or pivotal point in history. In regard to what will now be said, the religious confession to which a person belongs is of no consequence. For it can be substantiated from the Akashic Record that the day which represents the pivotal point in the evolution of mankind is 3 April in the year AD 33. Knowledge of the fact that the pivot of evolution lies at this point is an essential part of rosicrucianism.

What was it that really happened then? What happened was what can be called the crisis in the demon-world. And what does this mean? We know that in earlier times human beings possessed the faculty of primitive clairvoyance. This clairvoyance became progressively feebler, almost to the point of extinction. The fact is that hitherto the human being had been conscious mainly in the astral body and less in the ego. The crisis came about because of the darkening of ancient clairvoyance. Man's vision then extended only into the lowest regions of the spiritual world. The ego still lived in the astral world; but the beings and powers which the ego was able to behold deteriorated into greater and greater impurity. Man no longer had any vision of the good powers, but as he looked into the astral world he saw only these evil beings. The only means of salvation was the cultivation and development of the ego. The starting-point for this was what took place in the baptism by John in the Jordan. What was the experience of one thus baptized? He experienced in the first place the physical process of immersion in the water, which caused the separation of astral and etheric bodies from the physical body. This enabled him to perceive that a crisis was at hand in the world of the demons. And those who had been

220 ESOTERIC CHRISTIANITY

baptized knew: We must change our hearts! The time is at hand when the spirit is to stream directly into the ego. Such a person felt that these terrible astral beings were within him, continually penetrating into him.

Something had to come that transcends the astral, and this is the ego. Through the ego it will be possible for communities of human beings to gather together in freedom of soul, communities no longer determined by ties of blood. And now picture to yourselves someone possessed by demons of the most evil kind who know that they are facing a crisis. Picture to yourselves again that to such a person comes One whose mission it is to oppose the demons. What must the demons feel? They must feel extremely ill at ease! And so indeed it was: in the presence of Christ Jesus the demons were ill at ease.

Rosicrucianism contains the impulse through which the demons may and must be countered. Through this impulse the ego is to become supreme—but in this respect little progress has yet been made.

Returning to the point at which the lecture began, it is not difficult to realize that it will be harder for us as anthroposophists to make our voice heard in the world than it will be for any others. The adherents of other views of the world will have less persecution to suffer than anthroposophists. For nothing makes people more uneasy than to describe to them the true nature of the Christ. But our conviction is based upon the results of genuine occult science, and this conviction must be sustained with all the strength of which we are capable.

The Dawn of Occultism in the Modern Age

2. Kassel, 29 January 1912

Today we will lead on from the lecture of the day before yesterday to certain matters which can promote a deep personal understanding of anthroposophical life. If we survey our life and make real efforts to get to the roots of what happens in it, very much can be gained. We shall recognize the justice of many things in our destiny and realize that we have deserved them. Suppose someone has been superficial and thoughtless in the present incarnation and is subsequently struck by a blow of fate. It may not be possible, in a direct, outward manner, to connect the blow of fate with the thoughtlessness, but a feeling arises, nevertheless, that there is justice in it. Then again, looking back on our life, we find blows of fate which we can only attribute to chance, for there seems no explanation for them whatever. We can find these two categories of experience as we survey our life.

Now it is important to make a clear distinction between apparent chance and obvious necessity. When someone reviews his life with reference to these two kinds of occurrence, he will fail to reach any higher stage of development without striving for a very clear perception of everything that seems due to chance. We must try, above all, to have a clear perception of those things we have not wished for, which go right against the grain. It is possible to adopt a hypothetical stance and ask: How would it be if I were to take those things which I have not desired, which are disagreeable to me, and imagine that I myself actually really wanted them? In other words we imagine with all intensity that we ourselves willed our particular circumstances.

In regard to apparently fortuitous happenings we must picture the possibility of having ourselves put forth a deliberate and strong effort of will in order to bring them about. Meditatively as it were, we must induce this attitude to happenings which, on the face of them, seem to be purely fortuitous in our lives. Every human being today is capable of this mental exercise. If we proceed in this way, a very definite impression will gradually arise in the soul; we will feel as though something were striving to be released from us. The soul says to itself: 'Here, as a mental image, I have before me a second being; he is actually there.' We cannot get rid of this image and the being gradually becomes our 'double'. The soul begins to feel a real connection with this being who has been imagined into existence, to realize that this being does actually exist within us. If this conception deepens into a vivid and intense experience, we become aware that this imagined being is by no means without significance. We become certain that we did indeed once have the impulses of will within us which led to the apparently chance happenings of today. Thereby we reach a deeply rooted conviction that we were already in existence before coming down into the body. Every human being today can experience this conviction.

And now let us consider the question of the human being's successive incarnations. What is it that reincarnates? How can we discover the answer to this question?

There are three fundamental and distinct categories of experience in the life of the soul. Firstly our mental pictures, our ideas and thoughts. In forming a mental picture our attitude may well be one of complete neutrality; we need not love or hate what we picture inwardly, neither need we feel sympathy or antipathy towards it. Secondly there are the

moods and shades of feelings which arise alongside the ideas
or the thoughts; the cause of these moods in the life of feeling
is that we like or love one thing, dislike or abhor another, and
so forth. The third kind of experience in our soul-life are
impulses of the will. There are, of course, transitional stages,
but speaking generally these are the three categories.
Moreover it is fundamentally characteristic of a healthy life
of soul to be able to keep these three kinds of experiences
separate and distinct from one another. Our life of thought
and mental picturing arise because we receive stimuli from
outside. Nobody will find it difficult to realize that conceptual
life is most closely bound up with our present incarnation.
This, after all, is obvious when we bear in mind that speech is
the instrument whereby we express our thoughts; and speech,
or language, must, in the nature of things, differ in every
incarnation. We no more bring language with us at the
beginning of a new incarnation than we bring thoughts and
ideas. The language as well as the thoughts must be acquired
afresh in each incarnation. Hebbel once wrote something
very remarkable in his diary.[61] The idea occurred to him that
a scene in which the reincarnated Plato was being soundly
chastized by the teacher for his lack of understanding of Plato
would produce a very striking effect in a play! A person does
not carry over his thought and mental life from one incarnation to another, and he takes practically nothing of it with
him into his after-death existence. After death we evolve no
thoughts or mental pictures but have direct perceptions, just
as our physical eyes have perceptions of colour. After death
the world of concepts is seen as a kind of net spread out
across existence. But our feelings, our moods of heart and
feeling—these we retain after death, and we also bring their
forces with us as qualities and tendencies of soul into a new
earthly life. For example, even if a child's life of thought is
undeveloped, we shall be able to notice quite definite ten-

dencies in his life of feeling. And because our impulses of will are linked with feelings we also take them with us into our life after death. If, for instance, someone succumbs to a mistaken idea, the effect upon his life of feeling is not the same as if he devotes himself to the truth. For a long time after death we suffer from the consequences of false mental images and ideas. Our attention must therefore turn to the qualities and moods of feeling and the impulses of will when we ask ourselves what actually passes on from one incarnation to another.

Suppose something painful happened to us ten or twenty years ago. In thought today we may be able to remember it quite distinctly and in detail. But the actual pain we felt at the time has all but faded away; we cannot re-experience the stirrings of feelings and impulses of will which accompanied it. Think for a moment of Bismarck[62] and the overwhelming difficulties we know he had to face when he took his decision to go to war in 1866; think of what tumultuous feelings, what teeming impulses of will were working in Bismarck at that time! But even when writing his memoirs, would Bismarck have been conscious of these emotions and resolves with anything like the same intensity? Of course not! Man's memory between birth and death is composed of thoughts and mental pictures. It may be, of course, that even after ten or twenty years a feeling of pain comes over us at the recollection of some sorrowful event, but generally speaking the pain will have greatly diminished after this lapse of time; in thought, however, we can remember the very details of the event. If we now picture to ourselves that we actually willed certain painful events, that in reality we welcomed things which in our youth we may have hated, the very difficulty of this exercise rouses the soul and thus has an effect upon the life of feeling. Suppose, for example, a stone once crashed down upon us. We now try with all intensity to picture that we ourselves willed it so. Through such mental pictures—that we ourselves have willed the chance events in our life—we arouse, in the life of feeling, memory of our earlier incarnations. In this way we begin to realize that we are rooted in the spiritual world, we begin to understand our destiny. We have brought with us, from our previous incarnation, the will for the chance events of this life.

To devote ourselves in meditation to such thoughts and elaborate them, is of the highest importance. Between death and a new birth too, much transpires, for this period is infinitely rich in experiences—purely spiritual experiences, of course. We therefore bring with us qualities of feeling and impulses of will from the period between death and a new birth, that is to say, from the spiritual world. Upon this rests a certain occurrence of very great importance in the modern age, but one of which little notice is taken. The occurrence is to be found in the lives of many people today, but it is usually passed by unnoticed. It is, however, the task of anthroposophy to point to such an occurrence and its significance. Let me make it clear by an example.

Suppose someone has occasion to go somewhere or other and his path leads him to follow in the tracks of another human being, a child perhaps. Suddenly the person catches sight of a yawning chasm at the edge of the path along which the child is walking. A few steps further and the child will inevitably fall over the edge into the chasm. He runs to save the child, runs and runs, entirely forgetting about the chasm. Then he suddenly hears a voice calling out to him from somewhere: 'Stand still!' He halts as though nailed to the spot. At that moment the child catches hold of a tree and also stops, so that no harm befalls. If no voice had called at that moment the man would inevitably have fallen into the chasm. He wonders where the voice came from. There is no one at all who could have called, but he realizes that he would quite certainly have lost his life if he had not heard this voice; yet, however closely he investigates he cannot find that the warning came from any physical voice.

Through close self-observation many human beings living at the present time would be able to recognize a similar experience in their lives. But far too little attention is paid to such things. An experience of this kind may pass by without leaving a trace—then the impression fades away and no importance is attached to the experience. But suppose someone has been attentive and realizes that it was not without significance. The thought may then occur to him: 'At that point in your life you were facing a crisis, a karmic crisis; your life should really have ended at that moment, for you had forfeited it. You were saved by something akin to chance, and since then a second life has as it were been grafted on to the first; this second life is to be regarded as a gift bestowed upon you and you must act accordingly.' When such an experience makes a person feel that his life from that time onwards has been bestowed upon him as a gift, this means that he can be accounted a follower of Christian Rosenkreutz. For this is how Christian Rosenkreutz calls the souls whom he has chosen. Anyone who can recall such an occurrence—and everyone sitting here can discover something of the kind in their lives if they observe closely enough—has the right to say to himself: Christian Rosenkreutz has given me a sign from the spiritual world that I belong to his stream. Christian Rosenkreutz has added such an experience to my karma. This is the way in which Christian Rosenkreutz chooses his pupils; this is how he gathers his community. A person conscious of this experience knows with certainty that a path has been pointed out to him which he must follow, trying to discover how he can dedicate himself to the service of rosicrucianism. If there are some people who have not yet recognized the sign, they will do so later on;

for he to whom the sign has once been given will never again be free from it.

Such an experience comes to those who, during the period between their last death and present birth, were in contact with Christian Rosenkreutz in the spiritual world. It was then that Christian Rosenkreutz chose us, imparting an impulse of will which leads us now to such experiences. This is the way in which spiritual connections are established. Materialistic thought will naturally regard all these things as hallucinations, just as it regards the experience of Paul at Damascus as having been an hallucination. The logical conclusion to be drawn from this is that the whole of Christianity is based upon an hallucination, therefore upon error. For theologians are perfectly well aware that the event at Damascus is the foundation stone of the whole of subsequent Christianity. And if this foundation stone itself is nothing but an illusion, then, if thought is consistent, everything built upon it must obviously be fallacy.

An attempt has been made today to show that certain occurrences, certain experiences in life may indicate to us how we are interwoven in the spiritual fabric of world existence. If we develop our feeling memory then we live our way into the spiritual life which streams and pulses through the world. Theoretical knowledge alone does not make people true anthroposophists; those who understand their own life and the life of other human beings in the sense indicated today—they and they alone are true anthroposophists. Anthroposophy then becomes a fundamental force transforming our life of soul. And the goal of the work in our groups must be that the intimate experiences of the soul change in character, that through the gradual development of feeling memory we become aware of immortality. The true theosophist or anthroposophist must be certain that if he really desires it, if he applies the forces within him in all their strength, then he can utterly transform his character. We must learn to feel and experience that an immortal element holds sway in ourselves and in everything else. An anthroposophist becomes an anthroposophist because his faculties remain open and receptive his whole life long, even when his hair is white. And this realization that progress is always and forever possible will transform our whole spiritual life today.

One of the consequences of materialism is that human beings become prematurely old. Thirty years ago, for example, children looked quite different; there are children today of ten or twelve years of age who look almost like very old men and women. Human beings have become so precocious, especially the grown-ups. They maintain that lies such as that of babies being brought by the stork should not be told to children, that children should be enlightened on such matters. But this enlightenment itself is really a lie. Those who come after us will know that the souls of our children hover down as bird-like spirit forms from the higher worlds. To have an imaginative conception of many things still beyond our comprehension is of very great importance. As regards the fact in question it might be possible to find a better imaginative picture than the story of the stork. What matters is that spiritual forces operate between the child and his parents or teachers, a kind of secret magnetism must be there. We must ourselves believe in any imaginative picture we give to the children. If it is a question of explaining death to them, we must point to another phenomenon of nature. We can say: 'See how the butterfly flies out of the chrysalis. The same thing happens to the human soul after death.' Yet we must ourselves believe that the forces in the butterfly emerging from the chrysalis present us with a true image of the soul going forth from the body. The world-spirit has inscribed such a picture in nature to draw our attention to the process. It is tremendously important to be always capable of learning, of remaining young, independently of our physical body. And that is the great task of theosophy that has become anthroposophy: to bring to the world the rejuvenation which it needs. We must get beyond the banal and the purely material. To recognize soul and spirit as powers operating in life—this must be the aim of the work in our groups. We must be permeated more and more with the knowledge that the soul can gain mastery over the external world.

The True Attitude to Karma

Vienna, 8 February 1912

I had good reason to emphasize at the end of each of the two public lectures[63] that anthroposophy must not be regarded merely as a theory or a science, nor only as knowledge in the ordinary sense. It is rather something that can be transformed in the soul into actual life, into an elixir of life. What really matters more than simply acquiring knowledge through anthroposophy, is that forces flow into us from anthroposophy which help us not only in ordinary physical existence but through the whole compass of life, including physical existence and the discarnate condition between death and a new birth. The more we feel that anthroposophy bestows upon us forces which strengthen and enrich life itself, the more truly do we understand it. When such a statement is made, people may ask: If anthroposophy is to be a power that strengthens and invigorates life, why is it necessary to absorb all this apparently theoretical knowledge? Why do we have to bother in our group meetings with all sorts of details about past planetary embodiments of the earth? Why is it necessary to learn about things that happened in the remote past? Why are we also expected to familiarize ourselves with the more intimate, intangible laws of reincarnation, karma and so forth? Many people might think that anthroposophy is just another kind of science, on a par with the many sciences existing in outer, physical life.

Now in answering this question, which has been mentioned here because it is very likely to be asked, we must put aside all considerations of comfort and convenience. Scrupulous self-examination is necessary to find whether or not such questions are tainted by that habitual slackness in life which we know only too well. People are often fundamentally unwilling to learn, unwilling to take hold of the spiritual because this is inconvenient, and so we must ask ourselves whether this fear of inconvenience and discomfort is creeping into such questions. Let us admit that we really do think occasionally that there might be an easier path to anthroposophy than all that is presented, for example, in our literature. It is often said light-heartedly that, after all, a person need only know himself, need only try to be a good and righteous human being, and then he is a sufficiently good anthroposophist. Yes, my dear friends, but precisely this gives us the deeper knowledge that there is in fact nothing more difficult than to be a good person, and that nothing needs so much preparation and hard work as attaining this ideal.

And the truth about self-knowledge is certainly not something that can be answered in a moment, as so many people would like to think. Today, therefore, we will consider certain questions which are often expressed in the way suggested above. We will think of how anthroposophy comes to us, seemingly, as a body of teaching, a science, although in essence it brings self-knowledge and the aspiration to become good and righteous human beings. And to this end it is important to study from different points of view how anthroposophy can flow into life.

Let us consider one of life's vital questions. I am not referring to anything in the domain of science but to a question arising in our everyday lives: that of consolation for suffering, for lack of satisfaction in life. How, for example, can anthroposophy bring consolation to people in distress when they need it? Every individual must of course apply what can be said about such matters to his own particular case. In addressing a number of people one can only speak in a general sense.

Why do we need consolation in life? Because something may distress us, because we have to suffer and undergo painful experiences. Now it is natural for us to feel that something in us rebels against this suffering. And we ask: 'Why have I to bear it, why has it fallen to my lot? Could my life not have been without pain, could it not have brought me contentment?' Anyone who puts the question in this way can only find an answer when he understands the nature of human karma, of human destiny. Why do we suffer? And I am referring not only to outer suffering but also to inner suffering due to a sense of failure to do ourselves justice or find our proper bearings in life. That is what I mean by inner suffering. Why does life bring so much that leaves us unsatisfied?

Study of the laws of karma will make it clear to us that something underlies our sufferings, something that can be illustrated by an example drawn from ordinary life between birth and death. I have given this example more than once. Suppose a young man has lived up to the age of eighteen or so entirely dependent on his father; his life has been happy and carefree, he has had everything he wanted. Then the father loses his fortune, becomes bankrupt, and the youth is obliged to set about learning something, to exert himself. Life brings him many sufferings and deprivations. It is readily understandable that the sufferings are not at all to his liking. But now think of him at the age of fifty. Because circumstances obliged him to learn something in his youth he has turned into a decent, self-respecting human being. He has found his feet in life and can say to himself: 'My attitude to the sufferings and deprivations was natural at the time; but now I think quite differently about them; I realize now that the sufferings would not have come to me if in those days I had possessed all the virtues—even the very circumscribed ones of a boy of eighteen. If no suffering had come my way I should have remained a good-for-nothing. It was the sufferings that changed my imperfections into something far better. It is due to the suffering that I am not the same human being I was forty years ago. What was it, then, that joined forces in me at that time? My own imperfections and my suffering joined forces. And my imperfections sought out the suffering so that they might be removed and transformed into virtues.'

This attitude can even arise from quite an ordinary view of life between birth and death. And if we think deeply about life as a whole, facing our karma in the way described in the lecture yesterday, we shall be convinced that our imperfections seek out our sufferings. The vast majority of sufferings are, indeed, sought out by the imperfections we have brought with us from earlier incarnations. And because of these imperfections a wiser being within us seeks for the path leading to our sufferings. For it is a golden rule in life that as human beings we constantly have within us a being who is much wiser, much cleverer than ourselves. The part of us we call 'I' in ordinary life has far less wisdom, and if faced with the alternative of seeking either pain or happiness would certainly choose the path to happiness. The wiser being operates in the depths of subconscious life to which ordinary consciousness does not extend. This wiser being diverts our gaze from the path to superficial happiness and kindles within us a magic power which, without our conscious knowledge, leads us towards suffering. But what does this mean: without our conscious knowledge? It means that the wiser being is prevailing over the less wise one, and this wiser being invariably acts within us so that it leads our imperfections to our sufferings, allowing us to suffer because every outer and inner suffering roots out some imperfection and leads to greater perfection.

234 ESOTERIC CHRISTIANITY

We may be willing to accept such principles in theory, but that is not of much account. A great deal is achieved, however, if in certain solemn and dedicated moments of life we try strenuously to make such principles the very life-blood of the soul. In the hurry and bustle, the work and the duties of ordinary life, this is not always possible; under these circumstances we cannot always oust the being of lesser wisdom—who is, after all, part of us. But in certain deliberately chosen moments, however short they may be, we shall be able to say to ourselves: 'I will turn away from the hubbub of outer life and view my sufferings in such a way that I realize how the wiser being within me has been drawn to them by a magic power, how I imposed upon myself certain pain without which I should not have overcome this or that imperfection.' A feeling of the peace inherent in wisdom will then arise, bringing the realization that even when the world seems full of suffering, there too it is full of wisdom! In this way, life is enriched through anthroposophy. We may forget it again in the affairs of outward life, but if we do not forget it altogether and repeat the exercise steadfastly, we shall find that a kind of seed has been laid in the soul, and that many a feeling of sadness and depression changes into a more positive attitude, into strength and energy. And then out of such quiet moments in life we will acquire more harmonious souls and become stronger individuals.

Then we may pass on to something else... but the anthroposophist should make it a rule to devote himself to these other thoughts only when the attitude that comforts him in his suffering has become alive within him. We may turn, then, to think about the happiness and joys of life. Someone who adopts towards his destiny the attitude that he himself has willed his sufferings will have a strange experience when he comes to think about his joy and happiness. It is not as easy for him here as it is in the case of his sufferings. It is easy, after all, to find a consolation for suffering, and anyone who feels doubtful has only to persevere; but it will be difficult to find the right attitude to happiness and joy. However strongly someone may bring himself to feel that he has willed his suffering—when he applies this mood of soul to his happiness and joy he will not be able to avoid a sense of shame; he will feel thoroughly ashamed. And he can only rid himself of this feeling of shame by saying to himself: 'No, I have certainly not earned my joy and happiness through my own karma!' This is the only cure, for otherwise the shame may be so intense that it almost shatters the soul. The only salvation is not to attribute our joys to the wiser being within us. This thought will convince us that we are on the right road, because the feeling of shame passes away. It is really so: happiness and joy in life are bestowed by the wise guidance of worlds, without our assistance, as something we must receive as grace, always recognizing that the purpose is to give us our place in the whole scheme of things. Joy and happiness should so work upon us in the celebratory moments of life, in moments of seclusion that we feel them as grace, grace bestowed by the supreme powers of the world who want to receive us into themselves.

While our pain and suffering bring us to ourselves, make us more fully ourselves, through joy and happiness—provided we consider them as grace—we develop the feeling of peaceful security in the arms of the divine powers of the world, and the only worthy attitude is one of thankfulness. Nobody who in quiet hours of self-contemplation ascribes happiness and joy to his own karma, will unfold the right attitude to such experiences. If he ascribes joy and happiness to his karma he is succumbing to a fallacy which weakens and paralyses the spiritual within him; the slightest thought that we have deserved happiness or delight weakens and cripples us inwardly. These words may seem harsh, for many who attribute suffering to their own will and individuality would like to be master of themselves, too, in the experiences of happiness and joy. But even a cursory glance at life will indicate that by their very nature joy and happiness tend to obliterate something in us. This weakening effect of delights and joys in life is graphically described in *Faust* by the words: 'And so from longing to delight I reel; and even in delight I pine for longing.'[64] And anybody who gives any thought to the influence of joy, taken in the personal sense, will realize that there is something in joy that transports us and erases our actual self.

This is not meant to be a sermon against joy or a suggestion that it would be good to torture ourselves with red-hot pincers or the like. Certainly not. To recognize something for what it really is does not mean that we must flee from it. It is not a question of running away from joy but of receiving it calmly whenever it comes to us; we must learn to feel it as grace, and the more we do so the better it will be, for we shall enter more deeply into the divine. These words are said, therefore, not in order to preach asceticism but to awaken the right mood towards happiness and joy.

If anyone were to say: 'Joy and happiness have a weakening, deadening effect, therefore I will flee from them' (which is the attitude of false asceticism and a form of self-torture)—such a person would be fleeing from the grace bestowed upon him by the gods. And in truth the self-flagellation practised by ascetics, monks and nuns in olden days was a form of resistance against the gods. We must learn to regard suffering as something brought by our karma, and to feel happiness as grace that the divine can send down to us. Joy and happiness should be to us the sign of how closely the gods have drawn us to themselves; suffering and pain should be the sign of how remote we are from the goal we need to attain as intelligent human beings. Such is the true attitude to karma, and without it we shall make no real progress in life. Whenever the world bestows upon us the good and the beautiful, we must feel that behind this world stand those powers of whom the Bible says: 'And they looked at the world and they saw that it was good.' But inasmuch as we experience pain and suffering, we must recognize what, in the course of incarnations, man has made of the world which in the beginning was good, and what he must contribute towards its betterment by educating himself to bear pain with purpose and energy.

What has been described are two ways of accepting our karma. In a certain respect our karma consists of suffering and joys; and we relate ourselves to our karma with the right attitude when we can consider it as something we really wanted, and when we can confront our sufferings and joys with the proper understanding. But a review of karma can be extended further, which we shall do today and tomorrow.

Karma does not reveal itself only in the form of experiences of suffering or joy. As our life runs its course we encounter—in a way that can only be regarded as karmic—many human beings with whom, for example, we make a fleeting acquaintance, others who as relatives or close friends are connected with us for a considerable period of our life. We meet human beings who in our dealings with them bring sufferings and hindrances to our path; or again we meet others whom we can help and who can help us. The relationships are manifold. We must regard these circumstances too as having been brought about by the will of the wiser being within us—the will, for example, to meet a human being who seems to run across our path accidentally and with whom we have something to adjust or settle in life. What is it that makes the wiser being in us wish to meet this particular person? The only intelligent line of thought is that we want to come across him because we have done so before in an earlier life and our relationship had already begun then. Nor need the beginning have been in the immediately preceding life—it may have been very much earlier. Because in a past life we have had dealings of some kind with this person, because we may have been in some way indebted to him, we are led to him again by the wiser being within us, as if by magic power.

Here, of course, we enter a very diverse and extremely complicated domain, of which it is only possible to speak in general terms. But all the indications given here are the actual results of clairvoyant investigation. The indications will be useful to every individual because he will be able to particularize and apply what is said to his own life.

A remarkable fact comes to light. About the middle of life the ascending curve passes over into the descending curve. This is the time when the forces of youth are spent and we pass over a certain zenith to the descending curve. This point of time—which occurs in the thirties—cannot be laid down with absolute finality, but the principle holds good for everyone. It is the period of life when we live most intensely on the physical plane. In this connection we may easily be deluded. It will be clear that life before this point of time has been a process of bringing out what we have brought with us into the present incarnation. This process has been going on since childhood, although it is less marked as the years go by. We have chiselled out our life, have been nourished as it were by the forces brought from the spiritual world. These forces, however, are spent by the point of time referred to. Observation of the descending line of life reveals that we now proceed to harvest and work over what has been learnt in the school of life, in order to carry it with us into the next incarnation. This is something we take into the spiritual world; in the earlier period we were taking something from the spiritual world. It is in the middle period that we are most deeply involved in the physical world, most engrossed in the

affairs of outer life. We have passed through our appren-
ticeship as it were and are in direct contact with the world.
We have our life in our own hands. At this period we are
taken up with ourselves, concerned more closely than at any
other time with our own external affairs and with our relation
to the outer world. But this relation with the world is created
by the intellect and the impulses of will which derive from the
intellect—in other words, those elements of our being which
are most alien to the spiritual worlds, to which the spiritual
worlds remain closed. In the middle of life we are, as it were,
farthest away from the spiritual.

A certain striking fact presents itself to occult research.
Investigation of the kind of encounters and relationships with
other human beings that arise in the middle of life shows,
curiously, that these are the people with whom we were
together at the beginning of our life, in our very earliest
childhood in the previous incarnation or in a still earlier one.
The fact has emerged that in the middle of life—as a rule it is
so, but not always—we encounter, through outward karmic
circumstances, those people who in an earlier life were our
parents; it is very rarely indeed that we are brought together
in earliest childhood with those who were previously our
parents; we meet them in the middle of life. This certainly
seems strange, but it is the case, and a very great deal is
gained for life if we will only try to put such a general rule to
the test and adjust our thoughts accordingly. When a human
being—let us say at about the age of thirty—enters into some
relationship with another ... perhaps he falls in love, makes
great friends, quarrels, or has some different kind of contact,
a great deal will become comprehensible if, quite tentatively
to begin with, he thinks about the possibility of the relationship to this person having once been that of child and
parent. Conversely, another very remarkable fact comes to
light. Those human beings with whom we were together in

earliest childhood—parents, brothers and sisters, playmates or others around us during early childhood—they, as a rule, are people with whom we formed some kind of relationship when we were about thirty or so in a previous incarnation; in very many cases it is found that these people are our parents or brothers and sisters in the present incarnation. Curious as this may seem, just let us try to see how the principle squares with our own life, and we shall discover how much more understandable many things become. Even if the facts are otherwise, an experimental mistake will not amount to anything very serious. But if, in solitary hours, we look at life so that it is filled with meaning, we can gain a great deal. Obviously we must not try to arrange life to our liking; we must not choose the people we like and assume that they may have been our parents. Prejudices must not falsify the real facts. You will see the danger we are exposed to and the many misconceptions that may creep in. We ought to educate ourselves to remain open-minded and unbiassed.

You may now ask what there is to be said about the descending curve of life. The striking fact has emerged that at the beginning of life we meet those human beings with whom we were connected in the middle period of life in a previous incarnation; further, that in the middle of the present life, we revive relationships which existed at the beginning of a preceding life. And now, what of the descending curve of life? During that period we are led to people who may also, possibly, have had something to do with us in an earlier incarnation. They may, in that earlier incarnation, have played a part in occurrences of the kind that so frequently occur at a decisive point in life—let us say, trials and sufferings caused by bitter disillusionments. In the second half of life we may again be brought into contact with people who in some way or other were already connected with us; this meeting brings about a shifting of circumstances, and a lot that was set in motion in the earlier life is cleared up and resolved.

These things are diverse and complex and indicate that we should not adhere rigidly to any hard and fast pattern. This much, however, may be said: the nature of the karma that has been woven with those who come across our path especially in the second half of life is such that it cannot be absolved in *one* life. Suppose, for example, we have caused suffering to a human being in one life; we could easily imagine that in a subsequent life we shall be led to this person by the wiser being within us, so that we may make amends for what we have done to him. The circumstances of life, however, may not enable compensation to be made for everything, but often only for a part of it. This necessitates the operation of complicated factors which enable such surviving remnants of karma to be adjusted and settled during the second half of life. This conception of karma can shed light upon our dealings and companionship with other human beings.

But something further can be observed when we consider the course of our karma, something that in the two public lectures I referred to as the process of growing maturity, the acquisition of a real knowledge of life. (We can use this phrase as long as it does not foster arrogance.) Let us consider how we grow wiser. We can learn from our mistakes, and it is the best thing for us when this happens, because we do not often have the opportunity of applying the wisdom thus gained in one and the same life; therefore what we have learnt from mistakes remains with us as strength for a later life. But the wisdom, the real knowledge of life that we can acquire, what is it really?

I said yesterday that we cannot carry our thoughts and ideas with us directly from one life to the other; I said that even Plato could not take his ideas straight with him into his next incarnation. What we carry over with us takes the form of will, of feeling; and in reality our thought and ideas, just like our mother tongue, come as something new in each life. For most thoughts and ideas live in the mother tongue whence we acquire them. This life between birth and death supplies us with thoughts and ideas which always come from this particular stage of earth existence. But if this is so, we shall have to say to ourselves that it depends upon our karma. However many incarnations we go through, the ideas that arise in us are always dependent upon one incarnation as distinct from the others. Whatever wisdom may be living in your thoughts and ideas has been absorbed from without, is dependent upon the way karma has led you to language, nationality and family. In the last resort all our thoughts and ideas about the world are dependent on our karma. Very much lies in these words, for they indicate that whatever we may know in life, whatever knowledge we may amass, is something entirely personal, and that we can never transcend the personal by means of what we acquire for ourselves in life. In ordinary life we never reach the level of the wiser being but always remain at that of the less wise. Anyone who flatters himself that he can learn more about his higher self from what he acquires in the world, is harbouring a comfortable illusion. This actually means that we can gain no knowledge of our higher self from what we acquire in the course of our life.

Very well, then, how are we to attain any knowledge of the higher self? We must ask ourselves quite frankly: What do we really know? First of all, we know what we have learnt from experience. This is all we know, and nothing else! A person who aspires to self-knowledge without realizing that his soul is only a mirror reflecting the outer world, may persuade himself that by penetrating into his own being he can find the higher self; certainly he will find something, but it is only what has come into him from outside. Laziness of thinking has no place in this quest. We must ask ourselves what happens in those other worlds in which our higher self also lives, and this is none other than what has been said about the different incarnations of the earth, and everything else that spiritual science tells us. Just as we try to understand a child's soul by examining the child's relationship to its surroundings, so must we ask what the environment of the higher self is. It is spiritual science that tells us about these worlds where our higher self is, in its account of Saturn and its secrets, of the Moon and Earth evolution, of reincarnation and karma, of devachan and kamaloca and so on. This is the only way we can learn about our higher self, about the self which transcends the physical plane. And anyone who refuses to accept these secrets is merely pandering to his own ease. For it is an illusion to imagine you can discover the divine in yourself. Experiences of the outer world alone are stored within you, but the divine in us can only be found when we search in our soul for the mirrored world beyond the physical. So that those things which can sometimes prove difficult and uncomfortable to learn are nothing else but self-knowledge. And true anthroposophy is in reality true self-knowledge! From spiritual science we receive enlightenment about our own self. For where in reality is the self? Is the self within our skin? No, the self is poured out over the world; everything that is and has been in the world is part and parcel of the self. We learn to know the self only when we learn to know the world.

What seem to be mere theories are, in truth, the ways to self-knowledge. A person who thinks he can find the self by staring into his inner being, says to himself: 'You must be good, you must be unselfish!' All well and good. But you will soon notice that he is getting more and more self-centred. On the other hand, struggling with the great secrets of existence, extricating oneself from the flattering self, accepting the reality of the higher worlds and the knowledge that can be obtained from them, all leads to true self-knowledge. When we think deeply about Saturn, Sun and Moon evolution, we lose ourselves in cosmic thought. 'In your thinking cosmic thoughts are living,'[65] says a soul who thinks anthroposophical thoughts; and adds: 'Lose yourself in cosmic thoughts!' The soul creating out of anthroposophy says: 'In your feeling cosmic powers are weaving,' but also adds: 'Experience yourself through cosmic powers!' not through powers which flatter. This experience will not come to someone who closes his eyes, saying: 'I want to be a good human being.' It will only come to those who open their eyes and their spiritual eyes also, and see the powers working and weaving beyond themselves, realizing that they are embedded in these cosmic powers. And the soul that draws strength from anthroposophy says: 'In your willing cosmic beings are working,' adding: 'Create yourself anew from beings of will!' And this will really happen if we grasp self-knowledge in this way. Then we shall really succeed in creating ourselves anew out of cosmic beings.

Dry and abstract as this may seem, in reality it is no mere theory but something that thrives and grows like a seed sown in the earth. Forces shoot out in every direction and become plant or tree. So it is indeed. The feelings that come to us through spiritual science give us the power to create ourselves anew. 'Create yourself anew from beings of will!' Thus does anthroposophy become the elixir of life and our view of spirit worlds opens up. We shall draw strength from these worlds, and when we have drawn these forces into our being, then we shall know ourselves in all our depths. Only when we imbue ourselves with world knowledge can we take control of ourselves and advance step by step away from the less wise being within us, whose way is barred by the Guardian of the

Threshold, and towards the wiser being, thus penetrating through all that is hidden from those who do not as yet have the will to be strong—which we can gain through anthroposophy.

Intimate Workings of Karma

Vienna, 9 February 1912

There was one point in the lecture yesterday about which I should not like misunderstanding to arise, but a conversation I had today indicated that this might well occur. It is of course difficult to formulate in words these matters connected with the more intimate workings of karma, and one point or another may well not be quite clear at the first time of hearing. In the lecture yesterday I said that we should regard our sufferings as having been sought out by the wiser being within us in order that certain imperfections may be overcome, and that by bearing these sufferings calmly we may make progress along our path. That, however, was not the point which might give rise to misunderstanding. It was the other point that happiness and joy must not be regarded as due to our own merit or individual karma, but deemed a kind of grace through which the all-prevailing spirit penetrates us. Please do not think that the emphasis here lies in the fact that joy comes to us as a mark of *favour* from divine-spiritual powers; the emphasis lies in the fact that these experiences are made possible through grace. That is what our attitude must be if we are to reach a true understanding of karma. Happiness and joy are given us by divine grace. Anyone who imagines that the happiness and joy in his karma indicate a desire on the part of the gods to single him out and place him above the others will achieve just the opposite. We must never imagine that happiness is allotted to us as a mark of favour or distinction but rather as a reason for feeling that we have been recipients of the grace outpoured by divine spiritual beings. It is this realization of grace which makes progress possible; the other attitude would hinder us in our development. Nobody should ever believe that joy comes to him because of special karmic privileges; he should far rather believe that it comes to him because he has no privileges. Joy and happiness should move us to deeds of compassion and mercy, which we shall perform more effectively than if we are suffering the pangs of sorrow. What brings us forward is the realization that we must make ourselves worthy of grace. There is no justification for the very prevalent view that one whose life abounds in happiness has deserved it. This is the very attitude that must be avoided, and is a misunderstanding I would not wish to arise.

Today we will extend and widen the scope of our studies of karma, and talk about karma and our experiences in the world, so that we may find how spiritual science can become a real life force within us. Observation of life and what happens to us will reveal, to begin with, experiences of two kinds. On the one hand we might say to ourselves: 'Yes, a misfortune has befallen me, but thinking about it, I can see that it would not have come my way if I had not been careless or negligent.' This realization, however, will not always be within the power of ordinary consciousness; many a time we shall find it impossible to see how the misfortune and the circumstances of our present life are connected. With regard to much that befalls us, ordinary consciousness can only conclude that it was pure chance, unconnected with anything else. We can make the same distinction in relation to undertakings which may either be successful or the reverse. In many cases we shall realize that failure was inevitable because of laziness, inattentiveness, or something of the kind, on our part; but in many others we shall be quite unable to discover any connection. It is a useful exercise to take stock of our own experiences and distinguish between things which have failed through no fault of our own, and others which succeed contrary to our expectations. We will try to get to the bottom of these matters, and of events which, on the face of them, seem to be due to pure chance, without any apparent cause, and also things we have done that are seemingly unrelated to our actual capacities. Let us look more closely at all these things.

We will proceed in rather a curious way. As an experiment, we will imagine that we ourselves have *willed* whatever may have happened to us. Suppose a loose tile from the roof of a house happened to crash down on us. We will picture, purely by way of experiment, that this did not happen by chance, and we will deliberately imagine that we ourselves climbed on that roof, loosened the tile and then ran down so quickly that we arrived just in time to be hit by it! Or, let us say, we caught a chill without any apparent cause; how would it be though, if we had given it to ourselves? Like the unfortunate lady who, being discontented with her lot, exposed herself to a chill, and died of it! In this way, therefore, we will imagine that things otherwise attributable to chance have been deliberately and carefully planned by ourselves. And we will also apply the same procedure to matters which are obviously dependent upon the faculties and qualities we happen to possess. Say some arrangement does not work out as planned. If we miss a train, for example, we shall not blame external circumstances but picture to ourselves that it was due to our own slackness. If we think of it in this way, as an experiment, we shall gradually succeed in creating a kind of being in our imagination, a very extraordinary being, who was responsible for all these things—for a stone having fallen upon us, for some illness, and so forth. We shall realize, of course, that this being is not ourselves; we simply picture such a being vividly and distinctly. And then, after a time, we will have a strange experience in connection with this being. We shall realize that though it is a creature we have only conjured up, yet we cannot free ourselves from him nor from the thought of him, and strange to say he does not stay as he is; he becomes alive and transforms himself within us. And then, when he has gone through this transformation, we get the impression that he really is there within us. And then we become more and more certain that we ourselves have had something to do with the things we constructed in imagination. There is no suggestion whatever that we once actually did them; but such thoughts do, nevertheless, correspond in a certain way with something we have done. We shall tell ourselves: 'I have done this and that, and I am now having to suffer the consequences.' This is a very good exercise for unfolding in the life of feeling a kind of memory of earlier incarnations. The soul seems to feel: 'I myself was there and prepared these things myself.'

You will readily understand that it is not easy to awaken the memory of previous incarnations. For just think what mental effort is required to recall something only recently forgotten; genuine mental effort is required. Experiences which occurred in earlier incarnations have sunk into the depths of forgetfulness and much has to be done if they are to be remembered. One such exercise has just been described. In addition to what I described in the public lectures, let me say here that one can notice a kind of memory arising in one's feeling: 'In former times you prepared this for yourself!'

Such principles should not be ignored, for if we follow them we shall find that more and more light will be shed upon life, so that we grow stronger and stronger. Once the feeling has arisen that we ourselves were there and carried out the deeds ourselves we shall have quite a different attitude to events confronting us in the future; our whole life of feeling will be transformed. Whereas formerly we may have experienced fear and all the other related feelings when something happened to us, we now have a kind of inner memory. And now when something happens, our feeling tells us that it is for a purpose; and that it is a memory of an earlier life. Life becomes much more tranquil and intelligible, and that is what people need, not only those who are sustained by a longing for anthroposophy, but those too who remain outside it. It is no excuse to say: 'How can earlier incarnations matter if we cannot remember them!' The right attitude towards earthly existence will certainly awaken memory, only it is a memory belonging to the heart, to the life of feeling, that must be developed, not the kind of memory that is composed of thoughts and concepts.

I considered it important during this particular visit to bring home to you how much can be given practical application, and how anthroposophy can become actual experience in those who actively pursue it.

Now in addition to what accrued in earlier incarnations other factors are also of importance in one's karma. We have a life between death and a new birth too, and this is by no means uneventful, it is filled with events and experiences. And the consequences of these experiences in the spiritual world appear in our earthly life, but in a peculiar form which often makes us inclined to attribute such occurrences to chance. Nevertheless they can be traced to significant experiences in the spiritual world.

I want to speak to you therefore of something which may seem remote from the first part of the lecture. But you will see that it is important for every human being and that what appear to be chance happenings may be deeply indicative of mysterious connecting threads in life.

I am now going to speak of an historical fact that is not preserved in history books but is in the Akashic Records. To begin with I have to draw your attention to the fact that the souls of all of us here now have been incarnated many times in earthly bodies, among the most diverse conditions of life, in ancient India, Persia, Egypt and Greece; again and again we have experienced different environments and conditions of existence, and there is purpose and meaning in the fact that we pass through one incarnation after another. Our present life could not be as it is if we had not lived through these other conditions. An extraordinary experience fell to the lot of people living in the twelfth and thirteenth centuries of our era, for very exceptional conditions broke in upon humanity at that time—roughly speaking not quite seven hundred years ago. Conditions were such that human souls were completely shut off from the spiritual world; spiritual darkness prevailed, and it was impossible even for highly developed individuals to achieve direct contact with the spiritual world. In the thirteenth century even those who in earlier incarnations had been initiates were unable to look into the spiritual world. The gates of the spiritual world were closed for a certain period during that century, and although people who in former times had received initiation were able to call up memories of their earlier incarnations, in the thirteenth century they could not themselves gaze into the spiritual worlds. It was necessary for people to live through that condition of darkness, to find the gates to the spiritual world closed against them. Highly spiritually developed human beings were, of course, also in incarnation at that time, but they too were obliged to experience the condition of darkness. When about the middle of the thirteenth century the darkness lifted, strange happenings occurred at a certain place in Europe. The name of this place cannot now be given, but sometime it may be possible to communicate it in a members' lecture. Twelve men in Europe of great and out-standing wisdom, whose spiritual development had taken an unusual course, emerged from the condition of twilight that had obscured clairvoyant vision. Of these twelve wise men, seven, to begin with, have to be distinguished from the others. These seven men had retained the memory of their earlier initiations and this memory, together with the knowledge still surviving, was such that the seven men recapitulated in themselves conditions they had once lived through in the period following the Atlantean catastrophe—the ancient Indian epoch of culture. The teachings given by the seven Holy Rishis of India had come to life again in the souls of these seven wise men of Europe; seven rays of the ancient wisdom of the sacred Atlantean culture shone forth in the hearts of these seven men who through the workings of world karma had gathered at a certain place in Europe in the thirteenth century and had found one another again. To these seven came four others. In the soul of the first of these four shone forth the wisdom belonging to the ancient Indian culture—he was the eighth among the twelve. The wisdom of the ancient Persian culture lived in the soul of the ninth; the wisdom of the third period—that of Egyptian-Chaldean culture—lived in the soul of the tenth, and the wisdom of Graeco-Roman culture in the soul of the eleventh. The wisdom of the culture as it was in that particular age—contemporary wisdom—lived in the soul of the twelfth. In these twelve men who came together to perform a special mission, the twelve different streams in the spiritual development of mankind were represented. The fact that all possible religions and all possible philosophies belong to twelve basic types is in itself a mystery. Buddhism, Brahmanism, Vedanta philosophy, materialism, or whatever it may be—all of them can be traced to the twelve basic types; it is just a matter of being quite exact. And so all the different streams of man's spiritual life—the religions, the philosophies and world conceptions that are spread over the earth—were united in that council of the twelve.[66]

After the period of darkness had passed and spiritual work

became somewhat possible again, a thirteenth came in remarkable circumstances to the twelve. I am telling you now of one of those events which take place secretly in the evolution of mankind once and once only. They cannot occur a second time and are mentioned not as an indication that efforts should be made to repeat them but for quite other reasons. When the darkness had lifted and it was possible to develop clairvoyant vision again, the coming of the thirteenth was announced in a mysterious way to the twelve wise men. They knew that the time had come when a child who had passed through significant and remarkable incarnations was to be born. Above all they knew that one of his incarnations had been at the time of the Mystery of Golgotha. It was known, therefore, that one who had been a contemporary of the events in Palestine was returning. And the birth of the child in these unusual circumstances during the thirteenth century could not have been said to be that of a person of renown. In speaking of previous lives there is a deplorable and only too widespread tendency to refer back to important historical personages. I have come across all kinds of people who believe that they were incarnated as some historical personage or figure in the Gospels. Quite recently a lady informed me that she had been Mary Magdalene, and I could only reply that she was the twenty-fourth Mary Magdalene I had met in my life. In these matters the greatest care must be taken to prevent fantastic notions arising.

History tells us very little about the incarnations of the thirteenth. He was born many times with great and profound qualities of heart. It was known that this individuality was to be born again as a child and that he was destined for a very special mission. This knowledge was revealed to the twelve seers who took the child entirely into their charge and were able to arrange that from the very beginning he was shut off from the outside world. He was removed from his family and cared for by these twelve men. Guided by their clairvoyance they reared the child with every care in such a way that all the forces acquired from previous incarnations were able to unfold in him. A kind of intuitive perception of this occurrence has arisen in people who know something of the history of spiritual life. Goethe's poem *The Mysteries*[67] has been recited to us many times. Out of a deep, intuitive perception Goethe speaks in that poem of the council of the twelve, and he has been able to convey to us the mood of heart and feeling in which they lived. The thirteenth was not brother Mark but the child of whom I have been telling you, and who almost immediately after his birth was taken into the care of the twelve and brought up by them until the age of early manhood. The child developed in a strange and remarkable way. The twelve were not in any sense fanatics; they were full of inner composure, enlightenment and peace of heart. How does a fanatic behave? He wants to convert people as quickly as possible; while they, as a rule, do not want to be converted. Everybody is expected immediately to believe what the fanatic wants them to believe and he is angry when this does not happen. In our day, when someone sets out to expound a particular subject, people simply do not believe that his aim may be not to voice his own views but something quite different, that is, the thoughts and opinions of the one of whom he is writing. For many years I was held to be a follower of Nietzsche because I once wrote an absolutely objective book about him.[68] People simply cannot understand that the aim of a writer may be to give an objective exposition. They think that everyone must be fanatically promoting his own view of the subject of which he happens to be speaking.

The twelve in the thirteenth century were far from being fanatics, and they were very sparing with oral teaching. But simply by living in communion with the boy, twelve rays of light, as it were, went out from them into him and were resolved in his soul into one great harmony. It would not have been possible to give him any kind of academic examination; nevertheless there lived within him, transmuted into feeling and sensitive perception, all that the twelve representatives of the twelve different types of religion poured into his soul. His whole soul reflected the harmony of the twelve different forms of belief spread over the earth.

In this way the soul of the boy had to bear a great deal, and consequently it worked in a strange way upon the body. And it is precisely for this reason that the process of which I am telling you now may not be repeated: it could only be enacted at that particular time. Strange to say, as the harmony within the boy's soul increased, his body became more delicate—more and more delicate, until at a certain age it was transparent in every limb. The boy ate less and less until he finally took no nourishment at all. Then he lay for days in a condition of complete torpor: the soul had left the body, and returned into it again after a few days. The youth was now inwardly quite changed. The twelve different rays of human outlook were united in one *single* radiance, and he gave utterance to the greatest, most wonderful secrets; he did not repeat what the first, or the second, or the third had said, but gave forth in a new and wonderful synthesis all that they would have said had they spoken in unison; all the knowledge they possessed was gathered into one whole, and when he uttered it, it was as though this new wisdom had just come to birth in him. It was as though a higher spirit were speaking in him. Something entirely and essentially new was thus imparted to the twelve wise men. Wisdom in abundance was imparted to them; and to each, individually, greater illumination concerning what he had hitherto known.

I have been describing to you the first school of Christian Rosenkreutz, for the thirteenth is the individuality known to us by that name. In that incarnation he died after only a brief earthly existence; in the fourteenth century he was born again and lived then for more than a hundred years. All those things again appeared in him that had developed in him in the thirteenth century. Then his life had been brief, but in the fourteenth century it was very long. During the first half of this later incarnation he went on great journeys in search of the different centres of culture in Europe, Africa and Asia, in order to gather knowledge of what had come to life in him during the previous century; then he returned to Europe. A few of those who had brought him up in the thirteenth century were again in incarnation and were joined by others. This was the time of the inauguration of the rosicrucian stream of spiritual life. And Christian Rosenkreutz himself incarnated again and again.

To this very day he is at work—during the brief intervals, too, when he is not actually in incarnation; through his higher bodies he then works spiritually into human beings, without the need of physical contact. We must try to picture the mysterious way in which his influence operates.

And I want to begin here by giving an example. Those who participate consciously in the occult life of the spirit had a strange experience from the eighties on into the nineties of the nineteenth century; they became aware of certain influences emanating from a remarkable personality (I am only mentioning one case among many). There was, however, something not quite harmonious about those influences. Anyone who is sensitive to influences from contemporaries living a great distance away, would, at that time, have been aware of something raying out from a certain personality, which was not altogether harmonious. When the new century dawned, however, these influences became harmonious. What had happened? I will tell you the reason for this.

On 12 August 1900 Soloviev had died—a man far too little appreciated or understood. The influences of his ether body radiated far and wide, but although Soloviev was a great philosopher, in his case the development of the soul was in advance of that of the head, the intellect; he was a great and splendid thinker, but his conscious philosophy was of far less significance than that which he bore in his soul. Up to the time of his death the head was a hindering factor and so, as an occult influence, he had an unharmonious effect. But once he died and the etheric body, separated from the brain, rayed out in the etheric world, he was liberated from the restrictions caused by his thinking, and the rays of his influence shone out with wonderful brilliance and power.

People may ask: How can such knowledge really concern us? This very question is an illusion, for the human being is through and through a product of the spiritual processes around him; and when certain occultists become aware of the reality of these processes, it is because they actually see them. But spiritual processes operate too in those others who do not see. Everything in the spiritual world is interconnected. Whatever influence may radiate from a highly developed Frenchman or Russian is felt not only on their own native soil, but their thought and influence has an effect over the whole earth. Everything that happens in the spiritual world has an influence on us, and only when we realize that the soul lives in the spiritual world just as the lung within the air, shall we have the right attitude.

The forces in the etheric bodies of highly developed individualities stream out and have a potent effect upon other human beings. So too, the etheric body of Christian Rosenkreutz works far and wide in the world. And reference must be made here to a fact that is of the greatest significance to many people; it is something that transpires in the spiritual world between death and a new birth and is not to be ascribed to chance.

Christian Rosenkreutz has always made use of the short

intervals of time between his incarnations to call into his particular stream of spiritual life those souls whom he knows to be ripe; between his deaths and births he has concerned himself as it were with choosing those who are ready to enter his stream. But human beings themselves, by learning to be attentive, must be able to recognize by what means Christian Rosenkreutz gives them a sign showing them that they may count themselves among his chosen. This sign has been given in the lives of very many human beings of the present time, but they pay no heed to it. Yet among the apparently chance happenings in a person's life, there is for many people one in particular that is to be regarded as an indication that between death and a new birth Christian Rosenkreutz has found him mature and ready; the sign is given by Christian Rosenkreutz on the physical plane, however. This event may be called the mark of Christian Rosenkreutz. Let us suppose someone is lying in bed—in other places I have mentioned different kinds of occurrence, but all of them have occurred—for some unaccountable reason he suddenly wakes up and, as though guided by instinct, looks at a wall that is usually quite dark. The room is dimly lit, the wall is dark, when suddenly he sees written on the wall: 'Get up at once!' It all seems very strange, but he gets up and leaves the house, and hardly has he done so when the ceiling over his bed collapses; although nobody else would have been in danger of getting hurt, he himself would inevitably have been killed. The most thorough investigation proves that nobody on the physical plane warned him to get up. If he had remained lying there he would certainly have been killed.

Such an experience may be thought to be an hallucination or something of the kind; but deeper investigation will reveal that these particular experiences—and they come to hundreds of people—are not accidental. A beckoning call has come from Christian Rosenkreutz. The karma of the one called in this way always indicates that Christian Rosen-kreutz bestows the life he may claim. I say explicitly: such occurrences occur in the lives of many people at the present time, and it is only a question of being awake to them. The occurrence does not always take such a dramatic form as the example quoted, but numbers of human beings nowadays have had such experiences. Now when I say something more than once during a lecture, I do so quite deliberately, because I find that strange conclusions are apt to be drawn from things that are half or totally forgotten. I am saying this because nobody need be discouraged who has had no such experience; this might not be the case, for if he searches he will certainly find something of the kind in his life. Naturally I can only single out a typical example. Here then we have in our life a fact of which we may say that its cause does not lie in the period of actual incarnation; we may have met Christian Rosenkreutz in the spiritual world. I have laid particular stress on this outstanding event of the call. Other events, too, could be mentioned, events connected directly with the spiritual world that occur during the life between death and a new birth; but in our spiritual context this particular event should be of special significance for us as it is so intimately connected with our spiritual movement.

Such an event surely indicates that we must develop quite a different attitude if we want to have a clear vision of what actually plays into life. Most human beings rush hectically through life and are not thoughtful and attentive; many people say that one should not brood but engage in a life of action. But how much better it would be if precipitate deeds were left undone and people were to reflect a little—their deeds, then, would be far more mature! If only the beckoning call were heeded with composure and attentiveness. Often it only seems as if we are dreaming or brooding, but it is precisely through quiet composure that strength comes to us—

and then we shall follow when karma calls, and understand its call. These are the things I wanted to call your attention to today, for they do indeed make life more intelligible.

I have told you of the strange event in the thirteenth century, purely in the form of historical narrative, in order to indicate those things which people must heed if they are to find their proper place in life and understand the beckoning call of Christian Rosenkreutz. To make this possible, the twelve needed to prepare and the thirteenth had to come. And the event in the thirteenth century was necessary in order that in our own time and hereafter such a beckoning or other sign may be understood and followed. Christian Rosenkreutz has created this sign in order to rouse people's attention to the needs of the times, to indicate to them that they belong to him and may dedicate their lives to him in the service of humanity's progress.

The Death of a God and Its Fruits in Humanity

Düsseldorf, 5 May 1912

I shall speak today of certain matters in a way that could not be used in public lectures but is possible when I am speaking to those who have been studying spiritual science for some considerable time.

The importance of what we shall first speak about will be evident to all serious students of spiritual science. Reference has frequently been made to this subject but one cannot speak too often of spiritual-scientific insights, for they must become actual forces, actual impulses, in people of the present and immediate future. I shall lay emphasis today upon one aspect of the significance of spiritual science for humanity in our time: the urgent need to impart *soul* to what we may call our 'world-body'.

A comparatively short time ago in the evolution of humanity it would not have been possible to speak, as we can speak today, of a 'world-body'. Looking back only a little into the historical development of mankind, we shall find that the idea of a world-body inhabited by the whole of humanity had not yet come to people's consciousness. We find self-contained civilizations, enclosed within strict boundaries. Guided each by their own folk-spirits, the Old Indian civilization, the Old Persian civilization, and so on, embraced peoples living a self-contained existence, separated from one another by mountains, seas or rivers.

Needless to say, such civilizations still exist. We speak, and rightly so, of Italian, Russian, French, Spanish, German culture; but when we look over the earth today, we also perceive unity extending over the globe—something by which peoples separated by vast distances are formed as it were into a single whole. We need think only of industry, of railways, of telegraphs, of recent inventions. Railways are built, telegraph systems installed, cheques made out and cashed in the same way all over the globe, and the same will hold good for discoveries and inventions yet to be made.

What is the peculiarity of this element that extends over the globe and is the same in Tokyo, Rome, Berlin, London, and everywhere else? It is all a means of providing humanity with food and clothing, as well as with ever-increasing luxury goods. During the last few centuries a material civilization has spread over the earth, without distinction between nation and nation, race and race. Greek culture flourished in a tiny region of the earth and little was known of it outside that region. But nowadays news flashes around the whole globe in a few hours—and nobody would doubt the justification of calling this material culture a global culture! Moreover it will become increasingly material and our earth-body more and more deeply entangled in it.

But those who realize the need for spiritual science will increasingly come to understand that no body can exist without a soul. Just as material culture encompasses the whole body of the earth, so must knowledge of the spirit be the soul that extends over the whole earth, without distinction of nation, colour, race or people. And just as identical methods are employed wherever railways and telegraph systems are constructed, so mutual understanding about questions concerning the human soul must soon come to unify the whole earth. The longings and questionings that will arise increasingly in people's souls demand answers. Hence the need for a movement dedicated to the cultivation of spiritual knowledge. Something comparable with cultural relations between different nations will then take effect on a wide scale, weaving threads between soul and soul over the whole earth. And what will weave from soul to soul will be an intimate, mutual understanding of what is sacred to individual souls everywhere: of how they are related to the spiritual world.

In a future not far distant, intimate understanding will take the place of what led in past times to bitterest conflict and disharmony as long as humanity was divided into regional civilizations which knew nothing of each other. But what will unfold on a universal scale over the globe as a spiritual movement embracing all earthly humanity, must unfold also between soul and soul. What a distance still separates the Buddhists and the Christians, how little do they understand of each other and how insistently do they turn away from each other on the circumscribed ground of their particular creeds! But the time will come when both Buddhists and Christians increasingly find that their own religion leads them towards a common spiritual science. And then complete understanding will reign between them.

That humanity is coming a little nearer to this mutual and intimate understanding can be discerned today in the fact that the science of comparative religion is also finding its place in the domain of scholarship. The value of this science of comparative religion should not be underrated, for it has splendid achievements to its credit. But what is really brought to light when the different teachings of the religions are set forth? Although it is not acknowledged, the basis of this science of comparative religion amounts to no more than expressing the most elementary beliefs, long since outgrown by those who have grasped the essence of each religion. The science of comparative religion confines itself to these elementary beliefs.

The aim of spiritual science, in contrast, is to seek something that lies beyond the reach of the scientific investigators—the essential truths contained in different religions. Spiritual science takes as its basic premise that mankind originated from a common godhead and that a primeval wisdom belonging to mankind as a whole and springing from one divine source has only for a time been separated and divided among the different peoples and groups of human beings on the earth, like separate rays of light. The aim and ideal of spiritual science is to rediscover this primeval truth, this primeval wisdom, uncoloured by this or that particular creed, and to give it again to humanity. Spiritual science is able to penetrate to the essence of the various religions because its attention is focused, not upon external rites and ceremonies, but upon the kernel of primeval wisdom contained in each one of them. It regards the religions as so many channels for the rays of what once streamed without differentiation over the whole of mankind.

When a professed Christian, knowing nothing beyond the external tenets of belief that have been instilled into the hearts of people through the centuries, says to a Buddhist: 'If you would reach the truth you must believe what I believe' ... and the Buddhist rejoins by declaring what *he* holds sacred, then no understanding is possible between them. But spiritual science approaches these questions in an entirely different way.

Those who can penetrate to the essence of both Buddhism and Christianity through methods leading to the development of the new clairvoyance come to know of sublime beings who have arisen within humanity and are called bodhisattvas. Herein lies the central nerve of Buddhism. But the Christian, too, hears of a bodhisattva who arises and works within humanity. He hears that one of these bodhisattvas—born 600 years before our era as Siddartha, the son of King Suddhodana—attained buddha-consciousness in the twenty-ninth year of his life. A Christian who is an anthroposophist also knows that a being who has risen from the level of bodhisattva to become Buddha need not appear again on earth in a body of flesh.

True, such teachings are also communicated to us by the scientific investigators of religions, but they can make nothing of a being such as a bodhisattva or a Buddha; the nature of such a being is beyond their comprehension; neither can they realize how such a being continues to guide humanity from the spiritual worlds without living in a body of flesh.

But as anthroposophical Christians, our attitude to the bodhisattva can be as full of reverence as that of a Buddhist. In spiritual science we say exactly the same about Buddha as a Buddhist says. The Christian who is an anthroposophist says to the Buddhist: 'I understand and believe what you understand and believe.' No one who has come to spiritual science through Christianity would ever dream, as a Christian, of saying that the Buddha returns in the flesh. He knows that this would wound the deepest, most intimate, feelings of the Buddhist and that such a statement would be utterly at variance with the true character of those beings who have risen from the rank of bodhisattva to that of Buddha. Christianity itself has brought him knowledge and understanding of these beings.

And what will be the attitude of the Buddhist who has become an anthroposophist? He will understand the particular basis of Christianity. He will realize that, as in the case of the other religions, Christianity has a founder—Jesus of Nazareth—but that *another Being* united with him. A great deal could be said about all that has been associated with the personality of Jesus of Nazareth through the centuries. But the Christian's view of the personality of Jesus of Nazareth differs from the Buddhist's view of the founder of his religion. In the East it would be said: 'One who is a great founder of religion has achieved the complete harmonization of all passions and desires, of all human, personal attributes.' Is such complete harmonization manifest in Jesus of Nazareth? We read that he was seized with anger, that he overthrew the tables of the money-changers, drove them out of the temple, that he uttered words of impassioned wrath. This is evidence to us that he does not possess the same qualities as are expected of a founder of religion in the East.

We could point to many other aspects of this question, but that is not what concerns us at the moment. The really significant fact is that Christianity differs from all other religions inasmuch as they all point to a founder who was a great *teacher*. But to believe that the same is true of Christianity would denote a fundamental misunderstanding. The essence of Christianity is not that it looks back to Jesus of Nazareth as a great teacher. Christianity does not originate in the realm of personality, but in a *deed*, in the event of the *Mystery of Golgotha*.

How could this be? It was because for three years there dwelt in Jesus of Nazareth a Being, whom—if we are to give Him a name—we call Christ. But a name cannot encompass the divine spirit we recognize in Christ. No human name, no human word, can express what is divine. In Christ we have to do with a divine impulse spreading through the world: the Christ impulse which at the baptism in the Jordan entered into Jesus of Nazareth. The very essence of Christianity lies in the Christ impulse which came to the earth through a physical personality, the physical personality of Jesus of Nazareth into whose mortal frame it entered. The Christ took this mortal frame upon Himself because the course of world-evolution is, first, a descent, and then again an ascent. At the deepest point of descent the Mystery of Golgotha takes place, because from it alone could spring the power to lead humanity upwards.

After the Atlantean catastrophe came the ancient Indian

epoch of civilization. The spirituality of that epoch will not again be reached until the end of the seventh epoch. The ancient Indian epoch was followed by that of ancient Persia, that again by the Egypto-Chaldean epoch. When we survey evolution, even in its external aspect, the decline of spirituality is evident. Then we come to Graeco-Roman civilization with its firm footing in the earthly realm. The works of art created by the Greeks are the most wonderful expression of the marriage of spirit with form. And in Roman culture, in Roman civic life, man becomes master on the physical plane. But the spirituality in Greek culture is characterized by the saying: 'Better to be a beggar in the upper world than a king in the realm of the shades.' Dread of the world lying behind the physical plane, dread of the world into which man will pass after death, is expressed in this saying. Spirituality has here descended to the deepest point.

From then onwards, mankind needed an impulse for a return to the spiritual worlds, which was given in the fourth post-Atlantean epoch through an event that far transcended the physical plane.

The Mystery of Golgotha was enacted in a remote corner of the earth, for the sake of no particular race or denomination. It took place in seclusion, in concealment. Neither outer civilization nor the Romans, who governed the little territory of Palestine where it occurred, knew anything of the event. The Romans were no followers of Christ—the Jews still less!

Who were present when the Mystery of Golgotha took place? Whom did the one who received the Christ into himself in his thirtieth year gather around him? Had pupils gathered around this Being as they had gathered around Confucius, Lao-tzu or Buddha? If we look closely we see that this is not so. Were those already His apostles who until the Event of Golgotha had been His disciples? No! They had scattered, they had gone away when the One whom they had followed entered upon the path of His passion. Only when, having passed through death, He gave them the certain knowledge of the power that had conquered death—only then did they become true apostles and carried His impulse to the peoples of the earth. Before then they had not even understood Him. Even Paul, the one who after the Mystery of Golgotha achieved most for the spread of Christianity, understood Him only after He had appeared to him in the spirit!

So we see that, unlike the other religions, Christianity was not, in essence, founded by a great teacher whose pupils then promulgate his teachings. The essential basic truth of Christianity is that a *divine impulse* came down to the earth, passed through death and became the source of the impulse which leads humanity upwards. When the individual personal element had passed through death, had departed from the earth—then and only then did the power which came upon the earth through Christ begin to work. It is not a merely personal *teaching* that works on, but the actual event that Christ was within Jesus and passed through the Mystery of Golgotha, and that from the Mystery of Golgotha a power streamed forth through the whole subsequent evolution of mankind.

That is the difference between what Christianity sees as the starting-point of its development and what the other religions see as theirs. When, therefore, we turn our attention to the beginning of Christianity, it is a matter of realizing what actually came to pass through the Mystery of Golgotha. Paul says, in effect: 'The descending line of evolution was caused through Adam, even before the Fall, before he was truly human, before he was a personality in the real sense. The impulse for the ascent was given by Christ.'

To feel this as a reality we must go deeply into the occult

truths available to mankind. To grasp the full significance of this fact, our understanding must be quickened by the deepest, most intimate, occult truths. Then we will realize why the loftiest thoughts and deepest truths of Christianity could not immediately be understood, even by its own adherents. To grasp the full meaning of this divine death and the impulse proceeding from it, to realize that such an event cannot be repeated, that it occurred at the deepest point of the evolutionary process and radiates the power which enables mankind henceforward to tread the path of ascent—could only be understood by a few. And so, in the centuries that followed, people clung to Jesus of Nazareth—for understanding of the Christ was as yet beyond their reach. Moreover it was through Jesus that the Christ impulse also made its way into works of art. People yearned for Jesus, not for Christ.

We ourselves are still living at the dawn of true Christianity: Christianity is only beginning to come into its own. And when people plead today: 'Do not take from us the individual, personal Jesus who comforts and uplifts our hearts, on whom we lean; do not give us, instead of him, an impersonal event' ... they must learn to realize that this is nothing but an expression of egotism. Not until they transcend this personal egotism and realize that they have no right to call themselves Christians until they recognize as the source of their Christianity the event that was fulfilled in majestic isolation on Golgotha, will they be able to draw near to Christ. But this realization belongs to a future time.

There may be some who say: 'Surely the Crucifixion should have been avoided!' Or who perhaps think that the Resurrection (of course we are not speaking of the resurrection of a *physical* body) might have been achieved without the Crucifixion. But this is simply a human opinion—no more than that. These people do not know the difference between an utter impossibility and a simple misunderstanding. For what came into the evolution of humanity through the Mystery of Golgotha could proceed *only* from the impulse of a God who had endured all the sufferings and agonies of mankind, all the sorrows, the mockery and scorn, the contempt and the shame that were the lot of Christ. And these sufferings were infinitely harder for a God than for an ordinary human being.

That the Mystery of Golgotha actually took place cannot be authenticated in the same way as other historical events. There is no authentic, documentary evidence even of the Crucifixion. But there is good reason why no proof exists, for this is an event which lies outside the sphere of the general evolution of mankind. The Mystery of Golgotha—and this is its very essence—is an event transcending the evolution of humanity.

The Mystery of Golgotha was concerned with the descending path which humanity has taken; and with what must lead it upwards again—with the luciferic influence upon mankind! Lucifer, together with everything belonging to him, is certainly not a human being. Lucifer and his hosts are *superhuman* beings. Lucifer did not desire to set mankind upon a downward path; his purpose was to rebel against the upper gods. He wanted to vanquish his opponents, not drag human beings down. Lucifer and all the lower gods of hindrance waged war against the progressive, upper gods; and from the very beginning of earthly evolution, man was dragged into this warfare. It was an issue that the gods in the higher worlds had to settle among themselves, but as a result of the conflict, human beings were drawn more deeply into the material world than they should have been. And now the gods had to create the balance; humanity had to be lifted upwards again, the deed of Lucifer made of no avail. This could not be achieved through a human being but only through a divine deed. This deed of a God must be understood in all its truth and reality.

If we ponder deeply about earthly existence, we find that its greatest riddle is birth and death. The fact that beings can die is the fundamental problem confronting humanity. Death is something that occurs only on the earth. In the higher worlds there is transformation, metamorphosis—no death. Death is the consequence of what came into human beings through Lucifer; and if the gods had done nothing the whole of mankind would have been more and more entangled in the forces which lead to death. And so a sacrifice had to be made by the gods: it was necessary that One from among them should descend and suffer the death that can be undergone only by the children of the earth. This was a deed which balanced out the deed of Lucifer. And from this death of a God streams the power which also radiates into human souls and can raise them again out of the darkness in which Lucifer's deed has ensnared them. *A God had to die on the physical plane.*

This is not a direct concern of human beings. They were mere spectators of an affair of the gods. No wonder that physical means are incapable of portraying this event, since it is an affair of the higher worlds, and falls outside the sphere of the physical world.

But the fruits of this deed which had to be wrought on the earth became the heritage of humanity, and Christian initiation gives human beings the power to understand it. Just as mankind could come forth only once from the lap of the gods, so could the overcoming of what was originally instilled into the human soul be achieved only once.

If the Christian who has become an anthroposophist were to speak of the nature of Christ to a Buddhist who has become an anthroposophist, the Buddhist would say: 'I should misunderstand you were I to believe that the Being whom you call Christ is subject to reincarnation. He is not subject to reincarnation—any more than you would say that the Buddha can return to earthly existence!'

Yet there is one fundamental difference. The Buddhist points to the great *teacher* who was the originator of his religion; but the true Christian points to a *deed* of the spiritual worlds, enacted in seclusion on the earth; he points to something entirely non-personal, having nothing to do with any specific creed or denomination. No single human being, to begin with, recognized this deed; it had nothing to do with any particular locality on the earth. *In majestic seclusion, divine power poured from this deed into the whole subsequent evolution of mankind.*

The task of a spiritual-scientific conception of the world is to seek for the truths contained in different religions. To seek for the kernel of truth in them all is the augury of *peace*. When an adherent of some creed truly understands his religion in the light of spiritual science, he will never force its particular ray of truth upon adherents of another religion. As little as the anthroposophical Christian will speak of the return of the Buddha—for then he would not have understood him—as little will the anthroposophical Buddhist speak of the return of Christ—for that, too, would be a misunderstanding. Provided personal bias is laid aside, the truth concerning Buddha and the truth concerning Christ never makes for discord and sectarianism, but for harmony and peace. This is a natural consequence of truth, which is the augury and source of peace in the world. At the highest level of truth, all nations and all religions on the earth can belong to Buddha the great *teacher*; and at the same highest level of truth, all nations and all religions can belong to Christ, the *divine power*. Mutual understanding augurs peace in the world. This peace is the soul of the new world-order. Anthroposophy must lead the way towards this soul, which shall reign throughout the world as the spiritual science common to all people in all cultures.

From the thirteenth and fourteenth centuries onwards,

such knowledge was cultivated in the rosicrucian schools. It was known there that such knowledge brings peace to the human soul. And in these rosicrucian schools it was known, too, that many a one who on earth cannot experience this peace, will find, after death, the fulfilment of his most treasured ideals—when he looks down to the earth and beholds peace spreading among the peoples and nations to the extent to which they open themselves to receive such knowledge.

As I have spoken here today, so did the rosicrucians speak in their small, enclosed circles. Today these things can be communicated to larger gatherings. Those to whom it has been entrusted to bear living witness through spiritual science to what streams into humanity from the Mystery of Golgotha know that every year at Eastertide, Jesus, who bore the Christ within him, seeks out the places where the Mystery of Golgotha was fulfilled. Whether actually in incarnation or not, every year he visits these places, and there his pupils who have made themselves ready can be united with him.

A poet—Anastasius Grün—felt the reality of this. In the poem 'Five Easters' he describes five such meetings of the Master with his pupils. The first, after the destruction of Jerusalem; the second, after the capture of Jerusalem by the Crusaders; the third—Ahasver, the Wandering Jew, lingering on Golgotha; the fourth—a praying monk, yearning and pleading for deliverance from his conqueror. For while sects of different kinds scattered over the earth are at strife among themselves, he through whom the greatest of all tidings of peace was brought to the earth looks again at the places that were the scene of his earthly deeds.

Four pictures are given in this poem of past visits of Jesus to the scene of his work on Golgotha. Then Anastasius Grün pictures another return to Golgotha, in the far future. He gives us a glimpse of a time when the power of peace will have prevailed on the earth, a peace based not on denomi-national Christianity, but on Christianity as it is understood in rosicrucianism. He sees children who, while they are at play, dig up an object of iron and do not know what it is. Only those who still possess some remote information about the wars waged between human beings in the distant past know that this object is a sword. In that age of peace the purpose of a sword is no longer known—it has been replaced by the ploughshare. Then a farmer digging in the earth finds an object made of stone ... Again it is not recognized. 'For a time this was banished from the earth,' say those who still have some knowledge, 'for people no longer understood it! Once upon a time they used it as a symbol of strife. It is a cross of stone—but now, when the impulse given by Christ Jesus for all future time gathers human beings together, *now* it has become something different!'

How does this poet, writing in the year 1835, describe this symbol of the true mission of the Christ Impulse? He describes it as follows:

Though known to none, yet with its ancient blessing,
Eternal in their breast it stands upright;
There blooms its seed abroad on every pathway,
A Cross it was—this stranger to their sight.

The Cross of Stone now stands within a garden,
A strange and sacred relic from days of old;
Flowers of every kind and twining roses
Climb upwards round it and the Cross enfold.

So stands the Cross, glorious with solemn meaning,
On Golgotha, amidst resplendent sheen.
Long since 'tis hidden by its sheath of roses;
No more, for roses, can the Cross be seen.*

---

* The whole poem consists of 108 verses, in five parts.

Address Given at the Opening of the Christian Rosenkreutz Group

Hamburg, 17 June 1912

We have gathered here to ask the blessing of those spiritual powers who oversee our spiritual scientific movement, to ask blessing for a working group which has, to its own deepest satisfaction, created a place of work that expresses our impulses of will through the most manifold symbols: that is, our will to humble ourselves before spiritual powers, to devote ourselves to them and serve them in the right way. Much spirit and soul work has been invested in furnishing and decorating these rooms in the right way. Surrounded by these symbols, members will always gain the right impetus for their work. But those who have hurried here to take part in this opening ceremony will take away with them a lasting memory; as will the ones too who send powerful impulses here, and for this purpose are united in spirit with those who have sought out this workplace for themselves.

That we stand within such a stream as our spiritual scientific movement must be seen as grace bestowed by spiritual powers: for this movement is a necessity of the future, and it has been granted to us to be the first to stand within this current that must flow into humanity's future evolution if it is not to grow arid and wither away. As an occultist one can see that such fertilization is absolutely necessary. Let us look on it as a grace and blessing that we may feel duty bound to offer a helping hand in this fertilizing process.

Waves of materialism arrived in the period between the sixteenth and nineteenth centuries—this too was a necessity, even though it could only bring us blessings needed in the physical world. Only few of the leading minds of recent times could understand that an ascent must once more spring from the necessary but downward pull of materialism's shackles.

The theosophical movement is a downpouring of spiritual forces and truths from higher worlds. Human beings are once more to know things that have been obscured for millennia.

If we wish to examine the nature of this movement in whose midst we stand, we can seek out its most significant characteristic. It is as if the finest and truest human spirit had worked in it, for three aspects—sensed in the right way—immediately give the idea of something that is completely in harmony with the needs of our time.[69] These three aspects say nothing less than that a spiritual movement is to be born in which everyone can take part. A stream of the most general human relevance is characterized by saying that this Society forms the core of developing brotherliness between all. This means no less than that there is no one on earth who could not become a member of this Society. But all over the globe the most diverse confessions and philosophies are spread. They cannot all be mistaken. Anyone who alleges this would be flying in the face of the wise powers who guide our world. What we must do, instead, is seek the objective core of all world views, and thus come to mutual understanding. The phrase 'No religion stands higher than the truth' is a motto that springs from such principles. The striving for truth can bring all people together, for it will nurture mutual understanding—and then the third principle is basically already included. But one could say perhaps that materialists are excluded from the Society. Yet this is only the case if their materialistic conviction is more pronounced than their search for the forces underlying all phenomena. It is not we who exclude materialists, for no earnest seeker has ever remained stuck in a materialistic point of view. Such a person only excludes himself, since he does not wish to seek the truth. Our movement needs no other principles: if everything is properly grasped the theosophical movement cannot be misused or corrupted, for it will embrace the great ideal of harmony and peace of soul. Let us be clear how peace and harmony can be spread across the globe.

The non-theosophist Christian will have little under-standing for what lifts the Buddhist to higher worlds. But the Christian who becomes a theosophist must make efforts to understand the Buddhist: he experiences this as a duty founded on the tenets of the theosophical movement which he acknowledges. The Christian will realize the significance of the life of Gautama Buddha on earth if he knows that a human being has to pass through countless incarnations before he can become Buddha. The Buddhist knows that after attaining Buddha-hood the Buddha no longer needs to return to the earth. In Christiania (Oslo) I made reference to the mission of Gautama Buddha, showing how this soul has a special task, to be fulfilled on Mars.[70] On earth the Buddha passed through a preparatory stage, in order to play a role amongst Mars people similar to that of Christ on earth. Not through a kind of Mystery of Golgotha, not by passing through death—for Mars people live in different conditions from people on earth. Thus the occultist is clear that the belief of Buddhists—that Gautama Buddha does not need to return to earth in a physical body—is fully valid. So we do not battle against their conviction, against what lies so close to their hearts, but go to meet them with the deepest interest.

If the Buddhist becomes a theosophist, he learns to see what is most holy to the Christian. He perceives that the fact of a certain individual passing through physical death embodies a world Mystery; that Christ descended from higher worlds to a single, unique incarnation, following which he would never again enter a physical body. He begins to understand that this Mystery re-establishes equilibrium in the battle between Christ and Lucifer. When the Buddhist learns this through theosophy, he tells himself: I understand the deepest sense of what the Christian means, I understand Christ's unique incarnation and see that He was never previously on earth before he found a body through Jesus of Nazareth.

If we give ourselves up to the principles I have stressed, we especially learn something that is wholly opposite to a certain fear common among Christians. People are anxious that their beliefs will shine less brightly if the merits of other faiths are illumined. But the Christian faith actually gains greater radiance when one brings esoteric light to bear on different religious faiths. Anyone who is anxious that his faith could be diminished by being placed alongside Buddhist belief should remember that there are still various unsolved questions for the Christian theologian: for instance, that an important issue is whether those who lived before the Mystery of Golgotha can still share in redemption through Christ. But if the Christian enlarges his perspective with what the Buddhist knows, he sees that the same souls lived in physical embodiment before the appearance of Christ as continue to return to earth after the Mystery of Golgotha. Now one might ask: What about the Buddha soul that incarnated for the last time six hundred years before Christ, and did not return?

Here too, occult research provides us with a satisfying answer. It shows us that the Buddha was sent ahead; that, belonging to a higher hierarchy, he was sent down with the Venus beings—so that one can rightly speak of the Buddha's mission to prepare for Christ. Every religion offers us a perspective for understanding every other, as long as none wishes to tyrannize over the other in an egotistic way. An orthodox Buddhist might perhaps wish to elevate his Buddha above all other beings—although no real Buddhist would do this. If someone wanted to practise a fanatical, limited Buddhism, he could teach that there can be no other being apart from Buddha who does not need to return to earth, and that the latter must therefore be the highest of all. This would set Buddhism vastly ahead of Christianity, giving the latter a subordinate position, so that one religion was opposed by the other. This however would be an un-theosophical deed, for theosophy or the science of the spirit is there to spread peace throughout the world, and, by understanding and studying the same truths to lead to knowledge of the importance of each one. For that reason let us bear in mind that we ought not to profess our principles in word alone, and then turn them into their opposite.

We must be filled with the conviction that the founding of a work and study group is not simply something to be pleased about, but that it goes hand in hand with a higher responsibility—especially when it invokes the name of the noble martyr whose manner of working asked, and will continue to ask, more endurance of him than of any other human being. I say 'human being', for what Christ suffered was suffered by a God. This is connected with the great dangers which truth will have to undergo in the future. If we christen this group with the name of 'Christian Rosenkreutz', we must be aware that it is hard to stay true to this particular loyalty. We take a vow of faithfulness for which we may perhaps not be strong enough. Nevertheless, no one should be forbidden from nurturing this loyalty in his soul, a loyalty that necessitates us taking a particular future direction. If we feel so strongly drawn to something that is already there that we make it into our own sphere of activity, we are appealing to previously strengthened powers of idealism. But when we found something new, the friend of all separatism, all supersensible self-obsession, looks over our shoulder: Lucifer gains hope at each new founding, but not when we link back to something old. Therefore Lord help us if we are not aware that 'Little folk never sense the devil, even when he's got them by the scruff'. But if we are of good will we can always loosen his grip.

To link our founding with the name borne by such a great martyr is a great yet dangerous moment. The founders themselves must vow not to undertake this lightly, but to hold fast in all faithfulness and with all strength to what they have vowed. Each founding of an anthroposophical working group involves a heavy burden of responsibility. If one considers how little the impulse given by Christian Rosenkreutz is still understood, one will be able to sense the enormous difficulties that lie in wait for those who think to follow in his steps.

No one contradicts oriental people when they speak in their own fashion of the Maitreya Buddha. But when the principle of Christianity—basically embodied in the three principles of the Theosophical Society—is at length found all over the globe, strong powers will arise to heap error upon error. And to Christian Rosenkreutz will belong those who can keep faith with him.

Already in our time we see how difficult it is to understand Christianity, and how little good will there is to grasp the core of Christianity. The principles referred to today, that hold sway like guiding stars within the spiritual scientific movement, will contribute both to a deepening and shaking up of things, to an impending avalanche. It is necessary to awaken a sense of responsibility, and it should be our particular task here to imbue ourselves strongly with this sense. Even in the most intimate circles various trials and tests will come to meet you!

By doing no more than mentioning the name Christian Rosenkreutz, we subscribe to the principle that no religion should be higher than our striving for truth. Christian

Rosenkreutz never demands any kind of personality cult, and takes pains to ensure that teachings are accessible to human reason and understanding. His teaching never requires blind faith in the masters. If we first use our own powers, the possibility will arise of applying truth to recognize the masters of wisdom and harmony of feelings. No one is asked simply to believe, for then belief in the masters would stand higher than the truth itself. If unconditional belief in a master should ever be demanded, the principles of the Theosophical Society would have been violated.

By applying certain methods one can recognize whether something is true or not. For instance, in the book *How to Know Higher Worlds*, it would have been an easy thing to write: 'These teachings were given through higher inspiration, etc., they come from the masters and so forth ...' But the principle of the theosophical movement is violated if the writer does not bear responsibility for what is written. If it is ever claimed that an author is not responsible for the book that has been written, you can be sure that the book does not contain truth but luciferic-ahrimanic deception. Nowadays the masters do not allow a writer to disclaim responsibility; therefore one is obliged to measure things against the yardstick of reason, and not simply take things on authority. Of course it is far easier to depend entirely on a personality cult, for reason and logic are harder taskmasters. Only those who examine and test what is given from the world of spirit can keep faith with Christian Rosenkreutz. So keep in mind that a working group is being set up here that wishes to keep faith—above and beyond whoever happens to be the teacher at any one time—with the principle of translating what flows down through Christ from worlds of spirit into what is humanly comprehensible.

If you vow to one another to think and strive in this way, then I may now call down the blessing of the spiritual beings in whom we do not need to believe, but in whose stream we know that we stand. May the good spirits—of whose existence I am as convinced as of the existence of all who sit here in physical embodiment—hold sway here and bless this work. Let this workplace be thus inaugurated. That which brings about our work in good spirit will be able to prevent the darkness that otherwise inescapably pours in over Christianity. May the masters of wisdom and harmony of feelings hold sway.

The Mission of Christian Rosenkreutz.
The Mission of Gautama Buddha on Mars

Neuchâtel, 18 December 1912

Friends have expressed the wish that I should speak today on the subject of last year's lecture,[71] when I described the initiation of Christian Rosenkreutz that took place in very special circumstances in the thirteenth century, and how, since then, this individuality has worked unceasingly throughout the centuries. Today we shall hear more about the character and the person of Christian Rosenkreutz as we study the great task of nurturing humanity's future which devolved upon him at the dawn of the intellectual age.

Anyone who, like Christian Rosenkreutz, appears in the world as a leading occultist, has to reckon with the conditions peculiar to his epoch. The intrinsic nature of modern culture, developed for the first time when the new natural science arrived on the scene with Copernicus,[72] Giordano Bruno,[73] Galileo[74] and others. Nowadays people are taught about Copernicus in their early schooldays, and the impressions thus received remain with them their whole life long. In earlier times the soul experienced something different. Try to picture to yourselves what a contrast there is between a person of the modern age and one who lived centuries ago. Before the days of Copernicus everyone believed that the earth remained at rest in cosmic space with the sun and the stars revolving around it. The very ground slipped from under man's feet when Copernicus proposed the doctrine that the earth moves with tremendous speed through the universe. We should not underestimate the effects of such a revolution in thinking, accompanied as it was by a corresponding change in people's life of feeling. All thoughts and ideas were suddenly altered from what they had been before the days of Copernicus. And now let us ask: What has occultism to say about this revolution in thinking?

Anyone who brings an esoteric perspective to bear on the kind of world conception derived from Copernican tenets will have to admit that although these ideas can lead to great achievements in the realm of natural science and in outer life, they are incapable of promoting any understanding of the spiritual foundations of the world and the things of the world; there has never been a worse instrument for understanding the spiritual foundations of the world than the ideas of Copernicus—never in the whole of human evolution. The reason for this is that all these Copernican concepts are inspired by Lucifer. Copernicanism is one of the last attacks, one of the last great attacks made by Lucifer upon the evolution of man. In earlier, pre-Copernican thought, the external world was indeed maya, but much traditional wisdom, much truth concerning the world and the things of the world still survived. Since Copernicus, however, man has maya around him not only in his material perceptions but in his very concepts and ideas. People take it for granted nowadays that the sun is firmly fixed in the centre and the planets revolve around it in ellipses. In the near future, however, it will be realized that the view of the world of the stars held by Copernicus is much less correct than the earlier Ptolemaic view.[75] The view of the world held by the school of Copernicus and Kepler is very convenient, but as an explanation of the macrocosm it is not the truth.

And so Christian Rosenkreutz, confronted by a world conception which is itself a maya, an illusion, had to come to grips with it. Christian Rosenkreutz had to save occultism in an age when all the concepts of science were themselves maya. In the middle of the sixteenth century, Copernicus' *Book of the Revolutions of the Heavenly Spheres*[76] appeared. At the end of the sixteenth century the rosicrucians were faced with the need to apply occultism to understanding the planetary system, for with its materially-conceived globes in space the Copernican planetary system was maya, even as concept. Thus towards the end of the sixteenth century one of those conferences took place of which we heard here a year ago in connection with the initiation of Christian Rosenkreutz himself in the thirteenth century. This occult conference of leading individualities united Christian Rosenkreutz with the twelve individualities of that earlier time and certain other great leaders of humanity. There were present not only individuals in incarnation on the physical plane but also some who were in the spiritual worlds; and the individuality who in the sixth century before Christ had been incarnated as Gautama Buddha also participated.

The occultists of the East rightly believe—for they know it to be the truth—that the Buddha who in his twenty-ninth year rose from the rank of bodhisattva to become Buddha, had incarnated for the last time in a physical body. It is absolutely true that when the individuality of a bodhisattva becomes a Buddha he no longer appears on the earth in physical incarnation. But this does not mean that he ceases to be active in the affairs of the earth. The Buddha continues to work for the earth, although he is never again present in a physical body but sends down his influence from the spiritual world. The *Gloria* heard by the shepherds in the fields was an intimation from the spiritual world that the forces of Buddha were streaming into the astral body of the child Jesus described in the St. Luke Gospel. The words of the Gloria came from Buddha who was working in the astral body of the child Jesus. This wonderful message of peace and love is an integral part of Buddha's contribution to Christianity. But later on too, Buddha influences the deeds of men—not physically but from the spiritual world—and he has co-operated in measures that have been necessary for the sake of progress in the evolution of humanity.

In the seventh and eighth centuries, for example, there was a very important centre of initiation in the neighbourhood of the Black Sea, in which the Buddha taught in his spirit body. In such schools there are those who teach in the physical body; but it is also possible for the more advanced pupils to receive instruction from one who teaches in an etheric body only. And so the Buddha taught pupils there who were capable of receiving higher knowledge. Among the pupils of the Buddha at that time was one who incarnated again a few centuries later. We are speaking, therefore, of a physical personality who centuries later lived again in a physical body, in Italy, and is known to us as St. Francis of Assisi. The characteristic quality of Francis of Assisi and of the life of his monks—which has so much similarity with that of the disciples of Buddha—is due to the fact that Francis of Assisi himself was a pupil of Buddha.

It is easy to perceive the contrast between the qualities characteristic of those who, like Francis of Assisi, were striving fervently for the spirit, and those engrossed in the world of industry, technical life and the discoveries of modern civilization. There were many people, including occultists, who suffered deeply at the thought that in the future two separate classes of human beings would inevitably arise. They foresaw the one class wholly given up to the affairs of practical life, convinced that security depends entirely upon the production of foodstuffs, the construction of machines, and so forth; whereas the other class would be composed of people like Francis of Assisi who withdraw altogether from the practical affairs of the world for the sake of spiritual life.

It was a significant moment, therefore, when Christian

Rosenkreutz, in the sixteenth century, called together a large group of occultists in preparation for the conference mentioned, and described to them the two types of human beings that would inevitably arise in the future. First he gathered a large circle of people, later on a smaller one, to present them with this weighty fact. Christian Rosenkreutz held this preparatory meeting a few years beforehand, not because he was in doubt about what would happen, but because he wanted to get people to contemplate future perspectives. In order to stimulate their thinking he spoke roughly as follows: 'Let us look at the future of the world. The world is moving fast in the direction of practical activities, industry, railways, and so on. Human beings will become like beasts of burden. And those who do not want this will be, like Francis of Assisi, impractical in outer life, and will develop an inner life only.' Christian Rosenkreutz made it clear to his listeners that there was no way on earth of preventing these two classes of people from forming. Despite all that might be done for them between birth and death, nothing could hinder mankind being divided into these two classes. As far as earthly conditions are concerned it is impossible to find a remedy for this division into classes. Help could only come if a kind of education arose that did not take place between birth and death but between death and a new birth.

Thus the rosicrucians faced the task of working from the supersensible world to influence individual human beings. In order to understand what had to take place, we must consider a particular aspect of the life between death and a new birth.

Between birth and death we live on the earth. Between death and a new birth man has a certain connection with the other planets. In my *Theosophy* you will find kamaloka described. This sojourn of man in the soul world is a time during which he becomes an inhabitant of the Moon. Then one after the other, he becomes an inhabitant of Mercury,

Venus, the Sun, Mars, Jupiter and Saturn, and then an inhabitant of the further expanses of heaven or the cosmos. It is not incorrect to say that between two incarnations on the earth lie incarnations on other planets, spiritual incarnations. Man at present is not yet sufficiently developed to remember, whilst in incarnation, his experiences between death and a new birth, but this will become possible in the future. Even though he cannot now remember what he experienced on Mars, for example, he still has Mars forces within him, although he knows nothing about them. One is justified in saying: I am an earth inhabitant, but the forces within me include something that I acquired on Mars. Let us consider those who lived on earth after the Copernican world outlook had become common knowledge. Whence did Copernicus, Galileo, Giordano Bruno and others acquire their abilities? Bear in mind that shortly before that, from 1401–1464, the individuality of Copernicus was incarnated as Nicholas of Cusa,[77] a profound mystic. Think of the completely different mood of his *Docta ignorantia*. How did the forces that made Copernicus so very different from Nicholas of Cusa enter this individuality? The forces that made him the astronomer he was, came to him from Mars! Similarly, Galileo also received forces from Mars that invested him with the special configuration of a modern natural scientist. Giordano Bruno too, brought his powers with him from Mars, and so it was with the whole of mankind. That people think like Copernicus or Giordano Bruno is due to the Mars forces they acquire between death and a new birth.

But the acquisition of the kind of powers which lead from one conquest to another is due to the fact that Mars had a different influence in those times from the one it exercised previously. Mars used to radiate different forces. The Mars culture that human beings experience between death and a new birth went through a great crisis in the earth's fifteenth and sixteenth centuries. It was as decisive and catastrophic a time on Mars in the fifteenth and sixteenth century as it was on the earth at the time of the Mystery of Golgotha. Just as at the time of the Mystery of Golgotha the actual ego of man was born, there was born on Mars that particular tendency which, in man, comes to expression in Copernicanism. When these conditions came into force on Mars, the natural consequence would have been for Mars to continue sending down to earth human beings who only brought Copernican ideas with them, which are really only maya. What we are seeing, then, is the decline of Mars culture. Previously Mars had sent forth good forces. But now Mars sent forth more and more forces that would have led us deeper and deeper into maya. The achievements inspired by Mars at that time were ingenious and clever, but they were maya all the same.

So you see that in the fifteenth century you could have said Mars' salvation, and the earth's too, depended on the declining culture of Mars receiving a fresh impulse to raise it up again. Things were somewhat similar on Mars to how they had been on the earth before the Mystery of Golgotha, when humanity had fallen from spiritual heights into the depths of materialism, and the Christ impulse had signified an ascent. In the fifteenth century it had become necessary for Mars culture to receive an upward impulse. That was the significant question facing Christian Rosenkreutz and his pupils—how this upward impulse could be given to Mars culture, for the salvation of the earth was also at stake. Rosicrucianism was faced with the mighty task of solving the problem of what must happen so that, for the earth's sake, the path of Mars culture should ascend once more. The beings on Mars were not in a position to know what would bring about their salvation, for the earth was the only place where one could know what the situation on Mars was like. On Mars itself they were unaware of the decline. Therefore it was in order to find a practical solution to this problem that the conference met at the end of the sixteenth century. This conference was well prepared by Christian Rosenkreutz through the fact that his closest friend and pupil was Gautama Buddha, living in a spirit body. And it was announced at this conference that the being who incarnated as Gautama Buddha, in the spiritual form he now had since becoming Buddha, would transfer the scene of his activities to Mars. The individuality of Gautama Buddha was as it were sent by Christian Rosenkreutz from the earth to Mars. So Gautama Buddha leaves the scene of his activity and goes to Mars, and in the year 1604 the individuality of Gautama Buddha accomplished for Mars a deed similar to what the Mystery of Golgotha had meant for the earth. Christian Rosenkreutz had known what the effect of Buddha on Mars would signify for the whole cosmos, what his teachings of Nirvana, of liberation from the earth, would signify on Mars. The teaching of Nirvana was unsuited to a form of culture directed primarily to practical life. Buddha's pupil, Francis of Assisi, was an example of the fact that this teaching produces in its adepts profound remoteness from the world and its affairs. But the content of Buddhism, which was not adapted to the practical life of man between birth and death, was of great importance for the soul between death and a new birth. Christian Rosenkreutz realized that for a certain purification needed on Mars the teachings of Buddha were pre-eminently suitable. As the Christ Being, the essence of divine love, had once come down to the earth to a people in many respects alien to his Being, so in the seventeenth century Buddha, the prince of peace, went to Mars—the planet of war and con-flict—to execute his mission there. The souls on Mars were warlike, torn with strife. Thus Buddha performed a deed of sacrifice similar to the deed performed in the Mystery of Golgotha by the bearer of the essence of divine love. To dwell on Mars as Buddha was a deed of sacrifice offered to the cosmos. He was as it were the lamb offered up in sacrifice on Mars, and to accept this environment of strife was for him a kind of crucifixion. Buddha performed this deed on Mars in the service of Christian Rosenkreutz. Thus do the great beings who guide the world work together not only on the earth but from one planet to another.

Since the Mars Mystery was consummated by Gautama Buddha, human beings have been able, during the period between death and a new birth, to receive from Mars different forces from those emanating during Mars' cultural decline. Not only does a person bring with him into a new birth quite different forces from Mars, but because of the influence exercised by the spiritual deed of Buddha, forces also stream from Mars into those who practise meditation as a means of reaching the spiritual world. When the modern pupil of spiritual science meditates in the sense proposed by Christian Rosenkreutz, forces sent to the earth by Buddha as the redeemer of Mars stream to him.

Christian Rosenkreutz is thus revealed to us as the great servant of Christ Jesus; but what Buddha, as the emissary of Christian Rosenkreutz, was destined to contribute to the work of Christ Jesus had also to come to the aid of Christian Rosenkreutz' work in the service of Christ Jesus. The soul of Gautama Buddha has not again been in physical incarnation on the earth but is utterly dedicated to the work of the Christ impulse. What was the message of peace sent forth from the Buddha to the child Jesus, described in the Gospel of St. Luke? 'Glory in the heights and on the earth—peace!' And this message of peace, issuing mysteriously from Buddha, resounds from the planet of war and conflict to human souls on earth.

Because all these things had transpired it was possible to avert the division of human beings into the two distinct classes, consisting on the one hand of people such as Francis of Assisi, and on the other of people living wholly materialistic lives. If Buddha had remained in direct and immediate connection with the earth, he would not have been able to concern himself with the 'practical' people, and his influence would have made the others into monks like Francis of Assisi. Through the deed of redemption performed by Gautama Buddha on Mars, it is possible for us, when we are passing through the Mars period of existence between death and a new birth, to become followers of Francis of Assisi without causing subsequent deprivation to the earth. Grotesque as it may seem, it is nevertheless true that since the seventeenth century every human being is a Buddhist, a Franciscan, an immediate follower of Francis of Assisi for a time, whilst he is on Mars. Francis of Assisi has subsequently only had one brief incarnation on earth as a child; and he died in childhood and has not incarnated since. From then onwards he has been connected with the work of Buddha on Mars and is one of his most eminent followers.

We have thus placed before our souls a picture of what came to pass through that great conference at the end of the sixteenth century, which resembles what happened on earth in the thirteenth century when Christian Rosenkreutz gathered his faithful around him. Nothing less was accomplished than averting the danger of humanity separating into two classes; thus human beings could remain inwardly united. And those who want to develop esoterically despite their absorption in practical life can achieve their goal because the Buddha is working from the sphere of Mars and not from the sphere of the earth. Those forces which help to promote a healthy esoteric life can therefore also be attributed to the work and influence of Buddha.

In my book *How To Know Higher Worlds* I have dealt with the methods appropriate for meditation today. The essential point is that in rosicrucian training, the human being is not torn away from the earthly activities which his karma require of him. Rosicrucian esoteric development can proceed without causing the slightest hindrance in any situation or occupation in life. Because Christian Rosenkreutz was capable of transferring the work of Buddha from the earth to Mars it has become possible for Buddha to exert the right influence on people from beyond the earth.

Again, then, we have heard of one of the spiritual deeds of Christian Rosenkreutz; but to understand these deeds of the thirteenth and sixteenth centuries we must find our way to their esoteric meaning and significance. It would be good if it were generally realized how entirely consistent the progress of theosophy in the West has been since the founding of the Central European section of the Theosophical Society.[78] Here in Switzerland we have had lecture cycles on the four Gospels.[79] The substance of all these Gospel cycles is contained in seed-form in my book *Christianity as Mystical Fact*, written twelve years ago. The book *How To Know Higher Worlds* describes the western path of development that is compatible with practical activities of every kind. Today I showed that a basic factor in these matters is the mission assigned to Gautama Buddha by Christian Rosenkreutz, by describing the significant influence which the transference of Buddha to Mars made possible in our solar system. And so stone after stone fits into its proper place in our western theosophy, for it has been built up in an inwardly consistent way; and everything that comes later harmonizes with what went before. Inner consistency is essential in any world view if it is to stand upon the ground of truth. And those who are able to draw near to Christian Rosenkreutz see with reverent wonder the consistent way he has carried out the great mission entrusted to him, which in our time is that of rosicrucian Christianity. That the great teacher of Nirvana is now fulfilling a mission outside the earth, on Mars—this too is one of the wise and consistent deeds of Christian Rosenkreutz.

A concluding observation

In conclusion, the following brief practical observation will be added for those who aspire to become pupils of Christian Rosenkreutz.

A year ago we heard how we may gain involuntary knowledge of having a certain relationship to Christian Rosenkreutz. It is also possible, however, to put a kind of question to one's own destiny: 'Can I make myself worthy to become a pupil of Christian Rosenkreutz?' It can come about in the following way. Try to place before your soul a picture of Christian Rosenkreutz, the great teacher of the modern age, in the midst of the twelve, sending forth Gautama Buddha into the cosmos as his emissary at the beginning of the seventeenth century, thus bringing about a consummation of what came to pass in the sixth century BC through the sermon of Benares.[80]

If this picture, with its whole import, stands vividly before the soul, if one feels that something streaming from this great and impressive picture wrings from the soul the words: O man, you are not merely an earthly being; you are in truth a cosmic being!—then one may rightly say and believe: 'I can aspire to become a pupil of Christian Rosenkreutz.' This picture of the relationship of Christian Rosenkreutz to Gautama Buddha is a potent and effective meditation.

And I wanted to awaken this aspiration in you as a result of what has here been described. For our ideal should always be to take an interest in the world; and then to find the way, through such study, to carry out our own development towards higher worlds.

APPENDIX

The Significance of the Year 1250

Lecture notes, Cologne, 29 January 1911

Why do we need a science of the spirit? As living beings on the physical plane we are on a path of descent. Our body is not the same as in ancient times, our bodies are less ensouled, less sustained by spirit. In ancient times the etheric body was active within us in the same way that the plant is permeated with water. Its nurturing forces imbued the physical body. Nowadays it has lost its power over the body, and we can only be saved by strengthening the spirit within us. When the astral body is permeated by spirit, then the human race will become healthier. It is destiny that the human physical body is in gradual decline, but the etheric body can become stronger and work upon it. But at the moment people are steering straight for decadence. The science of the spirit works to renew body and soul and make them healthier. An especially health-giving effect is exerted by what cannot be perceived by the senses or the brain alone. The world regards it as nonsense when we say that we should direct our thoughts to things that cannot be outwardly proven. But it is childish to want to subject the science of the spirit to present scientific methods of proof.

Our thinking about the outer world necessarily contains a destructive, reductive element, that works back harmfully on the physical body. Sleep heals this harm. Many phenomena of the cultural life of today have a destructive effect, especially screen images—which definitely harm the etheric body. Such images also arouse sensuality. True art can bring down into the sense world what comes from higher worlds. In the science of the spirit we work together with supersensible powers. Spirit knowledge is the only thing that gives us inner certainty. Any slave with inner spiritual certainty in the time of the Pharaohs and Egyptian priest-kings, had more certainty about life than many in our present age. Nowadays people strive for fixed stereotypes, for authority. But only one's own inner, wakeful activity can give the soul certainty. A spiritual scientific attitude sustains people and makes them happy, for what the science of the spirit gives offers them a solid point of reference in their inner lives, as necessary to the soul as daily bread to the body.

We stand on an earth that progresses towards dissolution. Gradually lakes and rivers will dry up. The face of the earth changes through such transformations. Geology alone tells us that we have already reached an epoch of disintegration. The well-known geologist Suess confirms that processes of decomposition are now taking effect in the earth rather than ones of renewal and growth. That has already been occurring throughout the last great evolutionary epoch of the earth, and specially intensely since the year 1250. Some researchers and people of genius in their own fields show the odd spark of insight: Burdach for instance. He has noticed a radical change since the Renaissance, but knows nothing about the change of direction of the earth's axis at the time the Spirits of Personality withdrew.

Various spiritual beings intervene in different ways at different times. This gives each epoch its own character, just as every stage of life has its own special task. It would have a destructive, undermining effect if one tried to introduce things that are not appropriate to our time—for instance ancient Egyptian teachings rooted in the atavistic clairvoyance of a people, that have survived in altered form as belief in a supersensible world. It is not what reason sees, not the outer things of the world, that are the objects of belief. Belief is strongly rooted in former experiences of the soul. The Spirits of Personality, the archai, are invisible, and yet they are there and take a hand in things. The archai intervened in a particularly strong way in the Egyptian-Babylonian period. The Spirits of Personality were at the time especially attracted to the earth sphere. Now things are different. Now they are not in the least attracted or sympathetic to what is happening on earth. They no longer intervene, not even in people's disposition of character. Since the year 1250 things have become different. In the thirteenth century a significant, important transformation of earthly conditions occurred, and from then on the archai ceased playing such a strong part in things. They withdrew to undertake deeds in the higher worlds. Previously their influence and activity was more directed to the earth itself. Such events must be properly understood, for since then other laws have held sway.

Adversaries—in this case retrograde Spirits of Personality—counter all progressive spirits in the cosmos. These adversaries, the bad Spirits of Personality, are now winning ground. This is connected with the change to the position of the earth's axis that occurred around 1250. Over the course of millennia the earth describes a cone-type movement, a dancing movement. Since the fifth, sixth centuries before Christ, the earth's axis has turned more and more. In scientific terms this is called the precession of the equinoxes, of the vernal point. Divisions between spring, summer, autumn and winter were different in the past as well, more regular.

Love of personality and all that is connected with it has both good and bad aspects. The Renaissance also brought this in its train, producing people who lived wholly in the realm of personality. All this was fairly extreme towards the thirteenth century, and long after, right up to the time of the Renaissance, both in those of artistic nature and people such as Cesare Borgia[81] and Pope Alexander VI. It was the same with the leaders of the crusades. In those days everything showed traits of the Spirits of Personality. The whole history of that time was imbued with the bad Spirits of Personality. People were as though possessed by these Spirits of Personality.

Souls incarnated in the thirteenth century knew that people could not get away from their personality, and the adversarial powers gradually rendered people as materialistic as possible. Those who were imbued with the bad Spirits of Personality could no longer look upwards to worlds of spirit. In those days connection with the spiritual world was created through faith and belief, and great importance was placed on this by Church scholastics. Belief and knowledge were strictly separated from one another. The effect of this continued through the centuries. Kant[82] was a last straggler from this time, and his adherents parroted what he said. But Luther still had a dim sense of the effect of the bad Spirits of Personality. He hurled his inkpot at the materialistic spirit of the times.[83]

This epoch is now past. We live in a time of the archangels, with thoughts that can reach upwards into the region where the archangels and their adversaries dwell. The adversaries of the archangels no longer imbue great personalities, as the archai did formerly. There are no longer great individuals who, like Leonardo da Vinci, are connected with the good Spirits of Personality or who, like Pope Alexander VI, are connected with the bad. Nowadays people are more schematic in their minds, and chase after abstract ideals. The influence of the archangels' adversaries leads to people being more and more possessed by ideas, opinions, feelings. This makes people into fantasists who are gripped by abstract ideals. They no longer love their own eternal ego, but are driven by all kinds of lusts and passions. They are rooted merely in their earthly personality and go into raptures about any old unreal fantasy. Yet it is only striving for the world of spirit that can endow the soul with real substance and content.

A secondary effect of the bad Spirits of Personality arises through wine. Wine becomes an adversary within one's own body. Anyone who wishes to push forwards into the world of spirit must consequently refrain from wine. But passionate anti-alcoholism and vegetarianism belong to partisan, partial ideals. The same is true of people's raptures about Greek physical education, Olympic games and so forth. Today's fad for cold showers belongs here too, and enthusiasm for what is only physically tangible, as well as for what is less physically tangible. This extends from the dreams of drunken people right through to the mad urge to commit crimes, for the adversaries of the archai work in this way in the sense world.

Each person must try to sense his place in the world, must experience something of what is storming in to humanity in the way that has been described. Weakness, uncertainty, loss of equilibrium will otherwise become the rule. People who swing between fantasy and materialism will never find their way. For instance there was a Wagner enthusiast—it is possible to be rapturous about Wagner and understand nothing of him—who went barefoot all the way to Bayreuth; then he became an ascetic, sleeping on a wooden board covered in gravel; finally he joined the Nietzsche camp as a Wagner-opponent. Weakness of soul is expressed in neurasthenia, to counter which an inner certainty is needed.

But we need something different from the people of the Middle Ages, for whom faith was sufficient. A child of seven needs something different from someone who is seven times seven. The science of the spirit can tear us away from the schema that passively does our work for us, without us becoming weak and rootless. The outer glory and edifice of our civilization will collapse all of a sudden. Present forms cannot remain, they will vanish without trace: time and spirit are stronger than man with his wishes and passions. The science of the spirit is a necessity and those who pursue it should be aware of its necessity.

The Seven Principles of the Macrocosm and their Connection with the Human Being

Lecture notes, Stuttgart, 28 November 1911

The macrocosm, the wider world, is as much involved in evolution as the microcosm, the smaller world of the human being. Just like the human being this macrocosm must develop its seven principles. These principles represent the totality of the hierarchies.

I. Seraphim
II. Kyriotetes, Dynamis, Exusiae
III. Archai, Archangeloi, Angeloi
IV. Son of Man

The following is the evolutionary sequence of the macrocosmic principles:

First macrocosmic evolutionary principle = Thrones
Second macrocosmic evolutionary principle = Cherubim
Third macrocosmic evolutionary principle = Seraphim
Fourth macrocosmic evolutionary principle = Christ

Or, in pictorial terms:
(see over page)

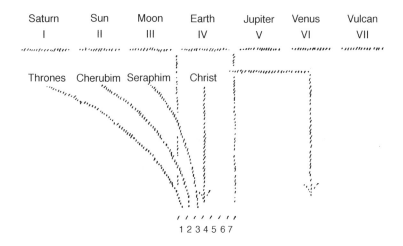

Saturn	Sun	Moon	Earth	Jupiter	Venus	Vulcan
I	II	III	IV	V	VI	VII

Thrones   Cherubim   Seraphim   Christ

1 2 3 4 5 6 7

For the earth, the root races are listed below as 1, 2, 3 etc. Schematically this gives:

1. Polar root race — repetition of the Saturn principle: Thrones
2. Hyperborean root race — repetition of the Sun principle: Cherubim
3. Lemurian root race — repetition of the Moon principle: Seraphim
4. Atlantean root race — Earth midpoint: Christ
5. Our root race — further evolution
6. Prefiguring of Jupiter evolution
7. Prefiguring of Venus evolution

The Christ principle thus evolves further through the Jupiter period, and will only be fully evolved at the midpoint of the sixth, the Venus epoch.[84]

From the middle of Atlantean times onwards, the Christ principle can only work in first, smallest beginnings. In the human being this occurs through an implanting of the disposition for the first seed of the ego. The first direct, true influence occurred in our time in the revelation on Mount

Sinai, where Christ revealed Himself to Moses in the guise of Jahve or Jehovah. Then Christ's direct connection with the earth came about at the baptism in Jordan, and the three years in the bodily sheaths of Jesus of Nazareth. The Christ impulse thus poured into humanity at the same time as the ego impulse. Christ therefore represents the macrocosmic ego.

The further evolution of the fifth, sixth and seventh principles on earth can thus only be possible as a kind of inner prefiguring. Man can receive no higher body than the physical body built up together with the fourth macrocosmic principle. Only on Jupiter will we receive the fifth, and on Venus the sixth body, and so forth. Thus in contrast to the Graeco-Roman period there is now something like an inner contradiction in human beings between spirit, soul and body, that is increasingly being felt the further evolution advances. Sensitive people can be aware of this contradiction already today.

Let us now use this schema to examine the adversarial influence of luciferic spirits. These come, of course, from a higher hierarchy than man: that of the angeloi or angels; but they did not complete their evolution on the Moon, where they passed through their 'human' stage. In their further evolution they therefore remained unable to find a connection with the fourth macrocosmic principle. Instead these luciferic spirits on the Moon evolved as it were a prefiguring of their fourth and fifth principles etc., but still without the macrocosmic fourth principle, without the Christ principle that was of course not yet there.

Let us look for a moment at the evolution of such luciferic spirits, who developed as far as the fifth principle on the Moon. These know nothing about the fourth macrocosmic principle, know nothing of Christ. It is difficult to express this in our language. One could say: they turn away, as though mocking the higher gods who endeavour to develop the

Christ principle in humanity, and call out to them: 'You can only give man the fourth principle; but we can endow him with the fifth'. That is indeed something higher that they have brought with them in a kind of prefiguring, as we do now in the fifth root race. But this lacks the macrocosmic fourth principle, Christ, of whom they know nothing at all. Thus they have matured early in a certain sense, are prefiguring something, but not in harmony with the cosmos. Normal evolution thus presents the luciferic spirits with something 'simpler', which they think is below them. And times will come when through the power of higher principles, of the fifth or even sixth principle, luciferic spirits will exert great influence on a humanity that falls prey to them.

Isn't it possible, today already, for us to have a true sense of the symptoms of this? In art and science and everywhere else we encounter a certain premature advance in evolution, which however seems to lack an inner core of truth, or harmony with what is eternal.

The leader of those spirits who have evolved six principles in this way, who therefore came close to perfection on the Moon, is the Antichrist, who can appear almost indistinguishable from Christ.

Nowadays already, the majority of humanity has fallen prey to this influence of luciferic spirits. This is why it is now necessary to nurture the inner gifts which man on earth can only receive through meditation. This is why spiritual science is necessary.

At the beginning of our fifth epoch, that is at the end of the Graeco-Roman period, in the thirteenth century, humanity was for a short period completely cut off from any clairvoyant capacity. This is why a great conference of the wisest people was held at the time, the 'College of the Twelve'. The first seven of these were the Holy Rishis, each one of whom embodied one of the seven Atlantean evolutionary stages.

Four other wise masters embodied the first four sub-races of our epoch: the Indian, the Persian, the Egyptian-Chaldean, and the Graeco-Roman. The twelfth represented all that followed. Among these twelve was a boy, the thirteenth, whom they took into their midst; and all twelve poured out their wisdom upon him in a particular way. As a result the body of the boy became wholly light-filled and shimmering. For a long time he had eaten nothing. He lived only a short while under this mighty influence, but during this time was able, through what he had taken up from all the others, to become their teacher, to instruct them in things that they themselves could not encompass singly. Specifically he could explain to them through his own vision the higher meaning of the Pauline event. Then he died and was reborn in the fourteenth century as Christian Rosenkreutz. He then lived for a hundred years, and since then has been the teacher not only of the twelve wise men, but of all humanity. He has the task of protecting humanity against the luciferic influence.

These luciferic influences are very powerful and will continue to grow significantly. One can rightly say of them: 'Little folk never sense the devil, even when he has them by the scruff'. In coming times the luciferic influence will become more and more prevalent.

The Starry Heaven Above Me, the Moral Law Within Me

Lecture notes, St. Gallen, 19 December 1912

Spiritual science teaches us that the processes in operation between death and a new birth are connected with conditions prevailing in the cosmos. The soul is subject to a very significant contrast. Changes may take place within us during physical existence, but not, in the same sense, during the period between death and a new birth. Suppose, for example, between birth and death we have been related in some way to a human being, or have shared experiences with a friend. And now, after his death, we have learnt from him something that was *not* a common experience between us on the earth. How is a relationship established after death? How can our feelings towards him give expression to sympathy or antipathy? When we ourselves have passed through the gate of death and are followed, later on, by someone with whom we had a certain relationship in physical life, this must necessarily remain unchanged for a long time after death; for after death we cannot add anything new to the old relationship. After passing into the spiritual world we are still subject to our own individual karma. The time when this karma can be transformed comes only in a new life and can only be adjusted or fully discharged in a new incarnation. An individual among the dead cannot, in spiritual existence, work upon the other dead in such a way as to change their life. But it is possible for someone still living on the earth to have an effect upon one who has passed through death. Take the following case as an example. Two human beings who love one another have different attitudes to spiritual science: one of them loves and the other hates it, and hence there is a spirit of opposition between them.

If the human being is able to speak of the freedom of his will, this is because ego-consciousness takes far deeper paths than does astral consciousness; in the depths of soul, therefore, a person often yearns for what, in his conscious life, he hates. How can we be of help to one of the dead? We must be united with him by a spiritual bond. We can help, for example, by quietly reading to him, uniting ourselves with him inwardly and lovingly, taking him with us through a sequence of thoughts, sending ideas and imaginations up to him in the higher worlds. Such services of friendship are always helpful. Reading in this way is of benefit. Although in earthly life the person may have been too indifferent, too easy-going, we can lighten his sufferings even if there was no evidence in his life that he longed for these things. Much blessing is often sent from the physical plane into the spiritual worlds, in spite of the great gulf which separates the life between birth and death from the life between death and a new birth.

Many living people will feel that they are intimately connected with the dead; they will also be conscious that they help the dead. The first souls with whom we come into contact after death are those with whom we had already formed close ties on earth, not those who were unknown to us on earth. A direct continuation of earthly life takes place after death. The soul is *inside* whatever it perceives, fills it through and through.

During the period of kamaloca, man's etheric form expands as far as the orbit of the moon. All human beings occupy the same space; they are not 'in each other's way' during the kamaloca period. After this period of moon-existence we inhabit the Mercury-sphere, then the Venus-sphere, then the sun-sphere; there we live within a sphere of higher spirituality, for the astral elements of the moon-sphere have been overcome. Life in each of the planetary spheres depends upon the mood and quality of soul acquired during the moon-period; the life of those who have developed moral fellow-feeling and compassion differs from the life of those who are egoists. The former open themselves to humanity. Above all we shall be able to form a connection with those with whom we were together in earthly life. The nature of these relationships will depend upon whether we have been a comfort or a source of trouble to others. A person of inferior morality will become a spiritual hermit; a truly moral person, on the contrary, a sociable inhabitant of the Mercury-sphere.

During the following Venus condition, we expand to the outermost circumference of the Venus-sphere. Someone who in earthly life had no religious feelings, who had received into himself nothing of the eternal, the divine, who during the Mercury-period had no bonds with other human souls, will become a hermit even during the Venus-period; but there too he is a sociable being if, during the Mercury-period he was together with other kindred spirits and warm mutual relationships existed between them. Atheists become hermits in the Venus-period; monists are condemned to live in the prison-house of their own souls, each one shut off from the other. A hermit has a dull, torpid kind of consciousness from which other human souls are excluded. A sociable being has a bright, clear consciousness which finds its way into the other being. Man ascends higher and higher into the world of the stars; but the more dimly he lives through these regions, the more rapidly he skims through the ages and therefore returns the more quickly to reincarnation—this applies, for example, to those who were criminals or idiots in their previous existence. On the other hand, the clearer consciousness has been in the world of the stars, the more slowly does the soul return to incarnation. Man must have been fully conscious out in the cosmos if he is to be capable of building and shaping the physical brain of his subsequent life. The condition of existence in which he becomes an inhabitant of the sun-sphere sets in about a century after death. During this sun-period it is possible to acquire a certain relationship to all human beings. If a person has consciously received the Christ impulse, the way to all other human beings is open for him. Since the Mystery of Golgotha, union can be achieved with the Christ impulse, the supreme spiritual power. But a person who has not received the Christ impulse remains a hermit, even in the sun-sphere.

When a human being with his aura is revealed to the clairvoyant during the moon-period of existence, a seed or kernel, enclosed in a kind of auric cloud, is perceived within the vast etheric body. This aura is dark and remains so, even during the Mercury-period. During the Venus-period, one side of the auric cloud lights up; and if, as clairvoyant, we then observe the human being, we perceive that someone who was previously moral and religious is able, from that time onwards, to have real contact with the beings of the higher hierarchies. If he was a good and moral person he lives in spiritual contact with higher beings during the Venus-period; if he was not good he cannot know or recognize these higher beings and is thus condemned to the pain of isolation.

Before the Mystery of Golgotha, in the first epoch of post-Atlantean culture, conditions were such that the throne of Christ was to be seen upon the sun. Those who had been good and moral in their lives found their way to the Christ in the sun sphere. In the age of Zarathustra, the Christ was already on His way to the earth and could not be found on the sun. Since the Mystery of Golgotha, Christ has been united with the earth. If, on earth, people have not received the Christ impulse, they cannot find Christ between death and a new birth either. When a person has become a sun-dweller and has taken the Christ impulse into himself, a multitude of facts, known as the Akashic Records of the sun, lie open before him. If, on earth, he had *not* found Christ, he cannot read the Akashic Records on the sun. We can learn to read this great script if, on earth, we have accepted the Mystery of Golgotha with warmth of heart—and then, on the sun, we are able to perceive the deeds of Christ on the sun through the millennia. Existence today is such that we are strong enough to become sun-dwellers. Later on we enter the sphere of Mars, then the spheres of Jupiter and Saturn and then, finally, the world of the fixed stars. On the path of return to earth, the ether body of man shrinks and shrinks in size—until it is so tiny that he can incarnate again in a new human embryo.

Up to the period of sun-existence, we stand under the leadership of Christ. From sun-existence onwards we need a leader whose task it is to guide us to the further realms of cosmic space. Lucifer now comes to our side. If we have fallen prey to him on the physical plane, it is bad for us; but if on the earth we have rightly understood the Christ impulse, then we are strong enough on the sun to follow even Lucifer without danger. From then onwards he has charge of the inner progress of the soul, just as on this side of the sun, Christ has had charge of our ascent. If on the earth we have received the Christ impulse, Christ is the keeper of our soul on the path to the sun. Beyond the periphery of the sun-sphere, Lucifer leads us out into the cosmos; *within* the periphery of the sun, he is the tempter.

If during the sun-period we have been armed with the Christ impulse, Christ and Lucifer guide us as brothers. Yet how differently similar words spoken by Christ and by Lucifer are to be understood! As a wonderful guiding light are the words of Christ: 'In you lives the spark of the Divine, ye are Gods.' (John, 10. 34). And then, Lucifer's words of temptation: 'Ye shall be as Gods.' (Genesis, 3.5). These similar utterances are at the same time in dire opposition! Everything depends upon whether here, on earth, man stands at the side of Christ or at the side of Lucifer.

Spiritual science gives us a deep and profound understanding of the world. A certain knowledge must come to us in the physical body. On the earth we must acquire understanding of Christ and Lucifer through spiritual science—otherwise we cannot pass consciously into cosmic space.

The time is now beginning on the earth when human beings must know quite consciously whether it is Christ or Lucifer who, after death, whispers these words into the soul. In the life between death and a new birth we must unfold a true understanding of Christ in order that we shall not be condemned to sleep-walk through the cosmos.

Spiritual science must be an influence, too, in little things. More and more it will become apparent whether or not forces of life have been acquired between death and a new birth. There will be human beings born with dried-up, withered bodies, because their antagonism to spiritual science renders them unable to gather life-forces from the cosmos. Understanding of spiritual science is necessary for the sake of earth-evolution itself! If people have opened their souls to the science of the spirit, the knowledge that before this life they were in a spiritual world, will bring them happiness. 'The starry heavens above me, the moral law within me'—this realization alone gives the world its greatness. Man says to himself: 'In the world of the stars I received the essence and content of my inner life; what I lived through in the cosmic expanse flashes up now within my soul. The existence of evil impulses in my soul is due to the fact that during my sojourn in the world of the stars I did not try to receive its forces or the spirit-power of Christ.' We have, indeed, yet to learn how to achieve union with the macrocosm. Today the human being can have only a dim premonition of what happens between death and a new birth.

He feels: In earthly existence I live within my soul and bear in my spirit the forces of the starry heavens.

If we meditate deeply on this concept it will become a great and mighty power within us.

Notes

Rudolf Steiner did not intend publishing the lectures of this volume, and he did not check them himself. Therefore he chose neither the name of the book nor the titles of the individual lectures. Those that have already appeared in print received their titles as publications of Marie Steiner.

Rudolf Steiner gave these lectures while still working with his anthroposophically orientated spiritual science within the Theosophical Society of those days, therefore he used the term 'Theosophy'. In accordance with instructions he gave at a later date many instances of this word have been altered to 'spiritual science' or 'anthroposophy'.

1   Helena Petrovna Blavatsky, née von Hahn (Ekaterinoslav, Southern Russia, 1831–1891 London), founded the Theosophical Society together with Col. H.S. Olcott in New York in 1875, its headquarters moving in 1879 to India (Adyar, near Madras).

2   *The Secret Doctrine, The Synthesis of Science, Religion and Philosophy.* Volume I, *Cosmogenesis*; Volume II, *Anthropogenesis*; London, 1888. A third volume was published from manuscripts by Annie Besant in London in 1897.

3   Max Müller: 1823–1900; one of the most important orientalists of the nineteenth century.

4   Paul Deussen: 1845–1919; philosopher and scholar of Indian culture.

5   See Rudolf Steiner, *Autobiography*, Anthroposophic Press 1999.

6   See Rudolf Steiner *The Anthroposophic Movement.* Eight

lectures in Dornach, 10–17 June 1923; Rudolf Steiner Press 1993.

7   See the Berlin and Stuttgart lectures *Reincarnation and Karma*, Anthroposophic Press 1992.

8   Ernst Haeckel: 1834–1919; German scientist. His remarks about Jeshu ben Pandira are in his work *Die Welt-rätsel* ('World Secrets'), Bonn, 1899.

9   Matthai was a pupil of Jeshu ben Pandira. See Rudolf Steiner's *The Gospel of St Matthew*, twelve lectures, Berne, September, 1910, Rudolf Steiner Press 1965.

10   See Marie Steiner's Foreword.

11   1899 marks the end of a period lasting from 3101 BC to AD 1899, which in Indian is called *Kali Yuga*, meaning 'The Dark Age'.

12   Vladimir Soloviev: 1853–1900; Russian philosopher. The three experiences mentioned by Rudolf Steiner are described by Soloviev in *Drei Begegnungen Moskau/London/Aegypten/ 1862–75–76* ('Three Meetings Moscow/London/Egypt/1862– 75–76') contained in the edition of poems by Vladimir Solo- viev translated into German by Marie Steiner, Dornach 1969. When Rudolf Steiner refers to Soloviev's vision of the future evolution of humanity arising out of these meetings, he means *The Antichrist*; Floris Books, Edinburgh, 1982.

13   Friedrich Wilhelm Joseph von Schelling: 1775–1854.

14   Georg Wilhelm Friedrich Hegel: 1770–1831.

15   Ernst Haeckel: See Note 8.

For above three notes, see Rudolf Steiner *The Riddles of Philosophy*, Anthroposophic Press 1973.

16   See Rudolf Steiner *The Gospel of St Luke*, ten lectures, Basle, September, 1909, Rudolf Steiner Press 1964.

17   Terminology in Eastern wisdom for the body of a Buddha after he has attained perfection. See the Gospel of St. Luke lecture cycle (previous note).

18   Gottfried Wilhelm Leibniz: 1646–1716. See Rudolf Steiner *The Riddles of Philosophy*, op. cit.

19   See the legend of Barlaam and Josaphat.

20   The second of Rudolf Steiner's four mystery plays, first per-

formed in Munich in the summer of 1911. See *Four Mystery Dramas* (1910–13); Rudolf Steiner Press 1997.

21 See the platonic dialogues 'Menon' and 'Protagoras'.

22 Celsus: Roman philosopher. In the middle of the second century AD he wrote *The True Word*, the first polemic against Christianity.

23 Urim and Thummim: Hebrew terms for morality and wisdom.

24 Arthur Schopenhauer, 1788–1860. See Rudolf Steiner's *Biographien und biographische Skizzen 1894–1905*, GA 33, in connection with Schopenhauer's interest in Buddhism.

25 The first of the three Rosicrucian mottos, meaning: 'from God we are born'; then comes: *In Christo morimur* = 'in Christ we die'; and *Per spiritum sanctum reviviscimus* = 'through the holy spirit we are reborn'.

26 Christian Rosenkreutz: A fourteenth century personality not given historical credence by external history but known to us from two anonymous rosicrucian legends *Fama Fraternitatis or Discovery of the Brotherhood of the highly commendable Order of the Rose Cross*, Kassel 1614; and *Confessio Fraternitatis or Confession of the commendable Brotherhood of the highly honoured Rose Cross*. According to these Christian Rosenkreutz was a German of noble descent who lived from 1378 to 1484. The name occurs for the first time in a document called *Chymical Wedding: Christiani Rosenkreutz. Anno 1459* written in 1604, handwritten copies of which were anonymously published in Strasbourg in 1616, the publisher being Johann Valentin Andreae who was inspired by Christian Rosenkreutz. See Rudolf Steiner: 'Die chymische Hochzeit des Christian Rosenkreutz', an essay in the periodical *Das Reich*, Munich, 1917/18; *Philosophie und Anthroposophie*, (collected essays) 1904–18, GA 35, Dornach 1965. See also Johann Valentin Andreae: *The Chymical Wedding of Christian Rosenkreutz Anno 1459*, Minerva Books, London.

27 Rudolf Steiner is evidently referring here, as he did in an earlier lecture (Berlin 16 December 1904) to an utterance of Count de Saint Germain handed down in literature according

to which he said in Vienna in 1790: 'I shall disappear from Europe towards the end of the century and proceed to the regions of the Himalayas. I shall rest; I must rest. In 85 years time I shall be seen daily.' (Quoted from Isabella Cooper-Oakley in the periodical *Gnosis* vol. 1, no. 20 of 15 December 1903). In the year 1875, that is, exactly 85 years after this utterance, the Theosophical Society was founded.

28   *Secret Symbols of the Rosicrucians in the sixteenth and seventeenth centuries*, 3 books, Altona 1785–88 (anon.). Book I contains an essay by Hinricus Madathanus Theosophus: 'Aureum Seculum Redivivum', which had already appeared in 1621.

29   Anagrammatic pseudonym of the paracelsist Hadrianus a Munsicht (Adrian von Mynsicht: Mynsicht is also an anagram of the surname Symnicht, originally Seumenicht, an alchemist) whose distinction it is to have been the first person to produce tartar emetic (or potassium antimonyl tartrate). He was born in Braunschweig the son of a pastor and lived from about 1590–1638. See C.S. Picht, 'Hinricus Madathanus', in *Die Drei*, Stuttgart 1927, vol. VII No. 4.

30   H.P. Blavatsky: *Isis Unveiled*, 2 volumes, New York 1877.

31   This place was not named later, either!

32   See Rudolf Steiner's lecture *The Mysteries, A Christmas and Easter Poem by Goethe*, Cologne, 25 December 1907: Rudolf Steiner Publishing Co., 1946.

33   See note 28.

34   Rudolf Steiner also mentioned the connection between these two figures in a lecture of 4 November 1904, in *A Christian Rosenkreutz Anthology*, Rudolf Steiner Publications 1968.

35   Gotthold Ephraim Lessing: 1729–81. In his work *The Education of the Human Race*, Lessing discusses the concept of reincarnation.

36+   In 1849 Maximilian Drossbach, 1810–84, wrote the article
37   'Wiedergeburt, oder die Lösung der Unsterblichkeitsfrage auf empirischem Wege nach den bekannten Naturgesetzen' ('Reincarnation, or the Solving of the Problem of Immortality by Empirical Means according to the known Laws of Nature').

Without disclosing his name he offered a prize of 40 ducats of gold for the best exposition of the idea expressed in this article. This prompted the writing of the article by Gustav Widenmann (1812–76) 'Gedanken über die Unsterblichkeit als Wiederholung des Erdenlebens' ('Ideas on Immortality as the Repetition of Life on Earth'), Vienna 1851, which won the prize. This short article was published anew in combination with an essay by C.S. Picht 'Das Auftauchen der Reinkarnationsidee bei dem Arzt und Philosophen Gustav Widenmann um 1850' ('The Emergence of the Concept of Reincarnation in Gustav Widenmann, doctor and philosopher, around 1850'), by Verlag Freies Geistesleben, Stuttgart, 1961.

38   Heinrich Khunrath: 1560–1605; medical doctor and the writer of a great number of articles on alchemy.

39   See Note 21.

40   Thales: 640 to circa 543 BC; first Greek philosopher.

41   Max Planck: 1858–1947; founder of quantum theory. *Die Stellung der neureren Physik zur mechanischen Naturanschaung* ('The position of modern physics with respect to the mechanical world outlook'), lecture given on 23 September 1910 at the 82nd session of German natural scientists and doctors in Königsberg, Leipzig, 1910.

42   Sigmund Freud: 1856–1939; founder of psychoanalysis.

43   Joseph Breuer, Viennese surgeon. See Rudolf Steiner *An Autobiography*, op. cit., and also lecture of 10 November 1917 in *Psychoanalysis in the Light of Anthroposophy*, Anthroposophic Press, 1946.

44   Gotthilf Heinrich von Schubert: 1780–1860; natural philosopher. *Die Geschichte der Seele* ('History of the soul') Stuttgart, 1839.

45   Johann Volkelt: 1848–1930; *Die Traum-Phantasie* ('Dream pictures') Stuttgart 1875. See also Rudolf Steiner *Riddles of Philosophy*, op. cit.

46   Secret Jewish order, about 150 BC to AD 70. See also Rudolf Steiner *The Fifth Gospel*, Rudolf Steiner Press, 1995.

47   Public lecture in Munich on 19 November 1911 'Von Para-

celsus zu Goethe'. There is no transcript of the lecture. See the corresponding lecture given in Berlin on 16 November 1911 in *Menschengeschichte im Lichte der Geistesforschung* ('Human history in the light of spiritual research'). GA 61 Dornach, 1962.

48 See Rudolf Steiner *From Jesus to Christ*, Karlsruhe, October 1911, Rudolf Steiner Press, London, 1973.

49 Henry Steel Olcott: 1832–1907; founder and president of the Theosophical Society from 1875 to 1907.

50 Edouard Schuré: 1841–1929; a French writer. His play was called *Die Kinder des Luzifer* 'The children of Lucifer'.

51 *Faust*, Part II, Throne-room scene.

52 It is not known who this was.

53 Ignaz Paul Vital Troxler: 1780–1866; was a doctor and practising educationalist in Basle and Bern. No one has yet found the passage referred to here.

54 The cycle *Occult Physiology* (Prague, March 1911); Prague, Rudolf Steiner Press 1983. However, there is no mention of Troxler in the available, incomplete transcript.

55 See note 35.

56 See note 32.

57 See note 26.

58 See note 36.

59 See note 1.

60 Arthur Schopenhauer: 1788–1860. See 'Die Welt als Wille und Vorstellung' ('The World as Will and Idea') in the 'Supplements' to the second volume, chapter 38, *Über Geschichte* (On History).

61 'After his soul journey Plato is now possibly being caned at school for—not understanding Plato.' Hebbel's diaries Nr. 1335.

62 Bismarck: *Gedanken und Erinnerungen* ('Thoughts and Memories'), 1898, 2 volumes.

63 Vienna 6 and 7 February 1912, on 'Death and immortality in the light of spiritual science', and 'The essence of eternity and the nature of the human soul in the light of spiritual science'.

These lectures were not printed. See the corresponding lectures given in Berlin, 26 October 1911 and 21 March 1912, in *Menschengeschichte im Lichte der Geistesforschung* ('Human history in the light of spiritual research'), GA 61, Dornach, 1962.

64 Goethe's *Faust*, Part I, Woodland and Cave.

65 Benedictus' words in Rudolf Steiner's second mystery play *The Soul's Probation*, Scene I.

66 See Rudolf Steiner *Human and Cosmic Thought*, 4 lectures Berlin, January 1914; Rudolf Steiner Press, London, 1994.

67 See note 32.

68 *Friedrich Nietzsche, Fighter for Freedom*, Rudolf Steiner Publications 1960.

69 The 'Three Principles' are:
1. To form the core of a common brotherhood of man, without distinction of faith, nationality, class, or sex.
2. To foster knowledge of the core of truth of all religions.
3. To research the deeper spiritual forces which slumber in human nature and the world.

70 See the ninth lecture, 11 June 1912, of the cycle *Man in the Light of Occultism, Theosophy and Philosophy*, Rudolf Steiner Press 1964. See also the lectures given at Neuchâtel on 18 December 1912 (in the present volume); and Berlin on 22 December 1912—the fifth lecture in the cycle *Das Leben zwischen dem Tode und der neuen Geburt im Verhältnis zu den kosmischen Tatsachen*, GA 141, Dornach 1997.

71 See the lecture at Neuchâtel, 27 September 1911 (in this volume).

72 Nicholas Copernicus: 1473–1543.

73 Giordano Bruno: 1548–1600.

74 Galileo Galilei: 1564–1642.

75 Claudius Ptolemy: circa AD 100 to 180; astronomer, mathematician and geographer in Alexandria.

76 *De Revolutionibus Orbium Coelestium, Libri VI*, Nuremberg 1543.

77 The relationship of these two individualities was presented in

greater detail in the lectures given in 1909, *Das Prinzip der spirituellen Ökonomie im Zusammenhang mit Wieder-verkörperungsfragen. Ein Aspekt der geistigen Führung der Menschheit* ('The principle of spiritual economy in relation to questions of reincarnation. An aspect of the spiritual guidance of mankind'), GA 109/111, Dornach, 1965. Nicholas of Cusa, 1401–64, wrote his work *De docta ignorantia Libri III* in 1440.

78   See Rudolf Steiner *The Anthroposophic Movement*, op. cit.

79   'Das Johannes Evangelium.' ('The Gospel of St. John'), 8 lectures, Basle, November 1907, in *Menschheitsentwicklung und Christuserkenntnis* ('Human Evolution and Knowledge of Christ') GA 100 Dornach, 1967; *The Gospel of St. Luke*, 10 lectures, Basle, September, 1909, Rudolf Steiner Press 1975; *The Gospel of St. Matthew*, 12 lectures, Berne, September 1910, Rudolf Steiner Press 1965; *The Gospel of St. Mark*, 10 lectures, Basle, September, 1912, Rudolf Steiner Press 1977.

80   Buddha's first sermon after his enlightenment: 'The eightfold path, the cause of suffering and the alleviation of suffering.'

81   Cesare Borgia: 1475–1509; the son of Pope Alexander VI (Rodrigo Borgia). Rodrigo Borgia was Pope from 1492 to 1503.

82   Immanuel Kant: 1724–1804.

83   Martin Luther: There is a well-known legend that during his stay in the Wartburg in Thüringen he threw an inkpot at the head of the devil who had appeared to him there. The ink-stain is said to be still visible on the wall.

84   This is presumably the seventh, not the sixth epoch (editor's note).

Index of Names

Hinricus, Madathanus Theosophus 46, 52

Jahve, Jehovah 305
Jerome 149
Jeshu ben Pandira 11f, 28, 39f, 44, 68, 87, 93, 107f, 112, 125, 143f, 149f, 184
Jesus boys, two 11, 22
Jesus of Nazareth 11f, 22, 24f, 25f, 37, 39f, 67, 81, 107, 126, 143, 149, 202, 205f, 265f, 273, 278, 285, 305
John of Damascus 23, 36, 41, 141, 208
John the Baptist 10, 12, 25, 25, 29, 82, 143, 157, 168, 219
Josaphat 23, 36, 41

Kant, Immanuel 300
Kepler, Johannes 284
Khunrath, Heinrich 65
Kyriotetes 303

Lao-tzu 267
Leibniz, Gottfried Wilhelm 23
Lessing, Gotthold Ephraim 55, 213, 217
Lucifer 91f, 194f, 196f, 205f, 209, 270f, 279, 281, 284, 305f, 312f
Luther, Martin 300

Mary Magdalene 208, 253
Matthai (Matthew) 11, 143, 149, 184, 207
Moses 35, 37f, 42, 127, 150, 155f, 305
Müller, Max vii

Nietzsche, Friedrich 254, 301

Olcott, Henry Steel 160

Paul 9, 25, 51f, 56, 66f, 90, 216, 227, 268
Planck, Max 133
Plato 223, 241
Ptolemy, ptolemaic 284

Rishis 24, 48f, 86, 250f, 306
Rosenkreutz, Christian 45f, 52f, 59f, 67f, 146f, 217, 226, 255f, 275f, 283f, 289f, 292f, 307

Saint-Germain, Count of 55
Sakya 107
Schelling, Friedrich Wilhelm Joseph 21, 23
Schopenhauer, Arthur 36, 85, 219
Schubert, Gotthilf Heinrich 135
Schuré, Edouard 197
Seraphim 303f
Shabbetai Tzevi 42
Siddhartha 36, 264
Socrates 27, 85, 140
Soloviev, Vladimir 21, 23, 27, 256f
Steiner, Rudolf viiif
Suddhodana (father of Siddhartha) 10, 22, 23, 36, 40, 264
Suess, Eduard 298

Thales 103
Thrones 303f
Troxler, Ignaz Paul Vital 206

Volkelt, Johann 135

Wagner, Richard 182, 301
Widenmann, Gustav 56, 217

Zarathustra 24, 86, 311